'Give me my scallop shell...'

The Confraternity of Saint James
1983 to 2003

Patricia Quaife

Bulletin 84

London • 2003

First published by the Confraternity of Saint James as no 84 of the Bulletin of the Confraternity of Saint James, London, December 2003.

ISBN: 1 870585 73 9

The Confraternity of Saint James – Registered Charity No. 294461

Company limited by guarantee registered in England and Wales No. 4096721

27 Blackfriars Road	Tel:	020 7928 9988
London	Fax:	020 7928 2844
SE1 8NY	Web:	*www.csj.org.uk*
UK	Email:	*office@csj.org.uk*

For Alfred Grover Quaife ARAM, 1894 to 1975

Contents

Preface

"What will you find there?"
"The past as a present."
Nadine Brummer, "Pilgrimage"

In January 1983 six people met and founded the Confraternity of St James. Twenty years later, some two thousand members are vigorously pursuing the objects of the Confraternity. This remarkable growth is an indication of the deep resonances that the pilgrimage to Santiago evokes in the people of our time. It is also a monument to the qualities of those six pioneers.

Among our founder members, Pat Quaife has served as Secretary, Chairman and Editor of the Bulletin, and many members of our Confraternity will find her prominent in their memories. I myself remember the detailed reply she sent to my hesitant enquiry about membership, the welcome and good cheer at my first CSJ event, and her leadership of both my first visit to Santiago and my first steps as a walking pilgrim. Now Pat has given us "the past as a present", to inform our present and inspire our future.

In order to thank her on behalf of the membership (and others who will read her work everywhere that St James is known) I have had the great pleasure of reading this lucid History. I find only one error in need of correction. In her Introduction, Pat calls the History her last tribute to the Confraternity. Somehow, I find that hard to believe.

WILLIAM GRIFFITHS,
CHAIRMAN OF THE CONFRATERNITY OF ST JAMES

Acknowledgments

It feels as if half the Confraternity has helped with this history; certainly all the founder members have, and a good proportion of other early members – who sent me fascinating accounts of their pre-1983 pilgrimage interests and activities. They include:

Ian Dodd, Peter Johnson, Robin Neillands, Mary Remnant and Jocelyn Rix (founder members); and Joaquín (Max) de Araoz, Katharine and the late Stephen Badger, Gosia Brykczynska, Mollie Coviello, Josie Eldred, Patric Emerson, Jim and Stella Hall, David Jarvis, John and Katherine Jenkins, Rosa McGregor, James Maple, Marion Marples, Elizabeth Marshall, Brian and Marijke Morris, Edwin Mullins, Aileen O'Sullivan, Richard Reece, Rosemary Rendel, Jean (Neilson) Rivington, Brian Tate and Rosemary Wells.

Their letters can all be found in full in the Founder and Early Members Archive, now in the Confraternity Library.

A number of members too have been generous, reminding me of developments in the more recent years and/or acting as 'readers' of different chapters. So my thanks also to:

Charo Carrión, Francis Davey, Laurie Dennett, Maurice and Marigold Fox, Paul Graham, William Griffiths, John Hatfield, Walter and Mary Ivens, William King, James Maple, Howard Nelson, Asumpta Oriol, Alison Pinkerton, Alison Raju, John Revell, Janet Richardson and Timothy Wotherspoon.

Three people in particular have enabled the history to 'see the light of day': Howard Nelson and James Hatts, whose skilful use of computers and new technology transformed my basic text (the last major effort of the Canon StarWriter mentioned later) into what you are reading today; and Marion Marples who scanned each chapter with an eagle eye and suggested many improvements. I am also grateful to John Revell for his proof-reading at short notice.

Much of the history was written in the Upper Reading Room of the Devon and Exeter Institution, a quiet haven in central Exeter, membership of which is a great pleasure.

My sincere thanks to everyone mentioned here – and to all Confraternity members for participating in the endeavours of the last 20 years.

PAT QUAIFE

Introduction

Twenty years, a quarter of the average life-span or even one-third of an adult life, is a good deal of time, however one looks at it. In terms of an organisation like the Confraternity of St James in which participation by members has always been a *sine qua non*, two decades of activity at the end of a century and the end of a millennium deserve to be recorded for posterity.

By happy chance – and quite unrelated to merit – I had the good fortune to be a founder member (1983), Secretary (1983 to 1988) and Chairman (1989 to 1994). Twelve years during which the Confraternity was central to my life and when I met and became friends with so many different and interesting people in this country and in the rest of Europe. Like other long-standing members, I have gained so much that not 'giving something back' to future pilgrims would be almost unnatural. I came to this history in 2002 after many years of editing the Bulletin and our *Camino Francés* guide, not to mention the rewarding and mainly fun-filled pilgrimages and visits to Spain, organised from 1985 to 1998. The history will be my last, and I hope lasting, tribute to the Confraternity. Writing it has not been easy, with so many events to record, pilgrimages to mention, people to remember, and decisions to be made on what to describe in detail and what to leave out for reasons of space. Inevitably some achievements have had to be omitted or a modest history would have swelled to encyclopaedic proportions (you may think it has already). If anyone feels they have not been given their due I beg forgiveness; no slight was intended. The seven chapters – with one exception – follow each other chronologically, from 1983 to 2003. The exception is the story of how the Refugio Gaucelmo came into being between 1987 and 1991. It deserved to be told in detail and would have overwhelmed any other chapter. Fittingly, as chapter 4, it stands at the centre of the history, preceded by the years 1983 to 1991 and followed by 1992 to 2002/3 – the jewel in the crown of the Confraternity. To long-standing members, I hope you will enjoy the recollections found in the earlier chapters, the events in which you participated, the history you helped to make. To newer members, I hope the account of the preceding 20 years will encourage you to explore the highways and byways of Europe's many pilgrim roads to Santiago de Compostela and to volunteer your services to help safeguard the future of the Confraternity for the next 20 years and beyond.

PAT QUAIFE

Chapter 1
In the beginning
1983

'From that time on [6 March 1983] I have had a very fond affection for the Confraternity as a whole and for each of its members, whether known or unknown'.

Max de Araoz

On 13 January 1983, Mary Remnant (whose birthday it was) invited five people to dinner at the Chelsea home she shared with her mother, Joan Remnant, and three cats. Like Mary, her guests already belonged to the French organization, the Société des Amis de Saint-Jacques de Compostelle, or were known to its long-standing Secretary, Jeannine Warcollier, who had supplied a list of names and addresses of the English members. The five had also already done the pilgrimage to Santiago de Compostela in different years and by various means:

> Ian Dodd (who worked then for the General Synod of the Church of England), in 1978 by train;
> Peter Johnson (who worked in insurance), in 1981 on foot from Vézelay;
> Robin Neillands (travel writer and publisher), in 1982 by bicycle from Bordeaux;
> Pat(ricia) Quaife (local government officer), in 1981 by bicycle from Vézelay;
> Jocelyn Rix (horticulturist), in 1982 on foot from Canterbury.

Mary herself had travelled to Santiago three times, the first being by public transport in 1967 as part of a Winston Churchill Travelling Fellowship to study the history of musical instruments as shown in the visual arts. The second time was in 1980, when she drove there (with another grant from the Churchill Trust) to plan her lecture-recitals about music on the pilgrimage routes; these have since been presented numerous times in Britain, France and Italy. Her third visit was for the feast of St James for the Holy Year of 1982.

The dual purpose of this convivial evening was to meet each other – over a delicious meal prepared by Joan Remnant – and subsequently to decide whether we should take up Jeannine Warcollier's suggestion of forming a British society of St James. Much enthusiasm for the idea was expressed by everyone present and midway through the evening Pat asked: 'What shall we call ourselves?' Rob said he very much liked the sound of the French *confrérie* and wondered what its English equivalent would be. 'Confraternity' replied Jocelyn, which led Peter to suggest 'Confraternity of St James'. This name was greeted with acclamation as highly appropriate for both linguistic and historical reasons. So the decision was made and it was as simple as that.

The rest of the evening passed very pleasantly with Mary introducing us to her specially-made organistrum (a large hurdy-gurdy, which needed two people to play it), based on the instrument depicted in the Pórtico de la Gloria of the cathedral of Santiago. Mary also drew our attention to an unpublished MA thesis on the pilgrimage to Santiago from Britain, written by one Constance Storrs and held at the University of London's Institute of Historical Research. We all agreed that we should try to discover her whereabouts as she might be a potential Confraternity member.

Pilgrim reminiscences inevitably occupied much time and we were intrigued to discover that each of us had met or corresponded with Jeannine Warcollier and that the paths of some of the six of us had also crossed in recent years (see Appendix 1). By the end of the evening the Confraternity had come into being, with six founder members and Joan Remnant as the first ordinary member. Three of the six happened to be cat-lovers, which immediately gave them another common interest.

If the initial decision had been easy, the second: how to publicize the existence of the newly-born Confraternity, to gain more members and generally establish a Committee and a programme of activities, was more difficult. It was agreed we would organize a public meeting in central London in early March and put notices in various churches as well as in sympathetic papers such as *The Tablet, The Catholic Herald* and *The Church Times*. The venue was to be the upstairs room of the Wren Restaurant at St James, Piccadilly, particularly suitable, we thought then, in view of the St James connection[1].

On Sunday 6 March, the six of us arrived in good time at the Wren, not knowing what or whom to expect. In the event 28 people came to the meeting, with Rob in the chair, and we were delighted that there seemed to be so much enthusiasm for starting the Confraternity, the name being universally approved. Peter had prepared a three-page handout consisting of a map of the pilgrim routes through France and

Spain, a page of general information on St James and the origins of the pilgrimage together with some ideas for future Confraternity activities. This was distributed to all present and a formal Steering Committee was set up, consisting of Rob as Chairman, Pat (who had access to a photocopier) as Secretary, Ian as Treasurer, and Peter with Joaquín (Max) de Araoz as joint archivists; Mary, with Peter Colesworthy, became an ordinary committee member. With only one exception, everybody present joined the fledgling society and paid Ian the agreed 1983 subscription of £2-50. Among these very new members was Marion Marples, who was to play such an important role in the future, although she did not suspect this in March 1983. Plans were also made in the latter part of the meeting for publicity, future events and a members' newsletter. The acorn had been planted in fertile soil and was to grow and flourish over the next 20 years.

★ ★ ★ ★ ★ ★

1983 was, naturally, a year of Confraternity 'firsts' in most of the fields of activity undertaken in later years. On 7 May the first CSJ visit was organized – appropriately to Reading – to see the ruins of Reading Abbey (founded by Henry I in 1125 and the seat of the cult of St James in England, where a possible relic of the Apostle in the form of a hand was prominent in the abbey's list of over 200 relics), and to St Peter's (Catholic) Church in nearby Marlow where a mummified hand is kept in the sacristy. The 17 participants included Jeannine Warcollier who had come over for the weekend especially from Paris. A very young James Hatts, then aged two and a quarter, the son of Marion Marples and her husband, Leigh Hatts, put in the first of countless appearances at Confraternity events. The most exciting moment of the day was in Marlow when Canon Griffiths, parish priest of St Peter's, ushered us into the sacristy and from a locked cupboard withdrew a glass case containing a blackened and mummified hand. Was it really the hand of St James, the first-century Apostle of Christ, we wondered, as Canon Griffiths gave us a brief history of the adventures of the relic over the years. He was clearly sceptical, but we felt the extraordinary story deserved further research. A welcome and lavish afternoon tea was then provided at the Bourne End home of Rob and Patsy Neillands, followed by two slide presentations: Rob on his cycling pilgrimage and Jeannine Warcollier on the Holy Year just past and the visit to Santiago in 1982 of Pope John Paul II.

In the meantime, the Steering Committee, which usually met at Mary Remnant's house in Chelsea, decided that to maintain contact

The Founding members, 13 January 1983
L-R: Ian Dodd, Peter Johnson, Jocelyn Rix, Rob Neillands, Patricia Quaife, Mary Remnant (photo: Mary Remnant)

George Grant arriving at the Tree of Jesse pillar, Santiago Cathedral, 24 July 1983

with and between members the Confraternity should produce a bi-monthly newsletter to be called the Bulletin. The first issue, dated June 1983, was typed by Pat Quaife on her portable typewriter, ran to four pages of A4 and included an account of the Reading visit and the announcement that both Jeannine Warcollier and José-Maria Ballesteros, director of the tourist office in Santiago, had agreed to become honorary members of the Confraternity. In addition, it was made known to members that on payment of an extra £2 it would be possible to become an affiliated member of the Société des Amis de Saint-Jacques and receive a publication in English, a four-page pilgrim passport and letters of safe conduct in French and Spanish for use on the Camino in emergencies.

June also saw the establishment of the Confraternity Library, a grand name for a small collection of books kept at the Secretary's house in East Finchley. The first of these, Elías Valiña Sampedro's classic spiral-bound *Guía del Peregrino* (1982), was presented to the fledgling library by José-María Ballesteros, friend and adviser in Santiago to pilgrims all over the world. The same pilgrims also have reason to be grateful to Elías Valiña, the scholar-priest of the mountain village of O Cebreiro. He, almost single-handedly in Spain, was responsible for the revival of interest in the Camino from the late 1970s onwards, not only with his books[2] and articles but also with his waymarking of the route across Spain with the famous and familiar yellow arrows. Some of the founder and other early members of the Confraternity had the pleasure of meeting him in Cebreiro during their pilgrimages.

Thanks to the publicity surrounding the 1982 Holy Year and the founding of confraternities in Italy and Britain (as well, of course, to the activities of the long-standing French Société des Amis de Saint-Jacques (1950) and the Amigos del Camino de Santiago de Estella (1962)), an increasing number of pilgrims from the UK was inspired to walk or to cycle to Santiago in the early years of the decade. Among these was the Confraternity's first pilgrim, George Grant of Rochester (Kent), who had joined in June 1983 following early retirement from his career in engineering. George, a Spanish speaker, was a highly accomplished cyclist, an Olympic triallist in his younger days, and had decided to start his pilgrimage from Santander in mid-July. As the existing guides to the Camino were only in French or Spanish at that time, the Secretary managed to produce a simple six-page prototype guide to the route in Spain from St-Jean-Pied-de-Port/Roncesvalles, with George and later pilgrims in mind. George was kind enough to say that he had found it very useful and on his return from Santiago supplied some helpful comments on it for the following year's edition. He thus initiated the 'feedback' system which has existed for all Confraternity guides ever since. The full account of George Grant's 1983 journey can be found in the Library; but in George's memory – he died in March 1997 – I would like to quote here three paragraphs from it, which to me epitomize the spirit of the Camino:

'The people one meets, all sharing this common goal, the testing road, the many kindnesses encountered and the final sense of achievement on reaching the shrine of St James, and heartfelt prayers of thanks at one's safe arrival, left a deep impression on me which I will never forget.

'I cycled with Jean-Marc Anglo (Société des Amis de Saint-Jacques) from Samos and met Jeannine Warcollier and a group from the Société once in Santiago and joined them in their travels, which proved most enjoyable.

'I was able to hear [on 25 July] the King, Juan Carlos, present the address in the Cathedral and in fact was sitting about 40 feet away, facing him and Queen Sofia.'

Back in London, a stream of new members was applying to join the Confraternity, due in no small measure to Mary Remnant's contacts and her now well-known lecture-recitals of early music illustrated with slides. Another useful reference point was the Catholic newspaper, *The Tablet,* which had published a short editorial piece on the founding of the Confraternity, following the inaugural meeting in March. Two early 1983 members, who were to play a prominent role in the future, Aileen O'Sullivan and Gosia Brykczynska, joined in March and April respectively. Aileen who worked at the Royal Hospital, Chelsea, had seen a notice about the March meeting, but had been unable to attend, while Gosia, then studying at Harvard University (USA), had seen the first *Tablet* piece while browsing in Harvard's School of Divinity Library. (She has been editor of the Bulletin since 2001.) Other 1983 members, in addition to those already mentioned, included Max and Rachel de Araoz, Stephen and Katharine Badger (he was to become Treasurer and Librarian), Laura Dyas, much beloved for her charisma and style, Patric Emerson, one of whose ancestors went on pilgrimage in 1201, Gerald McEnery, David Jarvis, Irene Lowson, James Maple (second Chairman and Chairman of the Rabanal Sub-Committee), Elizabeth Marshall, Rosa McGregor, daughter of a well-known Santiago family, P.J. McGarry, Stella Pigrome, Edwin Mullins, art critic and author of the popular 1974 book *The Pilgrimage to Santiago,* Richard Reece of the

Institute of Archaeology, University of London, Rosemary Rendel and Rosemary Wells, who would become Treasurer and later Covenants/ Gift Aid Secretary.

There must have been something in the air in 1983 because all those listed above or mentioned earlier were still members in 2002, as were five of the six founder members; more than double the number of people joining in subsequent years of the 1980s and still maintaining their membership.

Discovering the reasons for people joining the Confraternity, who or what influenced them, and their pre-1983 pilgrim activities and links, was always of interest in the early years, when the pilgrimage was little known. Before writing this history I contacted all the founder members and a selection of other early members who joined between 1983 and 1985, asking them about these points and also the reasons for their remaining as members for so many years. The answers were fascinating and are reproduced in full or in part in Appendix 1. Several people, including Mollie Coviello, Marion Marples, Edwin Mullins, Pat Quaife and Richard Reece learned of the pilgrimage in the 50s, 60s or early 70s through their academic studies or through a teaching contact. In turn a number of early members were influenced by books they had read in these decades including particularly Edwin Mullins's own book (and subsequent television programme), V. and H. Hell's *The Great Pilgrimage of the Middle Ages* ... (1966), Walter Starkie's *The Road to Santiago* ... (1957), Jonathan Sumption's classic study *Pilgrimage, an Image of Medieval Religion* (1975), as well as sources as diverse as the Michelin green guide to Spain and a Simenon detective story. Mary Remnant's lecture-recitals were also a source of knowledge and inspiration for members living all over the country. Family history or a family connection, or attendance at a St James church were also mentioned as were the influence of colleagues, travel and work in the travel trade. Once the Confraternity was well established, of course, there was more likelihood that new members applied partly or wholly because they had seen a reference to it in a travel book or article, had attended a well-publicized CSJ event, or had heard of it by word of mouth. The overwhelming reason given for remaining a member for up to 20 years was the success of the Refugio Gaucelmo project at Rabanal, which is the subject of Chapter 4.

A landmark date in the CSJ calendar of events was that of Wednesday 6 July when Mary Remnant gave her Santiago lecture-recital specifically for the Confraternity, 'Medieval Minstrels on the

Road to Santiago de Compostela' in the crypt of St James Church, Spanish Place, London W.1. Over 70 people were present, including nearly all the London members and their friends as well as Monsignor Frederick Miles, parish priest of St James, and John Wilkins, editor of *The Tablet*. Included in the slides was a selection of those Mary had taken on the Reading Abbey visit in May, thus giving a personal touch to the evening for some members of the audience. Towards the end of the performance copies were distributed of the words of two hymns from the twelfth-century *Codex Calixtinus* (or *Liber Sancti Jacobi*), 'Dum Paterfamilias' and 'Ad honorem Regis summi', which were enthusiastically sung by all present. In later years, with practice at subsequent lecture-recitals, some of these singers became the mainstay of the Confraternity Choir, performing far and wide under Mary's expert guidance.

Because our attention had been focused on this very successful event in early July, St James's Day, Monday 25 July, was not formally celebrated in 1983, although two founder members did meet for lunch at the Wren restaurant at St James. In later years St James's Day would be an important date in the Confraternity calendar.

London and the Home Counties were not the only venues where events connected with St James were organized in 1983, and CSJ members were invited to a Jacobean exhibition and weekend in northern France and to an important conference in Italy. In late April/early May Mary Remnant and Pat Quaife attended a weekend meeting in Chateau-Thierry (Aisne), a small town some 55 km north-east of Paris, where an exhibition entitled 'Sous le Signe de la Coquille: Chemins de Saint-Jacques et Pèlerins' had been organized at the Jean de la Fontaine Museum, with the assistance of the Centre Européen d'Etudes Compostellanes. Here, in the company of Jeannine Warcollier and a group of Amis de Saint-Jacques, we enjoyed not only the inauguration of the exhibition but also a colourful pilgrim procession and pageant of both horse-riders and walkers, appropriately dressed, through the streets of the medieval town. On the Sunday afternoon we were taken by coach to the Château de Condé-en-Brie where Mary gave her lecture-recital, in French, beginning and ending with 'Dum Paterfamilias' and other music from both the *Codex Calixtinus* and the thirteenth-century *Cantigas de Santa María*.

In Italy, Perugia was the venue for a late September conference on 'Pilgrimage to Santiago de Compostela and Jacobean Literature' organized by the University's Centro di Studi Compostellani, founded in 1982 by Professor Paolo Caucci von Saucken, who has a long academic and practical connection with the pilgrimage to Santiago. Earlier in the year the Confraternity had been invited to present a paper and initially Peter Johnson had offered to do some research on the topic of St James in English literature. However, work intervened and so Pat Quaife, who was having a sabbatical year, offered to continue what Peter had started. This gave her the chance of consulting Constance Storrs's thesis at the Institute of Historical Research and she very quickly realized what a valuable contribution it was to Jacobean studies in this country. Pat was unable to go to Perugia so Mary Remnant presented the paper in her place, with CSJ members Christabel Palliccia and Max and Rachel de Araoz in the audience. After some revision the paper was published by the Confraternity in 1984 as the first in a series of academic Occasional Papers.

Back in London Committee meetings had been taking place at regular intervals and by the end of the year two more Bulletins had been published, in September and November respectively, now with the familiar CSJ logo, designed by Peter Colesworthy's sister, Joy Dalton. Bulletin 2 was noteworthy for a useful pilgrim bibliography compiled by Peter Johnson while Bulletin 3 consisted of no fewer than 12 A4 pages; it included an article on the Perugia conference and visit to Pistoia by Mary Remnant and an announcement of the publication of a new book on the pilgrimage: *Holy Days and Holidays: the medieval pilgrimage to Compostela* by Horton and Marie-Hélène Davies and published by Associated University Presses, the first book to appear on the pilgrimage in the Confraternity's inaugural year.

Two more CSJ events brought 1983 to a close. On 22 October, an 'information meeting' was held in the Small Hall at St James, Spanish Place, with three very different – and entertaining – speakers: Edwin Mullins, whose readers were delighted to see (and hear) the author in the flesh, George Grant, our first pilgrim, and Dr David Thomas of the University of Bristol who was also a 1983 pilgrim, having cycled from St Malo. In contrast, on Sunday 11 December, a London Churches meeting was organized by Marion Marples (by now responsible for Confraternity publicity) with visits to St James, Garlickhythe in the City of London and St James, Spanish Place. This was the first of many occasions when the two Jameses were present: James Maple, a very new member attending his first meeting, and James Hatts, at two and three-quarters, a Confraternity veteran. Both would make significant contributions to the Confraternity in the future. They were promptly christened James the Great(er) and James the Less. For the first time also Marion's formidable organising skills came into play, as she first shepherded us on to the right bus from the City to the West End and then escorted us to one of the rare places open for tea on a Sunday afternoon.

The year ended with some 85 members enrolled, many of whom had come to know each other through Confraternity events. Whether people had done the pilgrimage or not there already existed a strong sense of fellowship, goodwill and shared interest in St James and the pilgrimage to Santiago.

NOTES

1   Some years later we discovered that the dedication of the church was probably St James the Less.

2   His most important academic work is *El Camino de Santiago, estudio historico-jurídico* (1971). He also edited and produced the *Boletin del Camino*, a small quarterly journal on the pilgrimage, the forerunner to the present *Peregrino* magazine.

Chapter 2
Laying Foundations
1984 to 1986

After a year with a Steering Committee running the affairs of the Confraternity, it was time to put its administration on to a conventional, democratic basis. This duly took place at the first Annual General Meeting held on Saturday 7 January 1984 at the Westminster Cathedral Conference Centre, which, in Pat's absence in Australia, was organized by Peter Johnson (who had recently taken over as Treasurer from Ian Dodd). The Steering Committee was determined that the AGM should be, as well as a business meeting, an entertaining event in the Confraternity calendar to which members would be attracted. At this inaugural AGM, chaired by Rob Neillands, the agenda, including the formal election of the 1984 Committee, was followed after tea by an illustrated talk by Jocelyn Rix on 'Personalities of the Pilgrimage'. Jocelyn had set off from Canterbury in April 1982 with no sleeping bag and no specific arrangements as to where she would sleep each night. Often 'controlled' by *gendarmes* in France in the late afternoon, she also encountered warm-hearted people who gave her a bed for the night in a variety of circumstances. One evening she was even left in charge of a house overnight and gave breakfast to the absent owner's dog and cat. In Saintes she slept on a camp bed in a convent bathroom, while in the Landes she met people who ferried her pack from one night's halt to the next and arranged places to stay with a sympathetic network of friends and relations. Reaching Santiago, with her brother Paddy, for the festivities for the Feast of St James, Jocelyn even carried a flag into the cathedral, representing all the pilgrims at the High Mass of 25 July[1]. The applause at the end of this delightful talk reflected the audience's appreciation of the quality of the first-ever AGM entertainment.

Earlier, during the business meeting, it had been reported that membership now stood at 95, of which some 30 were present, and that with an income in 1983 of £537 and expenditure of £525 (mainly on Bulletin printing and dispatch), there was, to the Steering Committee's collective relief, a surplus of £12 in the first year's accounts. Only one item did not go smoothly: the Constitution. A draft had been prepared, mainly by Peter Johnson and Rosemary Wells during the latter part of

1983 but, as Peter reported apologetically, it had unfortunately been lost in the post and would have to be sent to members for their comments a little later.

The only element missing from this inaugural AGM was a late-New-Year party, which would become a regular and much-enjoyed feature of future annual meetings, following the guest speaker or other entertainment. The first of these took place a year later at the 1985 AGM after a stimulating lecture by Dr Brian Kemp of the University of Reading on 'Reading Abbey and the Hand of St James'. Members attending were invited to contribute a dish of food or to pay £2-50 towards refreshments and it was agreed that the party rounded off the AGM very well and gave people time to talk to each other in a relaxed and informal manner. The pattern of 1985 was repeated in 1986 when, because of the popularity of the AGM and the increase in membership to 200, the larger venue of the John Marshall Hall at Christ Church, London SE1, was booked by Marion Marples who lived nearby. On this occasion Stella Pigrome, an early 1983 member, spoke on 'Life and Legends of St James', showing a fascinating variety of slides from medieval manuscripts, many from the Bodleian Library, Oxford.

Between January 1984 and December 1986 membership rose, almost effortlessly, from 95 to 275, thanks to references to the Confraternity in books and articles, personal contact by Committee and other members, and publicity for events organized by Marion Marples. In this respect 1984 was notable for three reasons: firstly we were honoured that H.E. the Spanish Ambassador, D. José Joaquín Puig de la Bellacasa, accepted our invitation to become (honorary) President of the Confraternity; secondly two distinguished scholars accepted honorary membership: Professor George Zarnecki CBE and the Marquis René de la Coste-Messelière, founder and president of both the Centre Européen d'Etudes Compostellanes and the Société des Amis de Saint-Jacques de Compostelle; and thirdly two well-known university professors of Hispanic Studies became members: Professor Derek Lomax of the University of Birmingham and Professor Brian Tate of the University of Nottingham, both of whom made outstanding contributions to the Confraternity in later years. They were joined in 1985 by Dr Richard Fletcher of the University of York's Department of History, and by our first American member, the art historian Dr Annie Shaver-Crandell of the City University of New York. Another welcome 1985 member was T. A. Layton, author of *The Way of Saint James*, published in 1976, and a real benefactor of the Confraternity over the next few years.

Other prominent new members who would make an enormous contribution to the Rabanal hostel project in particular as well as to the administration of the Confraternity, were Walter Ivens and Laurie Dennett, the former becoming the first Membership Secretary in 1988 and the latter becoming Chairman in 1995 after a number of years as a committee member and Vice-Chairman. Paul Graham, William Griffiths and Sue Morgan also joined, Paul later playing an important role on the Rabanal Sub-Committee, William becoming Vice-Chairman and Chairman, and Sue organising numerous events in Bristol.

Until August 1986 enquirers about Confraternity membership were sent a one-page information sheet describing the aims and background of the organization, together with a membership application form (1986 subscriptions being £5 for individuals and £7-50 for joint members). The aims listed differ little from those of the Confraternity of 2003:

- to undertake and promote research into the history of the pilgrimage in Britain and to foster further studies of related history, art, architecture and music;
- to identify, preserve and safeguard monuments and works of art in Britain connected with St James and the pilgrimage to Santiago;
- to provide a programme of activities for members and future pilgrims;
- to provide practical information on the pilgrimage routes in France and Spain particularly for those intending to travel on foot or by bicycle;
- to join in any all-European efforts to re-establish authentic pilgrim paths in Europe;
- to welcome pilgrims from other countries.

During 1984 the Committee continued working towards becoming a registered charity for which a formal, approved Constitution would be needed. The draft that had been lost in the post duly reappeared and the (first) Constitution was agreed and adopted at the 1985 AGM. An initial approach was then made to the Charity Commission in the course of 1985, followed by a formal application. The Commission required further evidence of the Confraternity's educational role and various minor amendments to be made to the Constitution. These were ratified at the 1986 AGM. Charitable status was finally granted on 19 August 1986, under registration number 294461. Apart from giving the Confraternity a publicly recognized identity – or official respectability – as a non-political, non-sectarian and non-denominational charity, the fact of being a charity also provided protection for members' funds and enabled subscriptions to be covenanted for four years and the relevant income tax to be reclaimed, a valuable source of income in future years.

In 1985 following Peter Johnson's move to France, Rosemary Wells became Treasurer and also played an important part in drafting the Confraternity's introductory publicity leaflet. This was published, with the coveted charity reference number, in late August 1986, thanks to the generosity of T.A. Layton who sponsored its printing, and from that time on it was sent by the Secretary to all enquirers.

Throughout these early years events were being organized for members and their guests on a regular basis and, just as in 1983, there were a number of significant 'first' occasions. The most ambitious of these was the first formal Confraternity visit to Santiago de Compostela, organized by the Secretary Pat Quaife in October 1985. The aim of the visit was to provide an opportunity for members who were unable, for whatever reason, to walk or cycle to Santiago, to enjoy a leisurely visit to the city, to see the Cathedral, churches and other monuments, and to soak up its unique atmosphere. While this objective may sound worthy and solemn, in reality the nine members who went in 1985 all had a rewarding and often very amusing time. Few members spoke Spanish then and the visit would not have been possible without the help of José-María Ballesteros of the Santiago Tourist Office. He has good English and French and made all the arrangements for us within Galicia, from the hotel on the Plaza de Galicia to a guided walking tour of Santiago and a day trip by bus to Noya, Muros, and Finisterre. We were even invited into his inner sanctum behind the public part of the Tourist Office where he gave each of us a very fine Xunta de Galicia poster depicting either castles, monasteries, *hórreos* (the traditional raised, granite grain stores), or St James – the choice was ours – and a small gramophone record of the Galician poem 'Don Gaiferos' (with text). In addition, he presented us with a most beautiful book on the Cathedral of Santiago, now in the Library. We were unable to reciprocate in kind, so invited him to our final dinner at the Trinidad restaurant. Here, Irene Lowson (an early member, 1983) unexpectedly whipped out a jar of home-made marmalade from her bag and presented it, to applause from the group, to a beaming Señor Ballesteros.

The guided walking-tour was a huge success, our guide being the scholarly and multi-lingual D. José Proupín, a Santiago resident of long standing, who knew the city inside-out, and who took us to places that were new to everybody. The afternoon ended with coffee or hot chocolate in the lounge of the Reyes Católicos, the first time that any of us, except Mary Remnant, had entered its hallowed portals.

Another highlight was Cathedral Mass on the Thursday when the *botafumeiro* was in action, especially for the Confraternity. Mary was given the honour of sprinkling the incense on to the embers before it swung from end to end of the transepts, with smoke billowing in front of us. We then descended to the crypt of the cathedral for a special exhibition of documents associated with its history and development. These included, to our delight, the famous twelfth-century *Codex Calixtinus* (which is not normally on display) open at a page showing 'the musically historic three-part hymn "Congaudeant catholici" by Magister Albertus Parisiensis'.[2]

The group also made its own music on 'memorable occasions by singing Aimery Picaud's *Ad honorem Regis summi* from the *Codex Calixtinus*. The first time was for Señor Suso between courses during dinner at his Bar at a moment when there were no other customers around. After the meal we repeated it, to the consternation of the new arrivals who all fled!'

To return briefly to 1984: from that year onwards St James's Day, 25 July, has always been celebrated in one way or another by members, often at a place with connections with St James. The first of these took place on 25 July 1984 in Clerkenwell, London EC1, where ten members, plus three-year-old James Hatts, met in the churchyard of St James for a damp lunch-time picnic, followed by a visit to the church. Here, the vicar informed us that the dedication was more likely to be St James the Less than the Great; 'Oh dear', we thought, 'shades of St James, Piccadilly; we really must get these London St Jameses sorted out.' We then visited the Clerk's Well which gave the area its name and where parish clerks gathered annually to perform their mystery plays. Nearby were several informative panels about the history of Clerkenwell which we thought might give us information on the dedication of the church, and were disappointed to find nothing about it. Subsequent St James's Day activities took place in St James's Park (an early evening picnic in 1985) and the City of London (a walk arranged by Marion Marples from All Hallows-by-the-Tower to the site of the former chapel of St James-in-the-Wall, in 1986).

The early years set the pattern for Confraternity events: January for the AGM, March and May for lectures and day trips, 25 July as described above for a St James's Day celebration, October for longer visits in this country or Spain and November or early December for a last lecture or short outing. Mary Remnant generously made her ground-floor sitting-room available as a venue for several 1984 meetings, although numbers had to be limited to 20. Appropriately, at the first of these (with Professor Brian Tate present) she spoke on the Perugia conference she had attended in September 1983 and was followed by Pat Quaife who read her paper on *St James in English Literature*. In the autumn, David Foster, a Waymark Holidays walking leader, gave a slide presentation on the route between le Puy and Conques, and later, in November, Kosti Simons, a Dutch Australian and founder of Pilgrims International,[3] spoke on his summer 1984 group pilgrimage across Spain to Santiago. On each of these occasions, the room was filled to capacity by enthusiastic members and the Committee agreed at the end of the year that Mary's hospitality must not be abused and that other London venues must be found.

In 1985 and 1986 we were able to meet in one of the two halls (large and small) of the crypt of St James, Spanish Place and in the Committee Room of the Westminster Cathedral Conference Centre, both conveniently central. In one or other location talks were given by T.A. Layton, wine-merchant and Hispanophile, Dr Richard Fletcher on his recently published book, *St James's Catapult; the life and times of Diego Gelmírez of Santiago de Compostela,* and Dr Annie Shaver-Crandell on 'The Pilgrim as Art Critic: the attitude of the author of the Compostella guide towards the art and architecture of the routes'. In March 1986 Max de Araoz, a Mexican member (1983) based in London, spoke on 'St James in Mexico and Latin America' which expanded our horizons much more widely than usual. A couple of years earlier Max had presented the Confraternity with a statute of St James, in wood, which he had carved himself and which often presided over meetings. In September 1986 members enjoyed an impressive audio-visual presentation of the Arles route (to Puente la Reina) by John Halliday and his sister Joanne Land, both keen travellers on pilgrim routes. The November lecture brought members closer to home: a joint slide presentation by Marion Marples and Pat Quaife on 'St James in London' which included a detailed discussion of the respective dedications (the Great or the Less) of St James's Palace and Park, St James Piccadilly, St James Clerkenwell and others. A surprise – and very welcome – visitor on this occasion was José-María Ballesteros who had foregone the pleasure of a World Travel Market cocktail party to attend a Confraternity event.

Apart from the autumn 1985 visit to Santiago, another ambitious event was organized in May 1984 in Reading and London. Taking place in London at the time was the superb English Romanesque exhibition at the Hayward Gallery, masterminded by the UK's leading expert on Romanesque art, Professor George Zarnecki, formerly Deputy-Director of the Courtauld Institute. The numerous Confraternity members who had already enjoyed it were delighted that Professor Zarnecki had accepted our invitation to give a special lecture at St James, Spanish Place on 5 May, his subject being 'A Twelfth-Century English Sculptor's Pilgrimage to Santiago'. Discussing the similarities in Romanesque carving between Kilpeck and Shobdon (Herefordshire), Aulnay (Poitou-Charentes) and Santiago de Compostela, he referred to the twelfth-century Wigmore Chronicle which relates how Oliver de Merlimond, steward of Hugh de Mortimer, lord of Wigmore (also in Herefordshire) made a pilgrimage to Santiago around 1130, probably with a sculptor in his retinue who had noted the patterns and motifs he had seen along the pilgrim routes and reproduced them at Shobdon and Kilpeck. At the end of his lecture Professor Zarnecki encouraged the Confraternity to take an interest in the twelfth-century Shobdon Arches, which were deteriorating rapidly due to their exposed position outside. Over 70 people were present, including Jeannine Warcollier and two other French visitors who, on the Friday evening, had attended Mary Remnant's lecture-recital in the Purcell room on 'Musical Instruments in English Romanesque Art'. Jeannine and friends also took part in the second Confraternity visit to Reading and Marlow on the Saturday. On this occasion we were lucky enough to be shown round the abbey ruins and the medieval section of the Reading Museum by Leslie Cram, curator of the museum and a fount of knowledge about Reading.

Another major exhibition took place in late 1985 in Ghent, Belgium. Unlike the English Romanesque in London, this exhibition, organized by Europalia, was devoted entirely to the pilgrimage to Santiago, as its name made clear: *Santiago, in Europe: One Thousand Years of Pilgrimage.* With typical generosity, Jeannine Warcollier invited the Confraternity to take part in a special European weekend she was arranging in Ghent in early November, the aim of which was to bring together members of all the European societies of St James, especially the newer ones founded in 1982 or later. A number of CSJ members took up the invitation, including Marion Marples and James Hatts. Heavy clouds and rain much of the time did not detract from the pleasures of Ghent where as well as enjoying the excellent and comprehensive exhibition[4] we visited the Cathedral to see Van Eyck's superlative altarpiece of the Mystic Lamb and one of the medieval *béguinages,* originally the residence of religious sisters, now used as almshouses. Marion also enjoyed Ghent's tram network as young James, at four by far the youngest member present, was already a transport enthusiast and demanded frequent journeys around the city.

Older visitors had the pleasure of meeting members of the two newly formed St James associations in Belgium: the French-speaking Association des Amis de Saint-Jacques and the Flemish Vlaams Genootschap van Santiago de Compostela. James Maple, a Committee member since 1984, had already met the founding president of the Walloon Association, Armand Jacquemin, on pilgrimage in the Pyrenees. Ghent gave more of us the opportunity to enjoy the company of Dr Jacquemin – an enthusiastic cyclist – and his charming wife Renée. They in turn introduced us to the Secretary, Jean-Pierre Renard, and to the General Secretary of the Vlaams Genootschap, Dom Willibrord (Jean-Marie) Mondelaers, a genial Benedictine who ran the society from St Andrew's Abbey in Bruges.

Visits to places of interest in England continued, including the first long weekend in Herefordshire in the autumn of 1984. Inspired by Professor Zarnecki's May lecture, we decided we must see some of the Herefordshire (and other) churches he had discussed. Kind members with cars drove those without wheels to our immediate destination, a large farm guest-house at Kingstone. From there we went out on the Saturday and Sunday to Kilpeck, Wigmore, Stretton Sugwas, Brinsop, Leominster, Shobdon, Rowlstone, and Llangua, each with its own connection to St James and/or the sculpture on the continental pilgrim routes. The state of the Shobdon arches, open to the elements on a green sward near the eighteenth-century church, was a cause of much interest and concern, which would be followed up in later years.

Mollie Coviello co-ordinated Bulletin contributions (no.9, Jan-Feb.1985) on the weekend, and wrote a concluding paragraph:

> 'It was perhaps fitting that our last church visit on the Sunday afternoon was to St James, Llangua (just in Wales, but still in the diocese of Hereford) … Inside the modest church was a splendid and colourful statue of St James. About three feet high, he is a sturdy figure with dark, curly hair and beard, staring into the distance as pilgrims do. His scallop shell was on his hat and on his feet he wore interesting maroon ankle

boots, the latter, according to the church booklet, having been especially studied (provenance unknown).'

The church of St James, Stoke Orchard, Gloucestershire, was the venue for a day pilgrimage by 16 members on foot from Cheltenham in May 1985. A stony, disused railway track took us directly from Cheltenham station to the church of St Michael and All Angels, the mother church of Stoke Orchard, in the village of Bishop's Cleeve, where the Royal Oak provided a hearty lunch in the old stables. A half-hour walk along quiet roads brought us to Stoke Orchard, a less attractive village than Bishop's Cleeve, but whose chapel-of-ease of St James is of great significance in the history of pilgrimage in this country. Its unique feature is the series of faded wall-paintings depicting the life of St James the Great based on Jacobus de Voragine's thirteenth-century *Golden Legend*.[5]

The subject-matter of the painting was not easy to identify, partly because at different times there have been no fewer than five successive schemes of painting in the church, from 1180-1220 (the life of St James) to 1723 (texts and the Royal Arms). The vicar, the Revd Chris Harrison, kindly presented us with E. Clive Rouse's and Audrey Baker's monograph *Wall Paintings in Stoke Orchard Church, Gloucestershire*, now in the Library. In subsequent years the Confraternity pressed the relevant authorities to take steps to preserve the paintings, and also contributed to The Friends of St James Stoke Orchard.

October 1986 found a 25-strong group in Norfolk, based in a Norwich hotel, notable for the presence of Basil, a large and friendly tabby cat. Saturday morning was free for people to explore the city, including the Cathedral and some of the 31 medieval churches still standing, including a St James church now used as a puppet theatre. Our first exodus from Norwich, in a convoy of seven cars, was to St Faith's Priory at Horsham St Faith, four miles north of the city. Now a private home, the Priory was originally a Benedictine house, founded as a cell of Conques. The story of the priory is depicted in thirteenth-century wall-paintings, together with a Crucifixion scene discovered in 1924 and a large crowned female figure; we preferred the attribution to St Faith rather than to the suggested alternative of St Margaret of Scotland. The first representation of a wheelbarrow completed this fascinating series of wall-paintings. In the afternoon the party divided into three groups to visit a number of churches, following a central, coastal or Walsingham option, with the groups asked to record the traces of St James they found in each church. The highlight of Sunday,

Church of St James, Stoke Orchard, Gloucestershire, January 1991
(photo: Patricia Quaife)

James Maple and Paul Graham at the first Practical Pilgrim Day
(photo: Patricia Quaife)

if not of the whole weekend, was the visit to St Helen's, Ranworth, on the edge of the Norfolk Broads. The church is well known for two special features: its incomparable painted screen – with a St James as well as a panel showing James and John as children, with their mother Mary Salome – and the *Sarum Antiphoner*, a medieval service book containing 19 illuminated miniatures. The rector allowed us to look at it outside its case and even to turn over each of its many pages. At this point we were grateful that Alain Arnould from Bruges was in the group. He was spending a post-graduate year at the Warburg Institute of the University of London, specializing in the study of medieval manuscripts, and gave us an impromptu talk on how the Antiphoner would have been produced and illuminated. We found no St James but were pleased to see a number of medieval musical instruments which Mary Remnant photographed.

Back in London, a historic Confraternity event took place on 24 April 1986, the brainchild of James Maple who had been elected Chairman earlier in the year. This was the first ever Practical Pilgrim session, organized by James, where experienced pilgrims dispensed information and advice to those making the journey later in the year. Cyclists and walkers converged on the South Bank's Jubilee Gardens from all points of the compass, including North Wales, with George Grant, the Confraternity's first 1983 pilgrim, coming up specially from Kent. Also present at his first CSJ event was Walter Ivens who was to cycle to Santiago later that year. A pilgrim support vehicle was provided by Stephen Badger who, with his daughter Penelope, dispensed biscuits and cups of tea brewed on their pilgrim stove. At the end of the afternoon it was agreed that Practical Pilgrim should be an annual fixture, and not always in London.

One of Rob Neillands's brainwaves, developed by Marion Marples with help from Stephen Badger and Rosemary Clarke, was the creation of a pilgrim footpath from Reading Abbey to Southampton, where medieval pilgrims could have taken ship for Galicia or Bordeaux. Bulletin 10 (March 1985) included an appeal from Marion for information on pre-historic trackways, Roman roads, abandoned villages and any existing pilgrim routes or centres at or between Reading, Basingstoke, Winchester and Southampton. Alan Janes and Frank Reavey responded to this appeal and in mid-September the project took off, with a walk from Reading to Mortimer; participants checked museums, churches and footpaths as they went. In May 1986 a second stretch of the Path was walked, nine miles from Mortimer to Pamber Priory, via Silchester and the Roman town of Calleva, led by Marion and her husband Leigh Hatts, who, with young James, had piloted the walk a week earlier.

While some members were in Hampshire, a new (1986) member, Laurie Dennett, originally from Toronto but based in London, was on a much longer pilgrimage, from Chartres to Santiago. She was raising funds for multiple sclerosis research (her mother had MS) and reporting twice a week on her progress on a Canadian radio programme. Despite enduring the coldest and wettest summer France had known for 40 years, she was not deterred from her objective and enjoyed much better weather on the other side of the Pyrenees. At O Cebreiro she was warmly welcomed by the priest D. Elías Valiña Sampedro and his sister who ran the mountain-top guest house or *hospedería*. Further into Galicia she was joined for the last few days of the pilgrimage by the Canadian High Commissioner, Roy McMurtry, and they reached Santiago on 10 June. On this occasion Laurie raised £33,000 in the U.K. and subsequently wrote a well-received book, *A Hug for the Apostle*, published by Macmillan of Canada in 1987.

Other pilgrims in these years included Chairman Rob Neillands, cycling again in 1984, but this time from le Puy (his book *The Road to Compostela* was published in 1985), and Amanda Bath of Bristol who by arriving on 16 April was the first English pilgrim to reach Santiago that year. Two other Bristolians, Shaun and Seamus McLoughlin, the latter aged 12, cycled together from St Malo. Shaun was a BBC radio producer and he and Seamus later made a delightful radio programme, *The Field of the Star*. Down-to-earth extracts from Seamus's diary, read by him, and music by Mary Remnant all contributed to the programme.[6] Another pair of 1984 pilgrims were Brian and Marijke Morris, riding their tandem from Santander, the first Confraternity tandem pair to make the journey. James Maple celebrated his CSJ Chairmanship by cycling from Auxerre in July of that year, while the father-and-son combination of Francis and Marc Oeser cycled from Bordeaux the same month. Another 1986 cyclist was Walter Ivens, who on passing through the villages of the Maragatería, was moved to write in his diary:

> 'Seeing all those derelict villages – houses tumbling down – probably still lived in but nobody about, gave me a sense of guilt, because we supposed pilgrims pass by on one side with shame and an itch to take a photo to show off to others the primitiveness of the Camino. As modern pilgrims we take of

the route but I don't think we give enough back.'

This thought remained with him, to be given concrete expression in the Rabanal project which came to fruition five years later in 1991 (and is the subject of Chapter 4).

All these achievements, and others, were written up in the Confraternity Bulletin, the appearance of which slowly improved as the editor developed her skills and more up-to-date technology was used. Number 4, January 1984, was edited by Peter Johnson during Pat's absence in New Zealand, while no. 5 (like nos. 1 to 3) was produced on the portable typewriter mentioned in Chapter 1. The latter issue included an appeal by the editor for an electric typewriter at reasonable cost – the Confraternity could not then afford to buy a new machine – as her portable was being worn out by correspondence and Bulletins. Patric Emerson generously responded, offering an electric Smith-Corona he was no longer using very much, and was warmly thanked in Bulletin 6, the first to be produced on the new machine. Two years later, as finances improved, the Confraternity bought a brand-new Brother electronic typewriter, with a magical self-correcting mechanism which meant no more struggling with Tippex. So the look of Bulletin 17 (August 1986) marked a further improvement over earlier issues, while still being produced in double-sided A4 format, usually of 12 pages. However, no.19 (December 1986) was to be the last such issue, following much Committee discussion in 1986 on the style, name and content of the Bulletin.

Late in 1985 a ballot of members on the name of the publication took place, yielding a close result as between the existing Bulletin and *The Staff and Scallop*. On balance, it was felt that the latter, though picturesque, bore slightly too close a resemblance to the name of a public house. So the Bulletin it was, with the decision that in 1987 a smaller, A5 format, with a card cover, would be introduced. The contents, a mixture of articles, news, reports of meetings, list of new members and new publications, would be similar but it was hoped that contributors would provide photos, line-drawings or maps to illustrate their articles and make the Bulletin more interesting visually.

Even so, the years 1984 to 1986 saw a wide variety of articles and contributors to the Bulletin. These included the first listings by counties of churches dedicated to St James or where there might be a depiction of him in some form in a particular church. Bulletin 10 (March 1985) introduced the project of 'St James – Churches and Art' as one designed to fulfil two of the Confraternity objects: to identify, preserve and safeguard monuments and works of art in Britain connected with St James and the pilgrimage to Santiago, and to undertake and promote research into the history of the pilgrimage in Britain. Members were invited to visit and photograph St James churches in their area, to obtain a church booklet and consult their county library for further historical references. From this small beginning there developed the Confraternity's Research Working Party, which would be set up in 1989, chaired by Professor Derek Lomax.

Other Bulletin articles ranged from philately to France, Conques to the Médoc, Cornwall to Galicia and from art history to learning Spanish in Santiago de Compostela. One request for information that went unanswered appeared in Bulletin 7 (September 1984): an appeal for any information on the whereabouts of Constance Storrs, author of the 1964 thesis mentioned in Chapter 1. The A4 format Bulletins (nos. 1 to 19) are available in the Library.

However the Bulletin was not the only CSJ publication in the mid-Eighties. The *Pilgrim Guide to Spain* (i.e. the *Camino Francés*) was updated and published annually in March or April, thanks to contributions sent in by the previous year's pilgrims. From six pages in 1983 it increased to 12 or so pages in 1986 and was starting to be looked at enviously by pilgrims of other nationalities in Spain. In mid-1986 Patric Emerson's guide to the Paris/Tours route was published, with other French routes in preparation. 1984 saw the first of the Occasional Papers series, Pat Quaife's revised paper on *St James in English Literature*. And to encourage members' writing, T.A. Layton, who had accepted honorary membership of the Confraternity in 1985, offered a generous prize of £100 for the best essay annually on a given topic. The first joint winners of the T.A. Layton Prize in 1986 were Jocelyn Rix and Frank Turner (of Nottingham) who both reviewed Rob Neillands's book *The Road to Compostela*.

In the meantime Edwin Mullins's classic *The Pilgrimage to Santiago* (1974), much in demand by members, was becoming increasingly hard to find in bookshops and became out of print in 1984. But in late 1986 a Welsh member, John Humphreys of Port Talbot, made a remarkable discovery in a local bric-à-brac shop. In great excitement he telephoned the Secretary to say that he had just found a box of some 50 copies of *The Pilgrimage to Santiago* in mint condition at only 50p a copy and should he buy them for the Confraternity. The Secretary did not hesitate as there was no time to lose; she authorized John to buy them and send them on to her in London, with the cost and the postage to be reimbursed to him. The Committee although not consulted, was equally pleased with the discovery as it was possible not only to make a modest profit on copies sold on to members but also to satisfy general demand for an influential work on the pilgrimage.

NOTES

[1] For further details of Jocelyn Rix's pilgrimage, see Appendices 1 and 5.

[2] Mary Remnant, 'Santiago and Music' in Bulletin 14 (Feb. 1986), pp 11-12. Writing in 2003, Mary Remnant states: "It is now believed that the two upper parts are alternatives and that it was not actually a three-part piece".

[3] Pilgrims International was founded in 1983 to 'foster the joy of pilgrimage and to encourage pilgrimage as an act of Christian worship.' To these ends it organized non-profit-making international group pilgrimages to Santiago in the summer for several years, before Kosti Simons returned to Australia in 1987.

[4] The Confraternity Library has a copy of the 495-page catalogue (in French) of the Ghent exhibition. It includes 18 essays and a bibliography as well as an entry for each of the 634 items on display.

[5] The *Golden Legend* consists of a series of lives of the saints, incorporating legend, myth and history in equal parts.

[6] A cassette tape of the programme can be borrowed from the CSJ Library.

Chapter 3
Expanding Horizons
1987 to 1991

The five years from January 1987 to December 1991 were pivotal in the development of the Confraternity. If members had been asked in late 1991 to select the most significant on-going activity and the most important one-off event their answers would certainly have been, respectively, the 'hostel project' at Rabanal del Camino (León) and the international conference held in Suffolk in March 1990 on *Pilgrims from the British Isles to Santiago de Compostela in the Middle Ages*. European meetings also featured strongly in this period as the new Jacobean associations established in the early to mid-Eighties found their feet and organized a variety of activities. At the same time the regional Spanish associations were increasing in number, with a Federation of Associations of Amigos del Camino de Santiago being formed in 1987.

This chapter would be inordinately long if it were to include the complex story of the Rabanal project, the first phase of which covers the same period of 1987 to 1991. This will therefore be related in Chapter 4, making it appropriately the central section of this history.

For those who attended the conference at Hengrave Hall, Suffolk, two scholars of the pilgrimage will always be associated with it: Mrs Constance Storrs, author of the important 1964 London University thesis on medieval English pilgrims, and D. Elías Valiña Sampedro, whose life's work was referred to in Chapter 2. While Mrs Storrs was able to be present for part of the proceedings, very sadly, D. Elías, described as *el padre del Camino*, died before the conference took place.

In early 1988, after much searching, Mary Remnant had succeeded in finding the whereabouts of Constance Storrs. She was living quietly in retirement in the Suffolk village of Badwell Ash, near Bury St Edmunds, with her husband Francis and their friend, Dr Susan Tracey. While Mrs Storrs was delighted to be 'discovered' and very interested to hear of the existence of the Confraternity, she had told Mary firmly that she would never go back to London under any circumstances.[1] It was this conversation that raised the idea that the planned Confraternity conference should take place near Constance Storrs's home. An obvious venue was the nearby Hengrave Hall, run as a retreat and conference centre, and happily the Confraternity was offered a weekend booking for 16 to 18 March 1990.

In the meantime in Spain, at an international conference in Jaca (Aragón) in September 1987 that he himself had organized, Elías Valiña had been succeeded as Comisario-Coordinador by Ángel Luis Barreda Ferrer of the Palencia Amigos, based in Carrión de los Condes. In addition, the modest but valuable *Boletín del Camino* published by D. Elías since 1985 was soon to be replaced by the more ambitious *Peregrino* magazine. Despite his disappointment and subsequent illness in 1988 and 1989, Elías Valiña quietly continued his work as priest of O Cebreiro, preparing a new edition of his guide to the Camino and acting as friend and adviser to all the pilgrims who were so well received there.[2] During 1989, as preparations for the Hengrave conference intensified, the Confraternity hoped that he would recover in time to be able to be present. Unfortunately, this was not to be and he died in Lugo on 11 December 1989, aged only 60. At the suggestion of a Committee member who knew D. Elías well, it was agreed that the conference, now just three months away, should be dedicated to his memory.

Seven European countries – apart from Britain – were represented at Hengrave Hall: Belgium, Ireland, France, Germany, Holland, Spain and Switzerland. Among the Spanish group was Elías Valiña's long-standing friend, D. Luciano Armas Vázquez, a priest from Lugo, who gave a moving appreciation in Spanish of the life and achievements of D. Elías. This was followed, on the Sunday morning, by a special Latin Mass in thanksgiving for his life, held in Hengrave Hall's own Church of Reconciliation, and celebrated by D. Luciano with the assistance of D. José Ignacio Díaz (editor of *Peregrino*) and other participants.[3]

An enormous effort had been made by the organizers, speakers and members generally to offer written translations, mainly into French and Spanish, of all the papers read at the conference as well as D. Luciano's contribution. The keynote speaker on Friday evening was Professor Derek Lomax on 'English Pilgrims to Santiago de Compostela': he was followed on Saturday and Sunday by Professor Brian Tate, Hilary Shaw (founder and Secretary of the Cornish Bredereth Sen Jago), and Dr Brian Kemp of the University of Reading. Marion Marples, one of the principal organizers of the conference, spoke on the Reading to Southampton footpath, while the conference concluded with a lively international Round Table, chaired by Pat Quaife. An honoured and welcome guest on the Saturday was Constance Storrs, then aged 79, who was able to meet other scholars of the pilgrimage 26 years after

Hengrave Hall Conference: Marion Marples, James Hatts, Patricia Quaife

Dr René de la Coste-Messelière and Br Anthony Brunning
(photo: Mary Ivens)

completing her own work on medieval English pilgrims.

The conference had its lighter-hearted moments as well. On the Friday morning, while still in London, a 30-strong party divided into four language groups, English, French, German and Spanish, and went in search of St James, visiting St James Spanish Place, St James Garlickhythe, All Hallows by the Tower and All Hallows, Staining (for the twelfth-century crypt of St James in the Wall). Later, on arrival at Hengrave Hall, the foreign participants were all struck by the beauty of its Tudor façade. Among these was Dr René de la Coste-Messelière of Paris who, unwinding himself from a small Renault driven by his compatriot, Colette Prieur, gazed at the Hall, which was bathed in sunshine, and was heard to exclaim loudly 'C'est superbe!' before unloading a battered suitcase. Odile Lutard, who chaired the Aquitaine regional association, had somehow managed to include in her luggage three magnums of claret as a gift to the conference from Jean Janoueix, one of the Aquitaine Vice-Presidents who owned a number of vineyards near Saint-Emilion. At Saturday evening's supper, thanks to French generosity, there was enough wine for well over 85 glasses.

A full evening's entertainment, presided over by James Maple, included a multi-lingual lecture-recital, *Music of the Pilgrimage,* orchestrated and presented by Mary Remnant. She had been at work for weeks prior to the event, dispatching music to the foreign delegates, rehearsing her English singers in London, and using any odd moments at Hengrave for last-minute rehearsals of the different language groups. The result was a delightful musical miscellany: James Hatts, then aged nine, played a young pilgrim with much aplomb while William Griffiths excelled in a dramatic recitation of the Middle English poem 'The Pilgrim's Sea Voyage and Sea Sickness'. Dr Armand Jacquemin, president of the Brussels-based Walloon association, borrowed young James's pilgrim hat and held the distinguished francophone group together in *la Grande Chanson.* While the English and German choirs acquitted themselves with credit, the Spanish, less well coordinated by Ángel Luis Barreda, were unable to achieve the same musical effect, but kept the audience in gales of laughter during the attempt.

The architectural delights of Suffolk were not neglected, with a Saturday afternoon visit to four medieval churches, organized by George McHardy, and a Sunday visit to Bury St Edmunds and its cathedral dedicated to St James, in time for choral evensong, The conference organizers spent the next week recovering from their efforts but were unanimous in feeling that it had all been very worthwhile.

★ ★ ★ ★ ★

By the start of 1987, the annual programme of lectures and visits, Bulletin issues, pilgrim guides and Practical Pilgrim days, was well established. Committee members were beginning to discuss the future of the organization and its relationship both to the Camino and to sister confraternities in Europe. Members of the two Belgian associations joined the 1987 and 1988 Annual General Meetings, braving the English Channel in January (this was before the advent of Eurostar trains). The 1988 (fifth anniversary) meeting was notable also for three other reasons: firstly, over a third of the 300-strong membership attended; secondly the Treasurer, Rosemary Wells, reported – for the first and only time – a deficit for 1987 of £100 ('so please pay your subscriptions promptly'); and thirdly, James Maple outlined the history of the Confraternity to date and ways of expanding its work. He mentioned several new and long-term projects, of which the idea of restoring a hostel on the Camino and thus helping to bring a village back to life was the most ambitious. Walter Ivens then distributed a Confraternity questionnaire to members, asking them to identify their interests, their preferences for future development and how they might be able to help in different areas. The questionnaire proved to be a valuable tool for finding out more about members' skills and expectations as well as a source of future assistance.

By the 1989 AGM, membership had risen to 400 and the previous year's deficit had been expunged. It was at this meeting that James Maple stood down as Chairman, after three years in that position. 'It is my belief', he said in his report, 'that the Confraternity will only continue to grow in strength if new members and new people become interested in running it.'

To an extent that had already happened. By mid-1988, it had become clear that the Secretary, Pat Quaife, needed to devolve certain tasks to other Committee members and volunteers. Stephen Badger therefore became Librarian as well as Treasurer, and the Library moved from East Finchley to Burbage Road, Dulwich. Walter Ivens became Membership Secretary, Amanda Bath took over publications and Susan Morgan became responsible for ties and sweatshirts, previously looked after by Patric Emerson and Anthea Hopkins. Anthony Brunning, with his computer skills, became mailing-list coordinator, producing Bulletin labels five times a year, while James Maple issued pilgrim records to members and George McHardy continued to look after the slide library. Pat Quaife remained as editor of the Bulletin, helped with dispatch from her sitting-room by Laurie Dennett and others.

This division of labour has remained largely unaltered – although with changes in personnel – since mid-1988, the only major difference being the acquisition of a Confraternity office in late 1994, from where information, Bulletins and publications are dispatched by a team of volunteers.

At the first Committee meeting of 1989 Pat Quaife was elected Chairman, Marion Marples Secretary and Stephen Badger Treasurer, a combination that was to last until the end of 1994. At the same time the two previous Chairmen, Rob Neillands and James Maple accepted invitations to become honorary Vice-Presidents.

Membership continued to grow, with 540 recorded at the 1990 AGM and 719 at the 1991 meeting. (Interestingly the surplus of income over expenditure grew at a very similar rate, from £513 in 1990 to £710 in 1991.) Among new members joining between 1987 and 1991, who would play a prominent role in Confraternity activities, were Anthony Brunning, Peter Tompkins and Timothy Wotherspoon, Phinella Henderson and Dr Miriam Hood (all 1987), Ronald R. Atkins of New York, John Durant, Doreen Hansen and Vincent Cowley (all 1988): Magdalena Stork de Yepes of La Coruña and four Confraternity couples, the Foxes (Maurice and Marigold), the Hatfields (John and Etain), the Mays (Joe and Pat) and the Nelsons (Howard and Jinty) joined in 1989 while Alison Raju and Janet Richardson joined in 1990, to be followed by Hilary Hugh-Jones in 1991.

In 1990 a change of Spanish Ambassadors in London meant a new Confraternity president. Our first president, D. José Joaquín Puig de la Bellacasa, who had always been most supportive of our activities, returned to Madrid and we invited his successor, D. Felipe de la Morena, to become the new President, a role which he willingly accepted.

While new members were being welcomed, the Confraternity was starting to lose some of its older supporters. In mid-1988 we learned of the death of our first benefactor, T.A. (Tommy) Layton, at the age of 78, who had suffered from Parkinson's Disease. Two years later and only five months after the Hengrave Hall conference Constance Storrs died of cancer on 24 August 1990. A Requiem Mass for her, attended by Mary Remnant, took place in Stowmarket on 13 September, the day an obituary notice written by Leigh Hatts appeared in *The Independent* newspaper. Our sadness was tempered by the fact that not only had she attended Hengrave in March but in May she had been told that the University of Santiago de Compostela had agreed to publish her thesis in English. (In fact, it was finally published in 1994 by the Xunta de Galicia.)

A year later, John Halliday of Warminster, a retired naval officer and author of the first edition of the Arles route guide, died after a short illness at the age of 79. He and his sister, Joanne Land, made a notable contribution to the Bristol Group, the genesis of which is described below.

★ ★ ★ ★ ★

Several working groups set up in the late Eighties enabled more members to take part in Confraternity affairs. One of these was the Research Working Party which first met at Birmingham University in May 1988 under the Chairmanship of Derek Lomax. He had recently become a member of the Council of Europe's specialist Santiago Committee and reported back on their Camino projects, including a major conference at Bamberg in the autumn of that year. Apart from keeping in touch with events in Europe, the main aims of the CSJ Working Party were to identify monuments relating to St James and the pilgrimage and to collect bibliographic material. Over the next couple of years a number of county coordinators were recruited to investigate a particular county from this standpoint. Meetings continued to be held at Birmingham twice a year and progress on different routes and counties reported in the Bulletin. The full title of the project became 'St James the Great and the Pilgrimage in Britain'.

By 1990/1, the Confraternity and its European sister associations were very aware that the first Santiago Holy Year for 11 years would be celebrated in 1993.[4] It would also be the first since the establishment of all the European Jacobean societies with the exception of the Société des Amis de Saint-Jacques (founded in 1950) and the Amigos del Camino de Santiago of Estella (founded in 1962). In order to prepare fully for this special year a further working-party, the 1993 Sub-Committee, was formed in late 1990; the results of its efforts are described in Chapter 5.

★ ★ ★ ★ ★

In the meantime members continued to go on pilgrimage to Spain. There were too many, between 1987 and 1991, to mention them all here, but one pair who attracted more attention than most, wherever they went, were Paul Graham and Charles (Carlos) Paternina who chose old-fashioned penny-farthings as their means of transport.[5] Carlos joined Paul at Burgos, they successfully completed their pilgrimage and Help the Hospices, their chosen charity, benefited by £94,000 from their long penny-farthing ride. Other noteworthy pilgrimages in 1988 included those of Michael Brown, who walked in medieval costume, of Canon Anthony Lathe and Archdeacon Michael Handley who listed in Bulletin 30 the 113 varieties of birds they saw as they cycled between Caen and Finisterre, and of Eileen and Peter FitzGerald who cycled from their Chichester front door to Santiago. These days fewer pilgrims go on pilgrimage on horseback than in the Middle Ages, but in August 1989 Robin and Louella Hanbury-Tenison hired a pair of matching Spanish greys, Duque and Guadalquivir, and rode to Santiago from Roncesvalles. Robin later recounted their adventures in his book *Spanish Pilgrimage: a Canter to St James,* published in 1990, and with Louella spoke at the 1991 AGM.

Two members who had already walked to Santiago were inspired to walk to Rome, Laurie Dennett in mid-1989, and Anthony Brunning in the summer of 1990. Their journeys were remarkable in that both left from their homes in London, and both raised large sums of money, through sponsorship, for multiple sclerosis research and for famine relief in Ethiopia respectively. Anthony, who was following the itinerary taken by Sigeric, Archbishhop of Canterbury 1000 years earlier in 990, literally walked to his new job in Rome, at the headquarters of the De La Salle order, where he was to spend several years.

All the departing Santiago pilgrims were armed with Confraternity accreditation. In the early years the Secretary would issue a simple certificate confirming membership and pilgrimage details, which could then be used as an itinerary sheet and for stamping along the way. This single sheet was developed by James Maple and Marion Marples into a 12-page pilgrim record using parchment-style paper, with a striking covered designed by Julia Ramos. The first stamp in many pilgrim records is that of the cathedral of le Puy or the monastery of Roncesvalles or other starting point. At an Embassy reception in March 1988 (see below), the First Secretary suggested to James that pilgrims might consider presenting their pilgrim records at the Embassy before setting out for Compostela, and receive the Embassy's official stamp and blessing.

In late 1988 it was decided to keep a register of all Confraternity pilgrim members, and a standard form was devised and sent to all those known to have walked or cycled or indeed ridden to Santiago. James Maple, whose idea this was, became the first keeper of the register, a task that was assumed in 1991 by Rosemary Clarke. Now the form is dispatched with the pilgrim record and people are asked to send it back, duly completed, to the Confraternity on their return.

As in earlier years Confraternity pilgrims made good use of our own guides to the routes in France and Spain. The fifth *Pilgrim Guide to Spain*, which benefited from the experiences of 1986 pilgrims, received an official ISBN number for the first time and so became known, through various bibliographical listings, to a potentially wider readership. The first guide to the le Puy route was also produced in 1987, edited by Alfred Peacock of Suffolk, while John Halliday produced the first part of his Arles route guide, from Arles to Castres, to be followed by part II, Castres to Puente la Reina, in 1988. John's sister, Joanne Land, was equally busy and in 1989 the Confraternity published her well-researched booklet on a possible English pilgrim route from Droitwich to Bristol. A second academic occasional paper was published in 1990: Derek Lomax's scholarly *The Order of Santiago*, the subject of his AGM lecture earlier in the year. In 1991 Alison Raju of Nottingham took over the editorship of the le Puy route guide, and the Hengrave Hall conference proceedings were launched at the AGM of that year.

The Bulletin, still edited by Pat Quaife, remained the principal means of communication with members, and became even more important as international membership increased. From no. 20 (March 1987) onwards, its format was reduced to a neater A5 size. The newsletter style of the early years developed into a members' journal, often with an editorial and longer, more academic articles. The special fifth birthday issue, no. 25 of January 1988 – complete with a laminated cover – is a case in point. Six distinguished members all willingly responded to a call from the editor and the articles by Richard Fletcher, Derek Lomax, Richard Reece, Mary Remnant, Brian Tate and Rob Neillands made this issue a particularly 'good read'. George F. Tull, an authority on City of London churches and county coordinator for Surrey and Sussex, wrote on 'The Long Quest for St James' in Bulletin 32, the first of many articles he contributed over the years. This issue also contained a central four-page detachable Pilgrim Blessing, provided by Anthony Brunning, and translated from the French by his colleague, the late Brother David Leo fsc. The Latin text of the medieval rite, dated 1078, is preserved in the Missal of Vich Cathedral, Barcelona and used at the Abbey of Roncesvalles to bless pilgrims at the end of the evening Mass.

Bulletin 39 (June 1991) – the last produced on the Confraternity's electronic typewriter – was a themed issue devoted to the relationship of Britain and Ireland with the pilgrimage, both medieval and modern, to Santiago de Compostela. Members were introduced for the first time to the fifteenth-century English pilgrim, William Wey, through James Hogarth's translation from the Latin of Wey's Itinerary to 'St James in Spain', a journey undertaken in 1456 from Plymouth to La Coruña. Bulletin 40 (December 1991) enjoyed a new look. A shell-patterned border, designed by Clare Venables, enhanced the cover while the contents were word-processed on the Confraternity's new and sophisticated Canon Starwriter 80, with its five fonts, five type sizes and numerous other advanced features.

Books and pamphlets written by members were also featured in the Bulletin at regular intervals. In 1988, shortly before she joined the Confraternity, Magdalena Stork de Yepes published in Spain *La Tierra de Santiago o Jacobsland*, which would later appear in English. Three Confraternity authors had books published in 1989: Mary Remnant with her *Musical Instruments: an Illustrated History from Antiquity to the Present*, Bert Slader with his *Pilgrims' Footsteps: a Walk Along the Ancient Road to Santiago de Compostela* and Hal Bishop with his guidebook *The Way of St James, the GR65, le Puy to Roncesvalles*. All these works, and many others, were added to the Library by Stephen Badger, who pursued an active acquisitions policy. A list of Library additions appeared in each Bulletin, which led to greatly increased use of the Library.

★ ★ ★ ★ ★

If members had much to read between 1987 and 1991, they also had a wealth of Confraternity and foreign events to attend. Some of these formed part of the regular programme of AGMs, lectures, Practical Pilgrim weekends or St James's Day celebrations; others were one-off happenings that took place in a particular year. For reasons of space they cannot all be mentioned individually, but a selection of the highlights of the period will give some idea of the range of activities.

At home, in March 1988, as part of the fifth birthday celebrations, the CSJ President, H.E. the Spanish Ambassador, very kindly hosted a reception at the Spanish Embassy in Belgrave Square. This was the first time that most members had been to the embassy, one of London's finest houses, and the hospitality of the Ambassador and his wife was much appreciated. The Chairman, James Maple, presented D. José with a signed copy of Brian and Marcus Tate's and Pablo Keller's *The Pilgrim Road to Santiago* (1987) in the presence of the authors and the photographer. London members had already met Brian Tate in November 1987 when he gave a lecture entitled 'Routes and Relics' at the Jesuit headquarters in Mount Street, Mayfair. Another interesting

London venue for lectures, used in 1987 and 1988, was Miranda House, Grafton Street, London W.1, the Cultural Centre of the Venezuelan Embassy. This well-restored town house was made available by Dr Miriam Blanco Fombona de Hood, the Cultural Counsellor at the Embassy, who became a Confraternity member in 1989. Jim Hall, author of the admirable 1974 work *Subjects and Symbols in Art*, was the first CSJ lecturer to speak at Miranda House, in September 1987, on 'Subjects and Symbols along the Road to Compostela'. New members' evenings were held in 1988 and 1989 in Soho's Grotto Club – not quite the daring venue its name might indicate, but the basement of the presbytery of the Church of Our Lady of the Assumption and St Gregory. Another church whose new purpose-built social centre the Confraternity would make considerable use of from 1991 onwards was that of St Alban's Holborn, where Marion Marples was a parishioner. Here in November 1991 Paul Graham, lawyer, viticulturist and pilgrim, presided over a meticulously organized Spanish Wine Tasting, one of many fund-raising events held in aid of the Rabanal appeal between 1988 and 1991.

Events were not of course restricted to London – a criticism sometimes made by members in earlier years. A gratifying feature of the 1987-1991 period was the development of three regional Confraternity groups, one on a more formal basis than the others, which gave members a greater choice of area and activity.

July 1988 saw the establishment of the first and most independent of these groups, the Bredereth Sen Jago, or Cornish Confraternity of St James, set up by CSJ members Hilary Shaw and Canon John Cotter (and others). Their first event, organized by Hilary, who became Secretary of the Bredereth, took place in mid-September: a tour of Lostwithiel, Goland and Fowey, to which CSJ members were cordially invited. Over the years, Bredereth members have ranged far and wide over Cornwall organising walks and pilgrimages and collecting information on St James in that county.

The less formal Bristol Group of the Confraternity was also set up in 1988, by Sue Morgan, John Halliday and Joanne Land, with the first event being held in Bristol. John and Joanne were the main speakers, on likely routes taken by English pilgrims through France and on West Country pilgrim routes respectively. The well attended meetings became welcome bi-annual events in the Confraternity calendar until Sue and Maurice Morgan moved to Wales. In 1991 two Leeds members, Ann and Simon Clark, organized a meeting and buffet lunch for North of England members at their home. This led to the formation of the Northern Group which was to arrange annual meetings in the north over the next few years.

Practical Pilgrim events, of which Marion Marples was the main organizer, took place at weekends in a variety of towns and cities: Reading (1987), Bristol (1988), Oxford (1989), Poole (1990) and Leicester (1991). Perhaps the most beautiful setting was Worcester College, Oxford; James Maple, a Worcester graduate, had obtained the consent of the Provost for Practical Pilgrim to be held in the college grounds, with their ancient trees and beautiful lake. The Confraternity children, who attended most events, James Hatts and Iona and Lorna Martin, enjoyed themselves as much as the older members who were busy exchanging information. On the Saturday afternoon Laurie Dennett led a walk round Oxford in search of St James. By happy chance the Ashmolean Museum was holding a small exhibition on pilgrimage which we visited briefly before going on to St Ebbe's church, Christ Church (Oxford's cathedral) and four college chapels where we admired depictions of St James in stained glass and stone as well as New College's painting of the saint by El Greco. In the evening we returned to Worcester College where Mary Remnant entertained us with her lecture-recital 'The Musical Road to Santiago de Compostela', to round off a very full day.

In Leicester in April 1991 Ted and Peggy Harper were the local hosts for Practical Pilgrim, held in the open spaces of Victoria Park, opposite the nineteenth-century church of St James the Greater. A shell-adorned tandem belonging to David and Diane Wesson was a particular attraction, as was James Maple's familiar tent, by now a veteran of Practical Pilgrim sessions. The afternoon was devoted to a walk round Leicester's heritage area, which includes the Tudor Guildhall, the cathedral and the ancient church of St Mary de Castro. Later, Ted and Peggy presented their audio-visual, 'The Way to Santiago' to a large and enthusiastic audience of St James parishioners and Confraternity members.

St James's Day was celebrated each year – mainly in London – even when 25 July fell on a weekday. Our furthest destination in the period 1987 to 1991 was Sandwich and Staple St James in Kent. The first port of call was the former pilgrim hospital of St Bartholomew on the outskirts of Sandwich, now a small square of almshouses clustered round a thirteenth-century chapel. From there, we made our way to Staple St James – where both vineyard and church awaited. After a picnic in the hay barn of Staple Vineyards, we enjoyed a guided sampling of three estate-bottled white wines before moving on to the medieval church of St James. The feature of greatest interest here was the elaborately decorated East Anglian font of around 1480, on one of whose panels stands a fine St James with scallop shell, scrip and other attributes. The last half-hour in Staple was spent in the churchyard reading out greetings from members unable to be present, including the now traditional Chairman's letter from James Maple.

Other St James's Day meetings included a 1989 visit to the Wallace Collection followed by Mass at St James, Spanish Place; a 1990 evening picnic in a north London garden (see Chapter 4) and in 1991 a return visit to the church of St Peter at Marlow. For this occasion the parish priest, Canon Griffiths, put the Hand of St James on display in the church for the duration of the special St James's Day Mass.

In 1988 St James's Day was the focus of a musical celebration on London's South Bank. A good turnout of members occupied the front rows of the Purcell Room where Mary Remnant presented a new version of her Santiago lecture-recital, well supported by Confraternity singers and members adept at turning the handle of the organistrum or playing different backing instruments. Later in the Queen Elizabeth Hall, Philip Pickett's New London Consort, together with a dance company, took the audience on another colourful musical journey through northern Spain. Visitors to London for this 25 July included Jeannine Warcollier from Paris and Joseph and Monique Theubet from Geneva, Joseph (a professional violinist) being the founding president of the Swiss confraternity, the Amis du Chemin de Saint-Jacques, Association Helvétique, set up earlier in the year.

★ ★ ★ ★ ★

Santiago itself was a Confraternity destination once again in October 1987. The week chosen happened to coincide with the Council of Europe's formal adoption of the pilgrimage as 'first European cultural itinerary' and thanks to Jeannine Warcollier the CSJ group was invited to attend the different events. On a grey Friday morning – 23 October – we waited in pouring rain at the Puerta del Camino, across the road from Santo Domingo de Bonaval, on the edge of the old city. Umbrella spokes hovered dangerously at eye level as Santiago residents squeezed through the crowd to cross into the city. Soon distant martial music became louder and the official party, led by the Secretary-General of the Council of Europe, took its place at the corner of Casas Reales and the Puerta del Camino. After two mercifully brief speeches, His

Serene Highness Prince Franz Joseph II of Liechtenstein stepped forward to unveil the first of the Council's direction markers: a blue and gold plaque in the form of a stylized scallop shell. The crowd then squelched along to the Cathedral for a special celebratory Mass, with the *botafumeiro* soaring the length of the transepts time after time. The next port of call was the Hotel de los Reyes Católicos for a formal welcome by the Mayor of Santiago and eight (yes, eight) speeches by political personages. These were followed by the Secretary-General's reading of the Council's formal Santiago de Compostela Declaration, recognizing the pilgrim route as the 'premier European cultural itinerary' and 'highly symbolic in the process of European unification'. Much later in the day we returned to the Cathedral for a multi-lingual pilgrim service in which Amanda Bath and William Griffiths took part, interpreting and offering a prayer respectively on behalf of the Confraternity. At the end of the proceedings the Confraternity singers, led by Mary Remnant, gave an impromptu performance of '*Ad honorem Regis summi*' – a final tribute to St James on an auspicious day.

After two visits to Santiago, the Committee decided in 1989 that members should be given the opportunity of seeing other towns and cities along the Camino. The obvious initial candidates were Burgos and León to which visits were led by Marion Marples and Pat Quaife respectively in 1989 and 1991.

Marion, not a Spanish speaker, admitted to much initial apprehension on the way to Burgos in October 1989 – would all her arrangements materialize, who would be able to speak Spanish for the group? In the event her fears were unfounded as transport arrangements all worked and Binnie Mobsby and Hazel Allport coped admirably with all the Spanish language requirements. Excursions took members south to Santo Domingo de Silos, eastward, along the Camino to San Juan de Ortega, where they were warmly welcomed by the priest, D. José-María Alonso, who ran the large pilgrim *refugio*, and who showed the group the forlorn state of the sixteenth-century hospital buildings and cloister. San Millán de la Cogolla, with its upper monastery of Suso and the tomb of the sixth-century San Millán, was another highlight as were visits to the monastery of Las Huelgas in Burgos and a convivial evening with Pablo Arribas Briones, president of the Burgos Amigos, at which he demonstrated how pilgrims would drink spirits to keep out the cold, setting them alight first to keep the witches away – the ritual of the *queimada*.

The León visit in 1991 was memorable ('unforgettable' was the adjective most of the 20 participants used) for two things. The first was our accommodation for the week: we had the enormous privilege of staying in the monastery of San Isidoro in the heart of León and taking part in the life of the community. The second was the inauguration, on Friday 25 October, by the Bishop of Astorga, of the Refugio Gaucelmo at Rabanal del Camino, in the company of a 15-strong CSJ working party, every resident of the village, and a host of specially invited guests from Spain, France, Germany and elsewhere. A full account of this historic day will be found in Chapter 4.

Spending a week in San Isidoro in October was not for wimps. Within its deep stone walls the temperature at night would drop to freezing or below and everyone quickly learned the word for 'blanket' *(manta)*; these were handed out by the guest-master, D. Francisco Rodríguez, from a huge box at the end of a winding corridor. Our bedrooms had plenty of space for the iron bedsteads but no heating and only cold water in the wash-hand-basins. The domestic haven was the *comedor* (dining-room) which was heated in the evening and which doubled as a meeting room after dinner. Another haven of warmth was the wide terrace-wall to sit out in the sun after lunch, with a splendid view of the great Romanesque tower of San Isidoro.

The only disappointment of the week was the closure of the Cathedral for a major exhibition on medieval music. However there was much else to admire in León, including the *parador*, church and archaeological museum of San Marcos. A day excursion to Astorga and Castrillo de los Polvazares produced some happy and unexpected meetings: first with Anthony Brunning, large rucksack on his back, who had flown from Rome to Madrid the day before and was on the point of walking the 18 kilometres or so to Rabanal; secondly with Alberto Morán, a key figure in the El Bierzo association, in the bar of the Hotel Gaudí; and thirdly, through a mixture of fluke and foresight, our bus met the Rabanal working party's mini-bus on the outskirts of Astorga, where a joyous encounter took place, including the husband-wife reunion of Walter and Mary Ivens. A second day-trip took us eastwards to Sahagún, the Mozarabic church of San Miguel de Escalada, with afternoon sun on the front arcade, and the Cistercian convent of Santa Maria de Gradéfes.

★ ★ ★ ★ ★

In alternate years, when Spain was not on the agenda, long weekend visits were arranged to different parts of the country: Herefordshire (for the second time) in 1988, Cornwall in 1990, and – as an extra and also a repeat – Norfolk in September 1991.

The Confraternity had visited Herefordshire only four years earlier but with so much of sculptural and architectural interest – with a Santiago connection – a repeat visit was organized in mid-October 1988. Kilpeck, Shobdon and Leominster were happily revisited, while we went also to Abbey Dore, Fownhope (with a Herefordshire school of sculpture tympanum), Kempley (frescoes of 1130-1140, including a pilgrim figure) and Dymock (carvings and Tree of Life tympanum). By now Marion's son James was seven and a half and, along with Alfred Peacock and George Tull, contributed a Bulletin account of the weekend:

> 'On Saturday I looked at Kilpeck church. We looked at about 6 churches and we had our lunch in a pub and we went to some more churches and we all had cream tea. Then we went along a single-track road to Ty Caradog, we overshot the drive and got stuck in a ditch. At Ty Caradog the farmer's wife cooked us a wonderful supper. I had triful [sic] for pudding. I got to bed at 12.00 p.m.'

Older members also enjoyed themselves, although Ted Harper who accidentally reversed his car into the ditch mentioned above, in the dark, had some anxious moments. Luckily it was possible to tow the car out of the ditch and drive cautiously on to the remote farmhouse of Ty Caradog, where a huge log fire and copious dinner made up for minor mishaps.

By October 1990 the Bredereth Sen Jago was over two years old and two of its leading members, Hilary Shaw and Rod Pascoe, combined to give a 15-strong Confraternity group a rewarding long weekend in Cornwall, based in Penzance and St Austell. After admiring the fourteenth-century bench-end of St James in the church of St Levan on the Penwith peninsula, walkers made their way along the coastal path, to nearby St Levan's Well and Baptistery, with views of the pounding sea. Later that afternoon stormy weather prevented a planned visit to St Michael's Mount but, wrote Marion Marples later, 'we made up for our disappointment by singing Nancy Rudden's recently composed Pilgrim Hymn at full blast from Chapel Rock – site of a medieval chapel where pilgrims could hear Mass in similar circumstances to ours:

> Centuries of pilgrim feet walk along the Way;
> Centuries of faith and prayer will strengthen us today,
> Refrain West to Compostela from every country came

Those who sought salvation, singing Blessed be St James'

Lostwithiel and Fowey provided more pilgrim experiences, especially the latter where 'standing on the North Gate carpark, it began to be possible to imagine pilgrims gathering here to sail to St James ... We traced the pilgrims' footsteps to the Town Quay and the jettied house at 9 South Street, near the church, where, pilgrims probably stayed.'[6] Sunday's explorations included the muddy site of St James's Chapel at Bellasize, the splendid church of St Neot, filled with fifteenth- and sixteenth-century stained glass, and the thirteenth-century Hospitaller church and Holy Well of St Cleer.

For the second Norfolk weekend in September 1991, some 20 members stayed at the University of East Anglia. After visiting the ruined St Benet's Abbey at Holme and taking a boat to the St James's Hospital chapel (now a barn) at Horning Hall, we were royally entertained by Julie Champeney, a Confraternity member living at Colton. She invited the whole group to afternoon tea in her house, The Malthouse, and in the evening, with her daughter Anna, gave a fascinating lecture on 'Pilgrims, Peasants and *Pallozas*: links with the past in modern Spain'. Earlier in the year Julie and Anna had visited O Cebreiro and a number of other remote villages in Galicia where they had studied in detail the round Celtic-type dwellings with thatched roofs known as *pallozas*. The interiors are (or have been) home to both humans and animals, as the slides demonstrated. On Sunday we descended on Little Melton, where Julie's brother Bob Brett lived and ran his Little Melton Light Railway. It was open to the public every fourth Sunday, and 22 September was the Confraternity's day for a Pilgrim Extravaganza to raise funds for the Rabanal appeal (see Chapter 4 for details of the afternoon).

★ ★ ★ ★ ★

If Confraternity events at home and in Spain were not enough, there was a wealth of conferences, meetings and symposia in Germany, Belgium, France and Spain to keep the most dedicated pilgrim delegate busy.

Among the most memorable of these was the first, a meeting for European pilgrims in Cologne, organized by Herr Herbert Simon and the Sankt-Jakobusbrüderschaft of Düsseldorf in March 1987. Confraternity members who attended were delighted to meet up with two Santiago personalites, José-María Ballesteros and the ebullient Señor Suso (or Jesús Quintela Montero – to give him his full name), known to pilgrims the world over. Elías Valiña was also there to speak

– in slow and easily comprehensible Spanish – on developments along the Camino, a talk which stood out for its clarity and precision. French translations had thoughtfully been provided of the papers given in German. Some relaxed sightseeing took us to a number of Cologne's beautifully restored Romanesque churches as well as the Cathedral where the heartier members climbed the 509 steps up to one of the towers for a stupendous view of the city.

A very different venue in September that year was the town of Jaca in Aragón, where the newly established Spanish Federation of Associations of Amigos del Camino de Santiago held its first international conference in late September, organized by Elías Valiña. Laurie Dennett represented the Confraternity at Jaca and recorded 'some excellent scholarly presentations', agreement on the pilgrim *credencial* and on the norms for administering *refugios*. But with the increasing 'political' significance of the Camino in Spain in terms of tourism and job creation, personal ambition sometimes overrode the ideals of the Jacobean movement, and 'the occasion proved painful and disillusioning for the man who had done most to bring it about ...'[7]

During this particularly busy period, both the Council of Europe – following its October 1987 declaration in Santiago – and the Spanish Federation of Associations organized conferences in quick succession. The first took place near Bamberg in southern Germany in September/ October 1988, a joint effort by the Council of Europe and the Deutsche Sankt-Jakobus-Gesellschaft e.V. based in Aachen. The venue, Schney Castle, was not the romantic edifice the seven Confraternity participants had imagined, but a very functional adult education and conference centre. The theme of the conference was the identification of routes to Santiago through countries other than France or Spain, with the keynote address given by Dr Klaus Herbers, Chairman of the Scientific Committee of the Deutsche St Jakobus-Gesellschaft, on 'Via Peregrinalis ad Sanctum Jacobum'. Non-German delegates were very glad of the simultaneous translations into English and French provided by Council of Europe interpreters.[8] The Bamberg conference also had a particular significance for the Confraternity, as the place where the Chairman, Pat Quaife, met the new Coordinator of the Spanish Federation, D. Ángel Luis Barreda Ferrer for the first time, to discuss what was to become the Rabanal hostel project. A third Council of Europe conference, in conjunction with the Centro Italiano di Studi Compostellani under its dynamic president, Professor Paolo Caucci von Saucken, took place in Viterbo, north of Rome in late September 1989.

With the conference theme 'Traces of the Santiago de Compostela Pilgrimage in European Culture', the Confraternity was represented by Professor Derek Lomax - a leading speaker - together with Anthony Brunning (in Rome for a job interview) and Laurie Dennett (on her way to Rome on foot).[9]

Two contrasting events in autumn 1988 and summer 1989 took place in Santiago de Compostela and León respectively. The first of these was a five-day symposium, organized by the Xunta de Galicia to celebrate the 800th anniversary of the completion of the Pórtico de la Gloria, the wonderful sculpted porch of the west front of Santiago Cathedral. Its full title: 'The *Pórtico de la Gloria* and the art of its epoch' makes clear its important art-historical perspective. Professor George Zarnecki presided over a session on architecture and interior decoration during the last building campaign of Santiago Cathedral, and also spoke on 'English art in the time of the *Pórtico de la Gloria*', while Mary Remnant attended presentations on music in Compostela in the time of the Pórtico and on the musical instruments depicted there. The León conference, entitled 'El Camino de Santiago: la hospitalidad monástica y las peregrinaciones'[10] took place in July 1989 in the monastery of San Isidoro, or Real Colegiata de San Isidoro de León, which itself provided splendid hospitality to the participants. For the week of the conference León became the cultural capital of the Camino, with some 42 papers presented by a series of distinguished speakers, mainly from the Consejo Superior de Investigaciones Científicas of Madrid and a number of Spanish universities. There was no sophisticated interpretation into English or other languages, so some of the foreign participants including Pat Quaife, the Confraternity representative, were glad to be able to read reports of the previous day's papers in the *Diario de León*.

No fewer than six international meetings took place in 1990, the Confraternity's own conference at Hengrave Hall in March being first in date order. Later events were held in Paris, Brussels, Estella, Speyer and Oviedo, too many even for the most dedicated pilgrim conference-goer. The only one where the Confraternity was not represented was that of Oviedo in early December, when the Principado de Asturias organized a conference on 'Las Peregrinaciones a Santiago de Compostela y San Salvador de Oviedo en la Edad Media'.

The Paris meeting – held in the imposing Hotel de Sully (the French 'Monuments Historiques') – in April had a special purpose: to celebrate the 40th anniversary of the founding of the Société des

Amis de Saint-Jacques de Compostelle. Jeannine Warcollier had invited a number of foreign representatives to speak, including Werner Streit from Cologne, Frank Claessen of the Dutch Confraternity and Pat Quaife from London, whose title was 'St Jacques Outre-Manche' or 'St James Across the Channel'. The three days in Paris passed in a whirl of lectures and entertainment, including a pilgrim walk through Paris led by Humbert Jacomet, an enthusiastic and deeply knowledgeable lecturer of the Monuments Historiques, a recital of pilgrim songs from the seventh to the twentieth centuries by Eusebio Goicoechea and María de los Angeles Vezón, a reception and guided tour of Paris's Hotel de Ville, a visit to the Tour Saint-Jacques and finally a visit to the Société's first office in the 20th *arrondissement*.

Two months later the two Belgian associations organized a day meeting in Brussels on 30 June, the hosts being Dr Armand Jacquemin and Dirk Aerts, representing the Secretary-General of the Vlaams Genootschap, Dom Willibrord Mondelaers, who was present but recovering after a long illness. The keynote lecture by Roel Jacobs, 'Brussels, a Town on the Road to Compostela', identified three authentic pilgrim routes into and through the city, after which we walked to the Flemish baroque church of Notre Dame de Bonsecours for the unveiling of a Council of Europe plaque on its façade. This church replaced the chapel of the former hospital of St James, close to the city ramparts. The day ended with an international Mass at Notre Dame, in Flemish, French and Spanish. The five Confraternity members who attended were overwhelmed by the tremendous hospitality of Brussels, notably from Armand and Renée Jacquemin but also from the Hotel de Ville and the Centro Gallego of Brussels.

After a short breathing-space, delegates assembled in Estella (Navarre) the second conference to be organized by the Federation of Spanish associations. Its title 'Camino de Santiago: Camino de Europa' and its theme, the revitalization of the Camino in a European context, emphasized both the cosmopolitan nature of the Camino and the need for services and hospitality to pilgrims along the way. Laurie Dennett gave a brief presentation in Spanish on the Rabanal project, which drew sympathetic applause from the audience and from Millán Bravo Lozano (who spoke later) the famous last words that such 'romantic projects' were likely to come to nothing! Round-table speakers included Odile Lutard on 'Pilgrims and Tourists', Professor Paolo Caucci von Saucken on the safeguarding of the Camino, backed up by Joseph Theubet of the Swiss Association who described how part of the route in Switzerland had been obliterated by a new road. The conference provided much food for thought at the beginning of a new decade – containing two Holy Years – when pilgrim numbers were increasing rapidly.

The last conference of 1990 at which the Confraternity was represented – by John Hatfield – was held in Speyer in Germany, organized by the Sankt-Jakobusbrüdershaft of Düsseldorf. Other delegates came from France, Belgium, Holland and Spain, the latter including the priest from Azofra where the Düsseldorf/Cologne group was helping rebuild a pilgrim refuge. In Speyer, commemorating two millennia of history, the (Catholic) Cathedral authorities had commissioned a statue of a St James pilgrim, placed in the main Maximillianstrasse opposite the Protestant church. Initially there had been strong opposition from the latter, overcome by much diplomatic effort on the part of the Mayor (a pilgrim himself) and the Cathedral. But there was another dimension to this conference, described by John Hatfield in Bulletin 37 (December 1990):

> 'One of the most poignant and moving aspects of the conference, held the weekend after the reunification of Germany, was the talk by the Auxiliary Bishop of Gorlitz, which is located at the eastern border of the unified Germany. He was accompanied by a large group of teenagers from all over the former German Democratic Republic, who last year had participated in the Pope's visit to Santiago. Herr Herbert Simon ... had met the Bishop there and had invited him to Speyer. Gorlitz Cathedral is dedicated to St James and was erected in 1900 in the place of a former St James's church. In medieval times, Gorlitz was on the pilgrim route from Silesia and Poland ... The hope was expressed that perhaps one day an international group of *Jacquaires* might revive the route by travelling eastwards, or starting there, as a symbolic gesture.'

★ ★ ★ ★ ★

In a history of the Confraternity of St James, why put so much emphasis on events in other countries? For two main reasons: first, the international nature of the Camino itself; and second the fact that the Confraternity is one of a network of European Jacobean associations whose aims and work, both practical and academic, are the stronger for being shared with one another.

To conclude this chapter, brief mention must be made of a variety of other events, at home and abroad, which had a direct or indirect connection with St James and the pilgrimage to Santiago.

January 1987: the discovery at Worcester Cathedral of the headless skeleton of a medieval pilgrim, buried at the foot of the south-east tower pier. The pilgrim, identified by a long staff bearing a cockle shell, was wearing knee-length leather boots and vestiges of leather outer clothes.[11]

January 1988: an exhibition of photographs of the Camino by Francis and Marc Oeser in their north London home.

March 1988: an exhibition of Pablo Keller's photographs taken for the book by Brian and Marcus Tate, *The Pilgrim Route to Santiago* (1987), held at the University of Nottingham.

July 1988: beginning of a connection with the church of St James, Garlickhythe, when Marion Marples and Pat Quaife give a lecture on 'St James the Great in the City of London' in St James Garlickhythe, during the City of London festival.

September 1988, the centenary of St James, Killorglin (County Kerry, Ireland) for which Aileen O'Sullivan prepared a travelling exhibition on St James and the pilgrimage.

Mid-1989: founding of the American association of St James, under the title of Friends of the Road to Santiago.

August 1989: Pope John Paul visited Santiago on the occasion of the fourth World Youth Day, addressing some 500,000 young people from all over the world on the slopes of Monte del Gozo.

September 1989: first of a series of biennial pilgrim reunions held by the Dutch association in Maastricht.

Late 1989: establishment of the Centre de Culture Européenne, Saint-Jacques de Compostelle, in the ancient royal abbey of St-Jean-d'Angély in the Charente-Maritime. The Centre is a non-profit-making foundation providing the opportunity for students aged 14 to 18 from different countries to share an educational experience of two weeks studying medieval European civilisation, with the pilgrim route as a unifying theme.

April 1991: 'Twelve Painters Take the Pilgrim Road to Santiago de Compostela', an exhibition at the Francis Kyle Gallery, Maddox Street, London W.1. Painters travelled the route in 1990, prior to the exhibition.

October 1991: the church of St James Garlickhythe was severely damaged by a crane arm and its counterweights crashing through the roof. There were no casualties, but the recently restored church suffered major damage to the floor, walls and roof, the counterweights having penetrated at least four feet into the medieval crypt.

November 1991: in preparation for the 1993 Holy Year, the Comite Pro Xacobeo '93 met for the first time, in London with representatives from the Xunta de Galicia, the Centro Gallego of London, the Universities of Oxford and Birmingham and the Confraternity.

NOTES

1 For further details, see appendix 2, 'The Quest for Constance Storrs', by Mary Remnant.

2 For an appreciation of Elías Valiña, see Laurie Dennett's 'Elías Valiña Sampedro, el Padre del Camino' in Bulletin 34, Feb. 1990, page 7; and her 'Elías Valiña Sampedro and the Camino de Santiago: an Appreciation' in Bulletin 69, March 2000, pp. 3-15.

3 The formal Conference proceedings are still available from the Confraternity Office for £5-50, plus p.&p.

4 A Holy Year occurs at regular intervals of six, five, six and 11 years, when St James's Day, 25 July, falls on a Sunday.

5 For further details, see 'To Spain by Penny-farthing' in Bulletin 26 (March 1988), pp. 3-5. A full account can be found in Paul Graham's *Santiago de Compostela: a Journey to Help the Hospices*, published in 1989 and available in the Library.

6 Marion Marples, 'Confraternity Autumn Visit to Cornwall', in Bulletin 38 (April 1991), pp. 15-17.

7 'Elías Valiña Sampedro and the Camino de Santiago: an appreciation' by Laurie Dennett (Bulletin 69, March 2000, p. 13).

8 See Bulletin 29 (November 1988) for a fuller account of the Bamberg conference. The conference proceedings, *The Santiago de Compostela Pilgrim Routes*, are in the Library.

9 The proceedings of the Viterbo conference, *Les Traces du Pèlerinage à Saint-Jacques de Compostelle dans la Culture Européenne*, are also in the Library.

10 The conference proceedings, under the same title and edited by Horacio Santiago Otero, can be found in the Library.

11 For a full account of this important discovery, see Helen Lubin, *The Worcester Pilgrim ...* edited by Philip Barker, 1990.

Chapter 4
'Giving Something Back'
A Project in the Montes de León

Woven intricately into the strands of Confraternity life between 1987 and 1991 was the Rabanal del Camino 'hostel' project. It came about in two linked ways: through the inspiration of one individual and as a response to the Confraternity's reflections on its future role and activities.

Walter Ivens's 1986 diary, written as he passed through the semi-deserted villages of the Maragatería (between Astorga and Foncebadón), has already been quoted in Chapter 2. On his return from pilgrimage and in the early part of 1987 he continued to think how past pilgrims might 'give something back' to the Camino – in its widest sense – and also benefit future pilgrims. At the September 1987 Committee meeting, he presented a paper in which he suggested 'that a purpose for the Confraternity would be to help in reviving one of these villages ... We could help to convert, with care, some of the old houses into a pilgrims' *hostal*, like the amenities and atmosphere at Cebreiro, but also with a shop to buy provisions. Hopefully the endeavour would attract more commerce/tourism and the village would come to life.' He then raised a series of questions about the size of the project, its cost, organization, fund-raising and so forth for the Committee to consider. The most important of these concerned the Spanish authorities: 'Is the idea practicable in the eyes of the Spanish authorities and would it receive their support? Before any talk of money/investment we need the blessing and moral and physical backing of an Elías Valiña ... Also needed later is full support from the local authorities and trust in a local builder.'

The Committee, chaired by James Maple, greeted the idea with enthusiasm as a potentially significant contribution to expanding the work of the Confraternity and to involving more members in its activities. A detailed questionnaire on the future, devised by Walter Ivens, was sent to members in November 1987 to ascertain their views. The second question: 'In what areas would you like the Confraternity to develop more fully?' included in the four options given: 'Helping to sponsor rebuilding of a hostel/hospice'. This generated much interest. Two months later, at the 1988 AGM and fifth anniversary celebrations,

James, in his Chairman's address, looked to the future and set out the proposal to restore a hostel somewhere along the Camino in Spain to help to bring a village back to life. It was at this meeting that the project formally came into being on the Confraternity side.

From the start, working in cooperation with the Spanish Associations of Amigos and with ecclesiastical and local authorities in Spain was regarded as essential. This took concrete form in April 1988 when a long letter outlining the project was sent both to D. Ángel Luis Barreda Ferrer, the recently elected national coordinator of the Spanish Associations, and to the editor of *Peregrino* magazine, D. José Ignacio Díaz. This letter was being drafted just at the time that *Peregrino* (no. 2, 2a epoca, Marzo 1988) was itself highlighting the deplorable state of some refuges along the Camino Francés, with Rabanal regarded as the worst case. The front cover of this issue consisted of a dramatic picture of the interior of the old schoolroom, including the broken doors on which pilgrims slept, lit by a makeshift candle, with the caption *¡De Vergüenza!* ('For Shame'). The editorial on page three was equally harsh, mentioning 'the crude and dreadful reality of accommodation for pilgrims in the Leonese village of Rabanal del Camino,' despite the fact that the Camino de Santiago had been declared a European Cultural Itinerary by the Council of Europe and was the object of an agreement by three central government ministries and five autonomous regional governments.

Later that year Ángel Luis Barreda wrote to Walter Ivens to say that he had held meetings with the Committee of the El Bierzo Association of Amigos, an active group based in Ponferrada, who had been considering the villages of Rabanal and Foncebadón (six kilometres beyond Rabanal) as possible sites for a refuge (or *refugio*). In the end their President, D. Luis Bacariza Naveira, persuaded the Committee to opt for Rabanal, where he had been the visiting doctor for some years. He was also on good terms with Chonina Alonso, a well-known matriarchal figure in the village who, prior to 1986, had run the Bar Santiago de Compostela on the main road and who had received thousands of pilgrims in her time. The Spanish associations in their turn applauded the idea, so Rabanal del Camino was agreed by all concerned. Ángel Luis Barreda's own enthusiasm for the idea was confirmed informally at the Council of Europe conference held in Bamberg in the autumn: there, he and the Confraternity Secretary, Pat Quaife, with Professor Derek Lomax acting as interpreter, were able to discuss the next steps to be taken, including working with the

El Bierzo Association. Ángel Luis also stressed the importance, in the Camino tradition, of the restored building – the former parish house of Rabanal – being a pilgrim *refugio* to which pilgrims staying overnight could make a donation, rather than a *hostal* which was essentially a commercial operation.

At this point a small amount of pilgrim history might be appropriate. Rabanal del Camino is the historic 'end of the ninth stage' of the *Pilgrim's Guide*, the fifth book of the twelfth-century manuscript compilation, the *Codex Calixtinus* or *Liber Sancti Jacobi*. It lies almost mid-point between Astorga and Ponferrada, two important pilgrim towns in western León, which are separated by some 50 kilometres. It was, and remains, a necessary stopping-point for pilgrims on foot. Over the last 25 years the permanent population of Rabanal has varied between 17 and 28, with an influx of visiting relatives in August.

By 1982, the Holy Year when Jocelyn Rix was on pilgrimage from Canterbury, 'Rabanal del Camino was', she wrote, 'a poor isolated village without even a public telephone ... Pilgrims were accommodated in the old schoolroom. I found the scouts frying bread and *chorizo* for their supper over an enormous camping-gaz stove. The scene was lit by candles for there was no electricity and, apart from the sight and sound of the modern blue gas, was almost medieval.'[1]

Four years later, in 1986, both Laurie Dennett (on foot from Chartres) and Walter Ivens (cycling from Paris) separately passed through the village, Laurie also spending an uncomfortable night in the same schoolroom. '... the floorboards had sprung free of their nails and the roof sagged. The place was filthy, thick with dust and the droppings of birds and bats. We peered about: there seemed nowhere level to unroll the sleeping bags. Three detached doors lay against one wall. These at least would hold the floorboards down. We arranged the sleeping bags on two of them, one on either side of our packs and the candle. The mountain chill was now so extreme that I put on everything I was not already wearing ...'[2]

Almost exactly three years on, in May 1989, Laurie, along with Paul Graham and Walter Ivens, returned to Rabanal in very different circumstances. The 1989 AGM had endorsed the setting-up of the Rabanal appeal, which would be administered by Paul who worked for a Spanish bank in the City; Ángel Luis Barreda had been in negotiations with the Bishop of Astorga, who was prepared to cede the parish house in Rabanal at a peppercorn rent to the El Bierzo Association; and the Association had removed debris of earth and stones which had accumulated in the house. Now it was time for all the parties to meet.

The Confraternity group went first to Ponferrada, where they met Ángel Luis Barreda, and office-holders from the El Bierzo Association, including D. Luis Bacariza, the Vice-President Eulogio (nicknamed El Greco) and the Secretary, D. Alberto Morán Luna, a youngish priest from the Basilica of Nuestra Señora de la Encina. It was agreed between the two associations that the Confraternity would be responsible for fundraising, with an initial target of £50,000, while El Bierzo would be responsible for organising the works programme and seeking gifts in kind from the local community.

In a Confraternity newsletter[3] of Summer 1989, Walter Ivens described their visit to Rabanal itself:

> 'On Monday morning we saw the plans of the site, had a friendly meeting with the Bishop of Astorga, and went on to Rabanal where we were given a superb Maragato regional lunch, organized by Chonina, **the** lady of Rabanal, who now has a new bar (the old one closed down ... in 1986) ... It was a lovely day and the setting of the village is beautiful. The building is perfect for conversion into a hostel. It is a two-storey, L-shaped house fronting the street opposite the church. Parallel to the wing of the L is a barn, making the whole virtually U-shaped, with a patio between and balconies along the L overlooking the patio. At the back there is a field and orchard of about 1000 square metres which can be used for camping, and the house can be renovated without spoiling its character, and turned into a hostel accommodating 30 to 50 pilgrims, as well as the camping facilities.'

Back in London, the Confraternity was holding detailed discussions with the Charity Commission regarding changes to the Constitution. Negotiations were protracted as it was unusual for a registered charity to undertake projects outside Britain, which would not be of obvious educational benefit to the public, as laid down in the Commission's rules. In order to meet its requirements, it was agreed that the *refugio* would have a room set apart as a library and study centre for pilgrims as students of the Camino. Thanks to the tenacity of Stephen Badger, CSJ Treasurer and Librarian, the Commission did finally agree to suitable minor changes to two clauses in the Constitution.

★ ★ ★ ★ ★

With both an agreement with El Bierzo and the revised clauses safely in the Constitution it was time to think of publicity and fund-raising for the Rabanal project. The Sub-Committee member with the most experience of fund-raising for worthy causes was Paul Graham who, with Laurie Dennett, soon produced a draft of a first leaflet, intended for wide distribution to members and their friends, to companies with a Spanish connection, and to charitable trusts. Entitled 'Where are all these people going?', the 'front cover' of the folded leaflet featured a map of the Camino in Spain being followed by an assortment of pilgrims, with Rabanal prominently marked just left of centre. Nearby was the answer to the question: 'They're following the Pilgrim Road to Santiago de Compostela, a route of unique historic, artistic and spiritual importance.' Other sections of the leaflet gave information about the Confraternity, an artist's impression of the rebuilt pilgrim hospice, and three further illustrated sides on 'The Road to Compostela', 'The Need for Shelter' and 'The Confraternity's Project'. A donation form and Freepost reply envelope, destined for Paul at his office, completed this initial appeal package.

For members, the appeal was also featured in the Summer 1989 Newsletter (in which Walter Ivens reported on 'The *Hostal* Project' (as it then was). The target of £50,000 seemed a very large sum at the time but, as Walter wrote, with much prescience, ' ... we can attain the target if we treat it in the pilgrimage sense and take it step by step ... Our membership is now nearly 500. In theory, if each member sets a target of £100 we would be there. The important thing is to set yourself a target, big or small, as the first step to achieving it.'

An immediate and encouraging reaction came from the late Alison Shrubsole, who lived in Rubite (Granada) and who had been on pilgrimage in the summer of 1989. She wrote to Walter Ivens in early August, saying: 'I was delighted to read your article in the Summer Newsletter ... I was in Rabanal in June, walking from León to Santiago, an unforgettable experience. Even though there are various moves afoot to breathe new life into Rabanal (we stayed for instance in newly-built rooms at the Bar Chonina) the idea of a *refugio* provided by the Confraternity is an excellent one and we were most interested to see the proposed building opposite the church.' Alison went on to offer some valuable observations on both fund-raising and the running of a hostel: '[we] noticed that the cleanliness and attractiveness of even the most modest *refugio* was in direct proportion to the amount of supervision it received. And the presence of someone like a youth-

The Parish House, Rabanal del Camino, León, March 1990
(photo: Patricia Quaife)

Refugio Gaucelmo restored, October 1996
(photo: Mary Remnant)

hostel warden ... will appear to be necessary if the idea of the library room – a delightful development – is to work well.... I wish you every possible success and pledge my support to your endeavours.' Another early correspondent with similar good advice was Aileen O'Sullivan, who had extensive experience of running a large retirement institution in London.

Bulletin 32 (August 1989) contained two pieces of good news. The first of these was an announcement that the Confraternity's President, the Spanish Ambassador, D. José Joaquín Puig de la Bellacasa, had offered to host a special reception to launch the Rabanal Hostel Appeal Fund at the Embassy in early November. The second concerned the first fundraising event of the appeal: Phinella Henderson's sponsored parachute jump in late October, her first ever. Sadly, on the day, the weather at Ipswich airport was far too windy and the jump had to be postponed for two weeks. She finally made her descent on 4 November, landed safely ('Gracias a Dios', to quote Alberto) and raised over £700 for the appeal. Other ideas and offers of direct practical help came from Francis Oeser, an architect, Peter FitzGerald, Ted Harper, James Maple, Maurice Morgan and Joanne Land.

To give further impetus to the Appeal, the Confraternity published ten issues of a special four-page newsletter, *Rabanal Hostel Appeal News*, between October 1989 and June 1991. This simple publication, distributed to members with their Bulletin, served several purposes: to keep the appeal in the forefront of people's minds; to report on fund-raising and rebuilding progress; and to acknowledge donors to the appeal. Issue no.1 of the Appeal News, which came out in late October, recorded donations of £4000 for the period September/ October 1989, from 66 individuals (53 of them members) and six companies: an encouraging start, representing nearly one-twelfth of the target sum.

This issue also introduced the idea of a Maragato pilgrim as the emblem of the appeal, the Maragatos historically being carriers or distributors of commercial goods. And, as George Borrow wrote in *The Bible in Spain* (1842), 'no-one accustomed to employ them would hesitate to confide to them the transport of a ton of treasure from the sea of Biscay to Madrid'. The 'ton of treasure' in the case of the appeal would, we hoped, be £50,000, to be collected by a Maragato pilgrim walking from Roncesvalles to Santiago – a distance of some 500 miles – with every £100 advancing our pilgrim one mile along the map of the Camino. Budding artists, including children, were invited to submit a three-inch Maragato pilgrim cutout in a competition to select the appeal emblem, in time for the Embassy reception.

10 November 1989 saw some 75 guests making their way to the Spanish Embassy in Belgrave Square, where they were warmly welcomed by the Ambassador and his wife. The majority were Confraternity members, with a sprinkling of charity and corporate guests. There was also a small Spanish delegation consisting of Alberto Morán, Secretary of the El Bierzo Association and specially invited for the occasion, and D. Jesús Jato, well known to many pilgrims for the *refugio* he ran, with his family, in Villafranca del Bierzo. After speeches by James Maple as Chairman of the Appeal and by the Ambassador, the youngest member present, James Hatts (then aged eight), presented Alberto and the Ambassador with a symbolic cheque for £4,500, representing the funds collected to date. The Maragato pilgrim competition had been won by John Durant of Bristol, a Hispanophile who had designed an impressively dressed figure beating a Maragato drum. His pilgrim was on display on a large-scale map of the Camino, along with photographs of the area, enlargements of the Appeal leaflet, and large colour photographs of the parish house in Rabanal.

★ ★ ★ ★ ★

Fund-raising continued in earnest throughout 1990 and 1991 with nearly every member making a contribution. A major donor, to whom the Confraternity is eternally grateful, was the Bernard Sunley Charitable Foundation which in January 1990, offered matching funding of £10,000, payable in four tranches of £2,500 once the Confraternity had raised £10,000, £20,000, £30,000 and £40,000. Their generosity meant that as early as late January 1990 the appeal fund stood at £12,770, shooting up to £26,625 by mid-June of that year.

One of the first individual donors, Ted Dickinson of Ripon, raised money by working on other people's gardens in his home town. Another was Adrian Wright who ran the 1990 London Marathon in 3 hours, 53 minutes and was sponsored for the Confraternity among other charities. Far away in St David's (Dyfed) Kathleen Timmis was taking visitors on pilgrim walks round the town while Bert Slader gave a lecture on the pilgrimage at Queen's University, Belfast. Both donated the proceeds of their efforts to the Appeal. On the literary/artistic side, Robin Hanbury-Tenison gave royalties from his book *Spanish Pilgrimage: a Canter to St James* and his wife Louella a number of pilgrim tee-shirts, bearing an attractive stencilled scallop-shell, which were eagerly bought by members at AGMs. Marion Marples designed a Rabanal mug, showing a cavalcade of pilgrims, which also sold well, as did a blue Confraternity tee-shirt every sale of which made 50p for the Appeal.

The Confraternity's own main promotion was a Rabanal raffle in 1990, organized by Mary Ivens, the Appeal Committee Secretary. Attractive prizes were on offer: a return flight to Spain given by Pax Travel, a touring bicycle by F.W. Evans Ltd., a beautiful hand-crafted quilt made by Louella Hanbury-Tenison, four cases of wine donated by C. & D.Wines of Beckenham and a number of travel books provided by Rob Neillands. With over 5000 tickets sold, the proceeds boosted the Appeal by a significant £2667. The raffle draw took place on St James's Day, 1990, during an early evening garden party at the Chairman's home in East Finchley. Stephen Badger, in his capacity as Treasurer, supervised proceedings and an unwonted hush fell as James Maple drew the first ticket. Most of the prizes went to non-members but a delighted roar greeted the news that a case of wine had been won by James himself who, as Chairman of the Appeal Committee, had worked so hard on the project.

The Appeal also struck a chord with St James's churches and schools. Special mention should be made of St James the Great R.C. Aided Primary School in Thornton Heath, Surrey. Patricia Chitty, a long-standing member who worked there, introduced the Head to the Confraternity when he was trying to find a suitable statue of St James for the school. Each New Year the school and parish organize a fund-raising One Family Dance in aid of different charities and in February 1991 a most generous cheque arrived for the Appeal.

The Hengrave Hall Conference held in March 1990 provided an opportunity for the Confraternity to present the Rabanal project to the foreign delegates for the first time. This produced an immediate response from Heinrich Bahnen, Secretary of the Aachen-based Deutsche Sanktjakobus-Gesellschaft, who pledged their support for the Appeal. He later wrote a piece for their journal, *Sternenweg,* inviting donations by eurocheque. Later in the year Marion Marples was invited by Heinrich and by the President, Dr Robert Plötz, to attend their AGM and conference in Münster and give a short talk about the hostel project. As Walter Ivens wrote in *Rabanal Hostel Appeal News* no.7, Marion's speech, in German, was well prepared and she received the unexpected reward of a spontaneous whip-round which raised over £700. Heinrich's article continued to bring in a response and the total figure for German donation came to well over £1300.

Other associations also responded generously to a letter sent by James Maple and Pat Quaife to all the European Jacobean groups. The Société des Amis de Saint-Jacques de Compostelle and *Peregrino* magazine sent donations directly and the Belgian Walloon Association sent the proceeds of a special tombola. The Centro Italiano di Studi Compostellani of Perugia promised a splendid gift of books, in response to a general appeal for books for the Rabanal library. These Professor Paolo Caucci von Saucken presented formally to Laurie Dennett and Pat Quaife at the Estella conference in September 1990. Later, in April 1991, Maryjane Dunn Wood, Secretary of the US Friends of the Road to Santiago, presented the Rabanal library with the famous – and highly appropriate - *Guide du Pèlerin de Saint-Jacques de Compostelle,* translated from Book V of the Latin *Liber Sancti Jacobi,* with the Latin and French texts side by side.

What of the Maragato Pilgrim in late 1990? In the summer Paul Graham had posted the Appeal leaflet to donors of his Help the Hospices penny-farthing ride to Santiago in 1989. This mailing brought a huge response and helped us reach a total of £33,000 by early September, taking the Maragato Pilgrim nearly to Astorga on the Camino map.

Back in London the Appeal fund was boosted in November 1990 and February 1991 by two most enjoyable musical events. The first of these was Mary Remnant's lecture-recital, 'The Musical Road to Santiago de Compostela', given at St Joseph's Hall, next door to the Brompton Oratory. This proved to be one of the most successful evenings in the Confraternity's fund-raising calendar, with James Maple and James Hatts (9) giving an expert performance on the organistrum. The church of St Giles, Cripplegate, in the City of London was the venue for a violin and piano recital of French and Spanish music given by Petronella Dittmer and John Martin three months later. The Appeal again benefited from the generosity of the performers.

By late June 1991 the fund stood at £44,720, the last tranche of the Bernard Sunley Charitable Trust having been received, and the pilgrim figure well into Galicia, between Portomarín and Palas do Rei. The target figure of £50,000 was tantalisingly close – would the last £5000+ come in time for a further payment to be sent to Spain for various works? Members' prayers were answered, at the very end of June, by another charitable trust, which asked to remain anonymous. Its donation was just the sum that was needed, a magnificent £5000 which enabled the pilgrim to reach Monte del Gozo, within sight of the spires of Santiago Cathedral, and the Confraternity to reach its target a couple of weeks later.

The administrative work involved in running the Appeal was both considerable and time consuming. Its main burden fell on Walter and Mary Ivens and on Paul Graham, the former two as project Co-ordinator and Secretary who answered countless letters and prepared the ten issues of *Rabanal Hostel Appeal News*, the latter as appeal Treasurer who, in addition to dispatching thousands of leaflets, also received and passed to the Ivens all the Freepost donations that resulted. Between them Walter, Mary and Paul dealt with 640 donations in the period October 1989 to June 1991, of which 617 came from individuals and 23 from companies, churches or trusts. A massive task – and an ongoing one – carried out with unfailing good-humour and efficiency.

June/July 1991 marked a watershed in the project: the £50,000 target met and the first wardens and pilgrims arriving. A second target of a further £25,000 had to be set to cover the proper restoration of the side of the *refugio* and the barn. It was decided that the *Rabanal Hostel Appeal News* had served its purpose, and that further progress reports on fund-raising, building, pilgrims, wardens and Rabanal news generally would revert to the main Bulletin.

Two more fund-raising events completed 1991, a Pilgrim Extravaganza at Little Melton, Norfolk, on 22 September and a Spanish Wine-Tasting presented by Paul Graham in early November, which has been recorded in Chapter 3. Vine Cottage was the Little Melton home of Julie Champeney's brother Bob Brett (also mentioned in Chapter 3), whose pride and joy was his Little Melton Light Railway which ran around the grounds. The railway, complete with volunteer staff, ticket office, points systems and stations, was open every fourth Sunday, with the proceeds going to a charity. Sunday 22 September was the Confraternity's day. Marion Marples efficiently organized CSJ members into their respective roles at the publications table, the produce table, the Rabanal display and different games, while Bob and helpers were getting the railway going. much to the pleasure of James Hatts (10) and other younger visitors. At 2 p.m. the public started to arrive – not, alas, in quite the numbers expected – but sufficient to keep the railway busy and to give all the stalls some custom. Teas were provided by Julie Champeney and helpers, with cakes becoming cheaper as the shadows lengthened. Thanks to an extra donation from a member unable to be present and a generous contribution from the railway operations, the Pilgrim Extravaganza raised a creditable sum and everyone had a happy time.

★ ★ ★ ★ ★

The years 1990 and 1991 were crucial in the rebuilding and conversion work on the parish house at Rabanal. They were equally important for the establishment of a good working relationship between the Confraternity and the El Bierzo Association, through a series of visits to Spain by members of the Appeal Committee and later the working groups who did hard physical labour on the house, barn and meadow.[4]

Laurie Dennett got 1990 off to a promising start, meeting El Bierzo colleagues in Ponferrada in January to discuss the plans for the house. Those that Alberto Morán had brought with him to the Embassy reception two months earlier were very impressive but, it was agreed, too ambitious for the Confraternity to fund, being costed at £125,000. On reconsidering the situation, El Bierzo came up with a more modest, first-phase plan prepared by a well recommended local builder, which would cost £22,500. Laurie, on her return, reported that the most dilapidated part of the house had collapsed further, including part of the roof, and that remedial works were becoming increasingly urgent. In March, Walter and Mary Ivens, Pat Quaife and Laurie visited Ponferrada and Rabanal to discuss the revised estimate with El Bierzo, and a timetable for the works. It was formally agreed to accept the Phase 1 plans, which involved virtually rebuilding the ruined front part of the house, providing an entrance hall, separate showers and WCs, a lounge or *salón,* the library room and stairs to the balcony to what would become the main dormitory. The Confraternity group was pleased to meet El Bierzo's builder, D. Rogelio Valcarce, who seemed genuinely interested in the project. He was able to start the Phase 1 works in mid-to-late April when the worst of the winter weather would be over, and would aim to finish by late July, with pilgrims able to sleep in the house, he hoped, from late June. It was confirmed that the Confraternity would pay for all the structural works while El Bierzo would be responsible for interior works, water supply, lighting, sanitary facilities and the provision of beds and other furniture.

Rogelio's timetable turned out to be on the optimistic side, as a third Confraternity group found when they visited Spain in early July 1990. Laurie Dennett, Paul Graham and James Maple were pleased with the progress made at Rabanal but it was clear that the house could not be ready to accommodate pilgrims that month after all.

Rogelio did promise, however, that the house would be at least wind- and watertight for the first working group visit in October. One of the group's concerns was that the building-stone and finish to be used on the front of the house should be in keeping with the vernacular architecture of the village. Rogelio responded by taking them on a tour of Maragato villages to show them different examples of stonework on buildings he had repaired or converted. At their final meeting with El Bierzo, both sides agreed on the phase 2 works to be carried out, and for which Rogelio would prepare estimates in the near future.

Soon after this meeting, the Confraternity learned, through Ted and Peggy Harper of Leicester, that Rabanal's infamous old schoolhouse was at last being renovated by the municipality for use as a temporary pilgrim refuge, together with a new house opposite. The spur to this long overdue project had apparently been Pope John Paul II's visit to Santiago in August 1989 for World Youth Day, when hundreds of thousands of young pilgrims had travelled the Camino and found Rabanal lacking in facilities, to say the least. Would two refuges in one small village be too many? we wondered. Probably not, was the answer, given the revival of interest in the pilgrimage and the next Holy Year of 1993 on the horizon. Ted and Peggy were also the first to meet the refuge's immediate next-door neighbours, Asumpta Oriol and Charo Carrión from Madrid, who would play such an important role in the next few years. Later in the summer, thanks to information and photographs received from other members, we learned that the exterior of the new part of the parish house had been completed, including the stonework, which was very attractive.

In September 1990 we heard with much sadness of the death, from cancer, of the President of the El Bierzo Association, D. Luis Bacariza, whose last public appearance had been at O Cebreiro, for the unveiling of a memorial bust to the late Elías Valiña. He was succeeded by D. Porfirio Fernández Rodríguez, head of a construction company, president of a number of local organizations and a local benefactor in the El Bierzo area. The October working group, consisting of John Durant, Jonathan Ingham, Walter Ivens, Joe May, Maurice Morgan and Roger Tisseau, were shown great hospitality by D. Porfirio and his wife, who served them with a typical Maragato dinner at their home in Compostilla.

A huge debt is owed by the Confraternity to the members of this first working group. Although good progress had been made with the building works there was a mountain of work to do in the meadow, patio and exterior generally. A first and vital question was whether it was possible to stay in the house. It would have been just possible, but under very rough conditions and not conducive to hard physical labour in mostly cold and wet conditions. St James was at hand however, in the shape of Alberto Morán, who solved the accommodation problem by putting the group in the house being built for his parents in Molinaseca. It had no interior doors at the time but it was warm and dry and partly furnished, and everyone was very comfortable. An article in Bulletin 37 (December 1990) gave readers a vivid picture of what the working group achieved:

> 'We cleared the garden of wooden beams, one of which even six of us failed to lift. We finally dragged it, using a primitive roller system, and added it to the pile in the paddock, about six tons in all. We pruned the dreadfully overgrown fruit trees using methods that Tarzan would have approved of. Meanwhile the two-foot high jungle of brambles and weeds was torn out by the roots. We removed from the pathway to the paddock the accumulated earth of years and got back to the original cobbles and ... we shifted a further pile of wood that will provide firewood for the hostel for years. All the clearing culminated in a bonfire that not only stopped Maurice Morgan working on his laid stone paving of the entrance, it stopped the builders working on the other side of the village! Joe May, whose bright idea it was, was deafened by the howls of protest in a variety of languages (and language).'

The work the group carried out was only part of the fruits of their visit. They established a definite presence in Rabanal and a very good relationship with the village. There were also meetings with the Bishop of Astorga and the El Bierzo Association to plan and to iron out the inevitable problems – all in Spanish, of course, with Walter Ivens leading the discussions, supported by the other Spanish speakers, Roger Tisseau and John Durant.

In addition the group was delighted to meet the immediate neighbours, Asumpta and Charo, who had been living next door since October 1989. The former related how on 2 December 1989, when they were in the church of Santa María close by, they had heard a noise like a bomb going off. On emerging, they realized that part of the parish house had collapsed. An enormous crack also appeared in Asumpta's bedroom, on the other side of the party wall. Following their representations to the Bishop of Astorga, his works foreman visited, cut a load-bearing beam which was on the verge of splitting and filled in the crack. The two Madrileñas, who spoke good English, were able to give the Confraternity group useful information about the village.

Perhaps best of all they were given a glimpse of the future through the arrival one day of John and Sarah, two young pilgrims from Scotland who had just walked from Astorga. Their first question was: 'How can we help?' A swift answer came: 'Shovelling the rubble out of the upper storey'. John set to with a will and some time later came the question of where they could stay for the night. The answer seemed obvious, so one of the small rooms was cleared and builders' insulation panels laid on the floor to make the base of a warm bed, and so they became the first pilgrims to stay in the hostel.[5] 'Their cheerful pilgrim faces and readiness to help demonstrated the worth of every bit of work that we had done', wrote Walter in his Bulletin article. 'It provided just a peep into the future of the hostel and showed us all how the project is not just a building, but a living entity that will benefit pilgrims and the local community far into the future.'

When Paul Graham and Walter and Mary Ivens visited Rabanal again in April 1991 they were thrilled to find that great progress had been made in the new building, including the installation of the *servicios,* which were in working order, tiling on floors both upstairs and downstairs, doors and windows in place and the walls and ceilings ready for painting. They estimated that the *refugio* would be ready by May/June, especially as a final pre-opening working group would be spending a week there putting the finishing touches to the building. By this time Rabanal had two bars, Chonina's on the main square receiving much custom from cyclists and Antonio's Bar/Mesón El Refugio on the Camino Real, just up from the church and a few seconds' walk from the *refugio*. Setting the pattern for the future wardens, Paul, Mary and Walter visited both and also had the pleasure of seeing Asumpta and Charo, the friendly and helpful neighbours first encountered in October the year before. Appeal Committee visits meant hard work as well: to meetings with El Bierzo colleagues was added on this occasion a series of newspaper and radio interviews, in which Walter dealt with numerous questions, stressing the cooperative nature of the project and the Confraternity's desire also to help bring more life to Rabanal.

Two other pieces of Rabanal news were reported in *Rabanal Hostel Appeal News*, no. 9 (April 1991). The first mention was made of a statue of St James being carved by the sculptor Beauford Linley for the empty niche on the façade of the house. This was being given anonymously in memory of Elías Valiña of O Cebreiro and would be installed in time for the inauguration ceremony in late October. Elías had visited the house at Rabanal in mid–1989 and commented in a note that it would need much work done on it. If anyone was qualified to comment he was, having laboured intensively to renovate and rebuild the church and *hospedería* at Cebreiro more than 30 years earlier. Members also learned that two couples, one Belgian, one English, and all four past pilgrims, had offered to be wardens for periods of two months, from June through to the end of September. The Belgian pair, whose names were not known at this stage, were in touch with *Peregrino* magazine, while David and Diane Wesson from Yorkshire had volunteered at the 1991 AGM to be responsible for the later period.

Before then, a second working group, led by Stephen Badger, spent an intensive week in Rabanal in early June. They had the exciting task of preparing the *refugio* for the first pilgrims and indeed receiving the first official pilgrims. Stephen, Amanda Bath, Roger Cocks, Martin Hockey, Jonathan Ingham and Joanne Land gave the house a thorough cleaning, tidied the garden, planted flowers, uncovered the old cobbled pathway down to the meadow, spread gravel in front of the entrance and made a stone tub for plants by the front door. They also put together 12 bunk beds (sleeping 24), with mattresses, mattress-covers and blankets, constructed shelving in the library and took the first steps towards establishing the library/study-centre. Early on they enjoyed an outing to a wholesale warehouse in Ponferrada with Alberto Morán and Porfirio Fernandez, to select cleaning equipment, paid for by El Bierzo.

A pilgrim record book, donated by Alberto, was placed in the front hall, alongside a second book, listing the donations made by pilgrims. (After much discussion in London and Ponferrada, it had been agreed not to make a set charge for the night but to invite pilgrims, in several languages, to make a contribution towards the maintenance of the *refugio*.) The first two places in the pilgrim record book, with a date of 8 June 1991, went, appropriately to two Spaniards who were doing much to revive the pilgrimage, José Ignacio Díaz, editor of *Peregrino* magazine, and Ángel Luis Barreda, Coordinator of the Spanish Federation of Associations. Their entry for that date eloquently sums up the spirit in which the *refugio* was conceived and developed:

'We have had the good fortune to be the first pilgrims on foot to be welcomed into this refuge. When we visited this place with Walter Ivens and other members of the Confraternity, we never imagined that this hopeful project would become a reality.

'Faithful to the spirit in which this refuge of Rabanal del Camino was born, we want it to be a place of welcome for pilgrims, a meeting point for those who come here from all over Europe, and hope that in the future it can become a study centre and place of rest for all those seeking the roots of European faith and spirituality. Thank you for your hospitality.'

Asumpta and Charo helpfully orientated the working group to village customs. They were shown where to throw rubbish, and given various other pointers on how to create a good impression locally. Joanne Land's flower-planting activities were much commented on and admired, according to the *Madrileñas* and by the end of the week the group was more or less considered to be *buena gente*. They patronized both bars in the village and on several days gave 'tours' of the *refugio*, mostly to visitors from other villages and towns.

The reaction of the people of Rabanal to the project was the first question the Bishop of Astorga put to the Confraternity group, and to Alberto and Porfirio, at their meeting with him on 10 June. Reassured on this point, the Bishop went on to say that he would be willing to bless and inaugurate the *refugio* on Friday 25 October, with a Mass at 12 noon, followed by a reception. This date meant that the CSJ group spending a week in León could be present, as well as an October Rabanal working group. Charo and Asumpta advised that it would be very important to invite the whole village to the event. The following day Alberto gave the house an informal blessing. After a prayer, and a song he had composed, holy water was sprinkled and a sprig of wild cherry placed in each room. It was a simple, moving ceremony and everyone felt that Walter and Mary Ivens and all those who had helped realize the dream were there in spirit.

The important question of the name of the *refugio* was jointly decided in early 1991. Antolín de Cela, the senior priest at Nuestra Señora de la Encina and an El Bierzo Committee member, put forward *Refugio Gaucelmo*, Gaucelmo being a late eleventh/early twelfth-century hermit who had lived in a cave or grotto near Foncebadón. Wanting to give practical and spiritual help to pilgrims on their way to Santiago, he obtained the support of the then Bishop of Astorga, Don Pelayo, and the approval of King Alfonso VI to build a church, hospital and refuge *(iglesia, hospital y alberguería)* in Foncebadón. This he achieved, with the help of fellow hermits, and the ruins can still be seen today on the outskirts of the village. It seemed fitting to everyone concerned that nearly 900 years later there should be another Refugio Gaucelmo, just down the road at Rabanal, again achieved with the support and blessing of the Bishop of Astorga. So 'Refugio Gaucelmo' it was, and the El Bierzo Association went ahead and ordered a solid brass plaque bearing that name to be affixed to the front of the house, for unveiling at the October inauguration.

There were, inevitably, problems of different kinds and not everyone in Rabanal was well disposed to the new *refugio*. The then village president had wanted to buy the property from the diocese for his private use and, having a family link with the new bar, was resentful of Chonina (whose bar had reopened in 1989) and her friendly relationship with the Confraternity. In addition, the priest responsible for the village, who had lived for a number of years in Astorga, made strong representations to the Bishop about his need for an office to receive parishioners and pilgrims in the refurbished house, which would have taken up a much-needed room on the ground-floor. Fortunately the Bishop managed to solve this problem by persuading the priest to accept a posting in Bolivia and the Confraternity heard no more about it. On the administrative side, the Town Hall *(ayuntamiento)* of Santa Colomba de Somoza, the local authority for Rabanal, put various obstacles in the way of the El Bierzo Association, taking a long time to approve the plans, and demanding excessive sums for local tax and for the water to be connected. (Rumour had it that the Mayor was keen to attract pilgrims to Santa Colomba and would not succeed if the Rabanal *refugio* went ahead.) This time it was Alberto who solved the problems, although not without the expenditure of much time and effort.

Even pilgrims posed problems at times, particularly groups, something we were not really prepared for. Soon after the departure of the June working group, the first wardens arrived, Etienne and Nelly van Wonterghem-Teirlinck who lived near Bruges and who were multilingual former pilgrims very much in sympathy with the idea of the *refugio*. All had gone well during their first two weeks with a flow of 123 pilgrims on foot and 42 on bicycles. A non-pilgrim visitor to Rabanal in mid-July was Pat Quaife, on her way from León to Santiago (not on foot), preparing for the León visit in October (see Chapter 3), and meeting with El Bierzo colleagues to finalize arrangements for the October inauguration. She was delighted to see the *refugio* looking so solid, welcoming and well cared for and found the contrast with 16 months earlier quite amazing. Putting her possessions on an upper bunk in the main dormitory she went off to meet Etienne and Nelly and check that they were happy for her to stay there. They persuaded her to take a bed in one of the small rooms, which she might or might not then have to herself. In the event around 7 p.m. a 12-strong group of walkers (all from the same country) arrived and were given beds mainly in the smaller rooms as most of the dormitory beds had already been taken. The group went off to the Bar El Refugio where they stayed for over five hours, returning around 1.30 in the morning, the men all in a state of great inebriation. They spent the rest of the night making an unbelievable amount of noise: heavy footsteps, banging doors, loud conversation and worst of all – being physically sick in the most audible fashion possible. Etienne spent much of the night coping with them, and sleep was impossible until 5 a.m. or so, by which time walkers were wanting to make an early start. This sort of thing had never happened before and Etienne and Nelly were mortified by the event, although it could not have been foreseen.

Both they and Pat discovered, independently, that the group was not a pilgrim one but on a walking holiday organized by a certain travel company, which was taking a lot of money from people and then using *refugios* along the Camino for their accommodation. This unfortunate incident immediately gave rise to a new Gaucelmo rule, that the *refugio* doors are locked at 11 p.m. (in addition to the 'no-smoking' rule and the request for silence after 11). It also precipitated an ongoing debate about the need for priority for individual pilgrims and how to deal with groups of different sizes – both walkers and cyclists – who could well have a supporting mini-bus or cars to carry luggage etc. Etienne undertook to write to the offending travel company to say their clients would not be welcome in the future and Pat contacted Ángel Luis Barreda about a Spanish tour operator that was also making blatant use of pilgrim refuges for holiday-makers.

Pat also had the pleasure of meeting Asumpta and Charo for the first time. They were so horrified by her account of her first night in the *refugio* that they kindly invited her to spend the next two nights with them. She was able to learn from them a great deal of useful information about life in Rabanal and the different personalities involved. At the end of her stay, Charo presented Pat with a most beautiful *Libro de Oro* that she, a book-binder by profession, had made for the Confraternity to record the names of donors to the Hostel Appeal, the wardens and working groups, past and future, participating in the *refugio*.

The Refugio Gaucelmo was extremely lucky with its inaugural wardens in 1991. Etienne and Nelly, with their multitude of pilgrim connections, were 'a gift beyond all reasonable expectations' wrote the second warden, David Wesson, in a letter from Rabanal to Mary and Walter Ivens.. 'Not only were they deeply experienced in the Camino, having walked it many times, … but they were ideal ambassadors. By the time I got here [in late July] they were obviously highly regarded in the village, and so that first and crucial bridge had been crossed. It is no longer 'the English refuge' but Refugio Gaucelmo as far as Rabanal is concerned, as Alberto Morán reported when I met him.' David continued to offer the warmth and care that pilgrims had enjoyed in the first two months, and the tradition of providing a simple breakfast for pilgrims to help them on the long road to Molinaseca or Ponferrada.

One of David's letters described a small ceremony at Gaucelmo in early September. His wife Diane had taken a series of photographs of St James on the Camino which had been framed and hung on the walls of the *salón*. The whole village was invited to the opening and David made a short speech to thank them for coming. Asumpta Oriol, replied in English on behalf of the village, saying that they had enjoyed themselves, that they admired the photographs, that they were impressed with the immaculate cleanliness of the house and that the *señora* was to be congratulated. At this point, David could not refrain from reminding them that for seven weeks *el señor* had kept it clean on his own.

Etienne, Nelly and David also kept meticulous pilgrim statistics, which have been continued by every warden since. In the first two months, from early June to 8 August, 1030 pilgrims stayed a night in the *refugio*, and made voluntary donations of over 200,000 *pesetas*. By the end of September the figure for pilgrims had risen to 1814, including 1515 walkers, 297 cyclists, two riders, two horses and a donkey called Peregrino. Twenty-eight different countries were represented, including New Zealand – the exact antipodes of Spain – the majority (over 1100) coming from Spain, followed by Germany, France, Belgium, Holland, England and Switzerland.

★ ★ ★ ★ ★

October was fast approaching, and the long-awaited inauguration on the 25th of the month. The 15-strong working group arrived by mini-bus, driven by Joe May or Walter Ivens, with a precious passenger behind the back seat: the statue of St James, snugly wrapped in foam rubber and blankets, and destined to be installed in its niche on the façade of the *refugio*. As John Durant wrote in his report in Bulletin 41 (January 1992) the working group's task in 1991 was much more complicated than it had been a year ago, with a range of skills required, including masonry, carpentry, diplomacy, calligraphy, accountancy, cookery, gardening and musical ability.

'On Tuesday muffled cries of shock were heard from the washroom as people experienced the effect of ice-cold water for their morning ablutions. Breakfast was in the kitchen with water heated on a calor gas stove which had only one ring working. After breakfast we went out into the cold sunlight to see what needed to be done before Friday and then had a meeting to decide who should do what. John Hatfield started clearing the well in the meadow. Joe began the task of readying the statue for its installation, drilling holes for retaining pegs in it and its niche. Walter cleared and started the old kitchen stove, Ken Thomas and Peter FitzGerald replaced the rotten boards in the kitchen floor, Marion Marples sorted out the library, Sue Morgan started writing notices in impressive script, and Ted Dickinson got his chainsaw working and began to make inroads on the huge pile of old timbers in the meadow. The others ... set about doing less dramatic but necessary tasks. The next day it was another fine, cold morning. A lorry with a crane appeared and Joe and the builder's foreman, Jesús, raised St James into his niche. Joe's careful preparations paid off, the pegs went into their holes without a hitch and the statue was bedded into concrete in which a Spanish and British coin had been placed. It was a very smooth operation, as it should have been in the hands of Jesús and Joseph, and elicited applause from the onlookers.' Preparations continued on Wednesday afternoon and Thursday, with Marion's recorder often heard as she rehearsed for the nerve-racking task of playing solo at the inauguration Mass. During Thursday afternoon there was a constant procession of group members going next door to Charo and Asumpta's house for a hot shower, a typical example of their kindness and generosity. Meanwhile a party led by Walter Ivens went into Astorga with Alberto to discuss final arrangements for the Mass with the Bishop and were surprised by his informality in opening the palace door himself when they rang the bell.'

Friday 25 October dawned warmer but cloudier. At Rabanal the day started at 6 a.m. for working group members. At San Isidoro the León group had a more leisurely start, setting off in their coach for Astorga and Rabanal at 10. There were three extra people on the coach by special invitation: the three Sisters from San Isidoro, who had been in León only a month and for whom this was their first excursion outside the city. At 11 a small procession left from the Cathedral in Astorga: the coach, the British Embassy car containing Sir William (the Military Attaché) and Lady Mahon, their son James, and Jane Rabagliati, First Secretary and Confraternity member, and the car of José Carlos Rodríguez and his wife, of the La Rioja Association, whom Pat Quaife had met at breakfast in a bar in Astorga.

The account which follows of the day's ceremonies and events is taken from an article by Mary Ivens and Pat Quaife which appeared in Bulletin 41 (January 1992).

'Rabanal was, of course, the focal point of the day and the convoy arrived at 11.45 to join the nearly full parking space in the main square outside Chonina's bar. A flock of sheep was crossing the road and disappeared up a path. Villagers and visitors were walking up to the *refugio* and to the church where all was ready for the special Mass. The Maragato and El Bierzo dancers arrived, dressed in their traditional costumes, the women wearing mainly black or red skirts covered with embroidered aprons, and silk scarves over their shoulders and heads. The men wore black breeches and jacket with bright embroidered sashes and black hats. Their castanets were decorated with coloured streamers which flew in the air as the clack, clack-a-clack noise sounded round the smaller square between the *refugio* and the church. The church bells had been summoning people since 11.30 with a strange, rhythmic cannon-fire of sound initially, followed at noon by 12 long clanging notes.

'The Bishop of Astorga, Monseñor Antonio Briva Mirabent, dressed in his scarlet and gold chasuble and mitre and assisted by Alberto Morán and seven other priests, began saying the Mass in the overflowing church. The tiny statue of St James had been moved from its usual place high on the south wall to a more prominent position to the left of the altar. The first sound was Marion's recorder leading us into the well-known hymn 'To Be a Pilgrim' which was followed by Bible readings in English and Spanish and bidding prayers. Two Taizé chants brought by Audrey Schmitt were included and Confraternity members were able to join in as the music had been distributed at the beginning of the week. In the gallery, Maximiliano, the Maragato piper-drummer, played at the consecration. Offerings were made by El Bierzo and Confraternity members: a pair of boots, a Spanish and an English book on the pilgrimage, some stones and pilgrim shells. The Bishop allowed Anglicans to take Communion, thus emphasizing the joint nature of the day's celebration.

'After the Mass everyone gathered outside the *refugio*, in the small square. Looking down on them from his niche on the upper wall of the façade was the new statue of St James, carved in Grantham from white Ancaster stone. He is a metre tall and represents a pilgrim St James with one foot forward, holding his staff and book and with a shell on his upturned hat. In his speech the Bishop made a reference to *'los Quijotes de Inglaterra'* not meaning that we were tilting at windmills, but that we were idealists, and that the ideal had become a reality. He then formally blessed the building and the statue, sprinkling holy water round the front elevation from a small ceremonial bucket. More speeches followed, mainly in Spanish from Jane Rabagliati of the British Embassy in Madrid, Walter Ivens, Alberto Morán and the representative of the Junta of Castile and León: two specially invited guests also spoke briefly: D. Jaime García Rodríguez, the Santiago Cathedral canon in charge of the Pilgrim Office there, and D. José Carro Otero, Xunta de Galicia Commissioner for Holy Year 1993 and himself a Maragato. Amanda Bath read a letter in English and Spanish from the Confraternity President, H.E. The Spanish Ambassador, D. Felipe de la Morena. She was followed at the microphone by Herr Herbert Simon from Cologne, who stressed how the example of Rabanal had inspired his own association to undertake restoration work at Azofra and Hospital de Orbigo. Finally the Bishop unveiled the brass commemorative plaque at the entrance, sweeping aside the Spanish flag which been covering it. This Alberto swiftly rescued so that it didn't touch the ground. In the meantime cameras had been clicking, video cameras whirring and the onlookers increasingly conscious of the cold creeping up their legs as the wind eddied round the square.

'With the end of the speeches came the turn of the Maragato musicians and dancers. To the sound of the pipe, drum and castanets, the dancers moved in circles, in couples, using centuries-old dance steps. Starting from the front square they slowly moved through the house and patio and into the meadow to eat and dance again in turn.

'Much work had been going on in the kitchen and the meadow. There three long trestle tables had been laid out, covered with plates of *tapas* and more filling dishes of hot sausages, *empanadas, tortillas,* 50

Ian Tweedie with Maragato dancer, Inauguration of Refugio Gaucelmo, 25 October 1991

Joseph May mending the roof of the Gaucelmo barn, 1998

loaves of bread and three kilograms of *chorizo*. Numerous bottles of local wine were opened (144 in fact) and the feast began. About 200 people enjoyed the meal, talking, laughing, even singing, in diverse European languages. The visitors were invited to dance – a great privilege – and several British members took the opportunity, notably Audrey Schmitt and John Fitzgibbon, the latter resplendent in his black and red cloak. Ian Tweedie, a member of the León group, was wearing his kilt and was a great hit with everybody. He was the subject of numerous photographs, one of which appeared the next morning on the front page of the local Astorga newspaper.

'Many people had travelled for days to be in Rabanal for 25 October. The first wardens, Etienne and Nelly van Wonterghem-Teirlinck, came from their home in Bernem, near Bruges, Herbert and Liliana Simon from Cologne and Brother Anthony Brunning from Rome, by plane, train and on foot. France was represented by Mademoiselle Jeannine Warcollier, who had brought a special letter from Monsieur René de la Coste-Messelière, President of the Société des Amis de Saint-Jacques, and Monsieur and Madame Mihatsch. Another letter had arrived from Ángel Luis Barreda, Co-ordinator of the Spanish Associations, who for reasons connected with his work, was unable to be present. But a number of other friends and colleagues from all along the Camino were there: Maribel Roncal from Cizur Menor, José Ignacio Díaz from Santo Domingo de la Calzada, Flora Ballesteros and Gustavo Alvarez (custodians of the Astorga Cathedral museum and formerly resident in Tunbridge Wells), Luciano Armas Vázquez from Lugo, Jesús Jato from Villafranca del Bierzo and Magdalena Stork de Yepes from La Coruña. Many members of the El Bierzo Association were present, including their President Porfirio Rodriguez. The feeling of friendliness and joy was palpable: one of the older men of Rabanal was quite overcome with emotion at the *vino español* because of the presence of the Bishop, the Press and visitors from Madrid, Santiago and abroad. Rabanal was famous.

'Back in the *refugio*, the Bishop signed the visitors' book and was given a tour of the building. A cosy log fire was burning in the hearth of the *salón*, the books with their new bookplates were admired in the library, and in the kitchen the old-fashioned range gave out a comforting warmth. After his tour the bishop was presented with a commemorative gift by Marion Marples. This was a copy in Spanish of Brian and Marcus Tate's and Pablo Keller's book, *The Pilgrimage to Santiago*, but with some special features. Dr Owen Gilbert had made a slipcase for it, edged with black leather, and given the book a purple marker ribbon, while Julia Ramos had designed and made a special large decorative bookplate in pale watercolours, with a suitable inscription. The Bishop seemed delighted with his gift, which was much admired by all who saw it.

'In the meantime the first spots of rain were ignored and the party continued. One happy member of the working group found Jesús Jato's *queimada* overwhelming and took to his bunk to sleep until it was time for dinner. Others who needed a quiet time retired to one of the two bars for coffee and just before 5 p.m. the rain came down in earnest. It sent some people homeward and sent the León group back to their coach for a quick look in fading light at Foncebadón and the Cruz de Ferro.

'Later the working group had supper in the two bars. The meal at Chonina's developed into a sing-song during which Walter Ivens revealed a hitherto hidden talent as expert on the castanets. Marion made a telephone call to Mary Remnant's house in London where, following a special Mass at the Brompton Oratory, an informal Rabanal party was in full swing with about 20 members and a representative from the Spanish Embassy. They had earlier sent a telegram to the Refugio Gaucelmo and were delighted to hear Marion speaking from Chonina's. That night the main dormitory of the *refugio* was crowded, with the working group members plus Phinella Henderson and Paul Graham who were also staying overnight and seven pilgrims, including three mystical dancers from Mexico.

'Before returning to Santander and Plymouth the working group enjoyed a large dinner at Alberto's parents' house in Molinaseca on the Saturday night, followed by a clearing-up day in Rabanal. Several bags of rubbish were taken to the village dump, and hundreds of windfall apples picked up from the meadow for the villagers to give to their pigs. That afternoon people who stayed in the hostel found themselves acting as guides to car-loads of sightseers who had read about the inauguration in one of the three different newspaper reports or heard about it on one of two local radio programmes to which Walter had contributed. Final dinners at the two bars and farewells were followed by drinks, dancing and singing at Charo and Asumpta's house. Next morning, alarm clocks went off around 5, the Refugio Gaucelmo was tidied for the last time in 1991 and a notice saying *CERRADO* fixed to the front door. The *refugio*, well and truly opened three days earlier, was left in the care of its winter warden, the plump kitchen mouse.'

★ ★ ★ ★ ★

If 25 October in Rabanal was the culmination of four years' work by numerous people, it was equally the start of a new phase in the life of the Confraternity, of the El Bierzo Association and of the village itself. Back in London, Appeal Committee members spent the last two months of 1991 planning more working groups (especially for the barn), more fund-raising and organising wardens for 1992.

At the end of the year, thanks to New York member, Ronald R. Atkins and the Washington-based International Center for Medieval Art (ICMA), an appeal for funds was launched for Rabanal in the USA. Ron Atkins wrote to both Confraternity and ICMA members on the subject of Rabanal, the success of the first phase of fund-raising and the work needed to complete the project. Eleven people offered their services as wardens. Rabanal was now an integral part of Confraternity activities and 1992 looked as if it too would be an interesting year.

NOTES

1   An extract from Jocelyn Rix's account of her pilgrimage, deposited in the CSJ Library.
2   Laurie Dennett, *A Hug for the Apostle* (1987), pp 181-2. A copy of this book can also be found in the Library.
3   Short newsletters were published when, for various reasons, it was not possible to produce a full Bulletin.
4   All participants, whether on an Appeal Committee visit or as a member of a working group, paid their own travel and subsistence costs.
5   There was a certain amount of competition between pilgrims as to who was the first to stay in the refuge. The different claims are set out in Appendix 3, 'Rabanal's First Pilgrims'.

Chapter 5
The 1993 Holy Year
prelude and aftermath

The inauguration of the Refugio Gaucelmo in Rabanal was, we realized, the start of a new era for the Confraternity. While 25 October 1991 had been the culmination of a huge amount of work by many people, the *refugio* would now be an on-going commitment in terms of its management, provision of wardens, maintenance and repairs and, very importantly, liaison with the El Bierzo Association and other organizations in Spain.

Over the next three years the Confraternity had two major preoccupations: the running of the Refugio Gaucelmo and the advent of the first Holy Year for 11 years. That of 1993 would be the first in the lifetime of all the European associations except for the Société des Amis de Saint-Jacques de Compostelle (founded in 1950) and the Amigos del Camino de Santiago de Estella (founded in 1962). Confraternity preparations for the Holy Year had been under way since mid-1991, with the setting-up of the 1993 Sub-Committee to plan a programme of events. The year was also the tenth anniversary of the founding of the CSJ in 1983, an additional reason for celebration.

However, Holy Years and anniversaries not withstanding, the established activities of lectures, visits to Spain, walks and pilgrimages, 'Practical Pilgrim' days or weekends and Bristol and Northern group meetings continued to take place through the three years. The Confraternity also worked with other organizations in the UK, notably the University of Reading, the Horniman Museum in London and the Bredereth Sen Jago in Cornwall. Further afield in Europe, members participated in the increasing number of events organized by our sister associations, most notably a 1993 colloquium in Toulouse and, in August 1994, a pilgrimage from Bayonne to Pamplona at the invitation of the Association des Amis de Saint-Jacques des Pyrénées Atlantiques.

On the domestic front three significant events occurred in the period 1992-1994: the arrival in London of a new Spanish Ambassador, D. Alberto Aza Arias, an enthusiastic pilgrim himself, who readily agreed to become Confraternity president; membership reaching 1000 in June 1994; and the acquisition of a London office in October 1994.

★ ★ ★ ★ ★

At the 1992 Annual General Meeting, held on 11 January in the new venue of the St Alban's Centre in Holborn, members were very aware of both the responsibility they now had for the *refugio* and the proximity of the 1993 Holy Year. Special guests at this AGM included Alberto Morán, Secretary of the El Bierzo Association, Etienne and Nelly van Wonterghem-Teirlinck, Gaucelmo's first wardens in 1991, Herbert and Liliana Simon from the Cologne/Düsseldorf association and Roger Tisseau from Paris who had been a member of Rabanal working parties. The post-AGM entertainment consisted – appropriately – of a presentation on Rabanal by James Maple, Chairman of the Rabanal Appeal Sub-Committee, Walter Ivens, Alberto Morán, David Wesson (the first English warden) and Roger Tisseau, together with a video of the inauguration made on 25 October 1991. Earlier in the afternoon Mary Remnant, who had contributed so much to the Confraternity, not only through her musical scholarship and lecture-recitals but equally in ideas and inspiration, accepted honorary membership of the Confraternity along with a huge bouquet of flowers. Three further friends of the CSJ and of Rabanal became honorary members at the same time: Alberto Morán and the Refugio's excellent neighbours, Asumpta Oriol and Charo Carrión.

With individual and joint membership having reached 850 by early 1992, some initial steps were taken that year to share the administrative load more widely. Committee members remained largely unchanged, but the role of Vice-Chairman was instituted, filled jointly by Laurie Dennett and Joe May, to provide cover in the absence of the Chairman. A vital part in the running of the Confraternity was already being played by John Hatfield as database manager, in succession to Anthony Brunning; he worked closely with Walter Ivens (Membership Secretary) and Marion Marples (Secretary) producing labels for the Bulletin and other mailings. John had also become Slide Librarian, taking over from George McHardy, and was busy expanding the service with the production of a comprehensive catalogue and an annual 'gaps list', the latter being given to departing pilgrims in the hope that their slides taken en route might fill some of the gaps. Early in 1993 Paul Graham became responsible for the dispatch of publications and Phinella Henderson devised a questionnaire on the future of the Confraternity, with the aim of encouraging greater participation by members in the affairs of the organization. This resulted first in a Committee reorganization in mid-1994 and second the recruitment of a small group of volunteers to help Marion Marples, whose secretarial remit was growing larger by the month.

At the 1994 AGM, Stephen Badger had been presented with a booktoken, bookplates (and a ball-point pen depicting a badger) to mark his 'retirement' as Treasurer after six years in office. As in most previous years he reported a healthy surplus for 1993, thus maintaining his reputation for careful stewardship of the Confraternity's funds. Phinella Henderson, who made notable contributions to the Holy Year and to the Rabanal appeal, also stepped down from the Committee. Newly elected members included Rosemary Clarke, Hilary Hugh-Jones, Howard Nelson and Timothy Wotherspoon, the latter also being elected Treasurer at the first Committee meeting of the year.

In June 1994 membership reached the magic figure of 1000, after the usual Spring fluctuation of those not renewing slowly being outnumbered by new members. Marion's role as provider of information and advice to members, enquirers, putative film-makers (the Camino was now becoming fashionable), writers, students, priests, parishes and schools, was fast growing unwieldy. In Bulletin 49 (March 1994) she appealed for help in finding a small office because at her home in London SE1 she was disappearing under large piles of paper and being fenced in by files. Fortunately, a solution was at hand in the shape of a one-room office on a short lease at 3 Stamford Street, SE1, a former Victorian hat factory that had been converted into offices for charities and local groups, and only a five-minute walk from Marion's home. The rent was affordable and the move took place in mid-October 1994, preceded by a great deal of work at the premises by Howard Nelson; thanks to his professional woodworking skills half of the office was fitted with shelving, enabling the growing Confraternity Library to be moved from Stephen Badger's home in Dulwich. The Librarian's role was then amicably shared between Stephen and Howard, the former remaining responsible for acquisitions and the latter for cataloguing and administration, helped by Liz Keay.

Just as importantly, Marion was at last able to train the group of volunteers to help in the office, especially with the dispatch of the CSJ information package, publications and Bulletins. John Davies in particular was a tower of strength and the new office, fitted with a fax machine and a telephone answering machine, was soon opened to members and the public every Tuesday from 11 to 3 and by appointment at other times. Another very useful form of assistance was provided by Joe May who gave advice on group pilgrimages to the increasing number of schools and parish groups and others who planned to go to Santiago.

A further set of volunteers, mentioned in Chapter 3, consisted of members of the Research Working Party, which met twice a year at the University of Birmingham. Since its inception in 1988 Professor Derek Lomax had chaired the Working Party, both during his last years as head of the Department of Hispanic Studies and his first year or so of retirement. It was therefore a great shock to learn of his untimely death from a heart attack on 12 March 1992, at the age of just 59 and only 18 months after he had retired. An obituary in *The Independent* concentrated on his academic and humanitarian achievements, but the paper did publish an addendum written by Pat Quaife about all he had done for the Confraternity since joining in late 1983. He was succeeded by Professor Brian Tate of the University of Nottingham, who served as Chairman until 2003.

July 1992 proved to be a happier month with four different events, two of an academic nature, a garden fete at the Horniman Museum in south-east London, and a visit to Winchester for a special Mass on St James's Day on the site of St James's burial ground. On 1 July, the Graduate Centre for Medieval Studies of the University of Reading and the Confraternity mounted a joint summer symposium on Pilgrimage, held at the University. Marion Marples opened the proceedings speaking on 'The Contemporary Pilgrimage to Santiago' and Mary Remnant closed them with an expanded version of her popular lecture-recital, 'The Musical Road to Santiago de Compostela'. In between, papers were given by Reading University staff on the protection of pilgrims in the Holy Land during the Crusades and shrines in late medieval Italy. Less than a week later, a U.S. member, Annie Shaver-Crandell of the University of New York, drew our attention to 'Some Less Pleasant Aspects of the *Pilgrim's Guide*' at a meeting in the St Alban's Centre, a fascinating lecture that encouraged many present to reread the *Guide* with a fresh eye.

1993 HOLY YEAR

This long-awaited year – the tenth in the life of the Confraternity – got off to a lively start on 23 January, date of the 10th AGM and of Bulletin 45, a special tenth birthday issue. At St Alban's Centre, over 150 members filled it to near capacity to celebrate the anniversary, the highlight of which was a light-hearted presentation of Ten Years of the Confraternity, orchestrated by Vice-President, James Maple. A variety of speakers, including James Hatts (11), reviewed the different activities that had taken place over the last decade. The most graphic was possibly Anthea Hopkins, describing Confraternity visits to Spain, and flourishing a pair of pink bedsocks she had once left behind in a hotel in Ponferrada. Mary Remnant concluded the pre-supper proceedings, conducting people vigorously through well-known songs from the *Codex Calixtinus*. As always members paid tribute to the refreshments team, spearheaded by Eileen FitzGerald and Stephen and Katharine Badger, whose efficient organization of food and drink meant that no-one was left hungry or thirsty.[1]

Earlier, Pat Quaife as Chairman had reviewd the events of 1992, with particular reference to the first full year's operation of the Refugio Gaucelmo, when 2677 pilgrims had received hospitality there. She also expressed concern about the major developments planned by the Xunta de Galicia for the Monte del Gozo area, the historic hill just outside the city of Santiago where pilgrims first see the towers of the Cathedral. In order to improve the Galician economy, the Xunta had promoted the Holy Year worldwide, in the hope of attracting millions of pilgrims and visitors to Santiago in 1993. In the event some six million did come, 100,000 or so on foot or by bicycle. The laudable aim of the Monte del Gozo development was to provide better facilities for pilgrims and other visitors to the city. In correspondence (along with nearly all our sister Jacobean associations) and at pre-1993 meetings in London organized by the Xunta, the Confraternity had voiced its anxieties about the enforced appropriation of the site and the scale of the development planned there: amphitheatre, restaurants, campsites, dormitory accommodation for pilgrims, etc. Despite Europe-wide protests at the scale of the project the bulldozers had moved relentlessly on with buildings now covering much of the site.

At the end of the meeting, to mark her fifth year as Chairman, Pat was presented with a copy of Walter Starkie's classic 1957 book, *The Pilgrimage to Santiago,* that came in a handsome slipcase made by Dr Owen Gilbert. She was also offered honorary membership of the Confraternity, which she was delighted to accept.

The Confraternity's Holy Year was centered on a series of seven special lectures given on Wednesday evenings in the crypt of St Etheldreda's Church in Holborn. The first of these was, very appropriately, given by Mary Remnant in mid-February on 'The Pilgrimage to Santiago and the Confraternity of St James', followed in later months by David Hugh Farmer, Alison Stones, Annie Shaver-Crandell, Brian Tate, David Stancliffe and Pat Quaife. A complete list will be found in Appendix 4.

Interspersed among the lectures were pilgrimages to Canterbury (for both walkers and cyclists) and to Santiago itself (along the *Camino Inglés* from La Coruña), an evening of words and music arranged by Phinella Henderson, a St James's Day weekend in Gloucestershire with a pilgrim service in St James, Stoke Orchard, and an ambitious week-long autumn visit to Spain, billed as 'Oviedo to Finisterre via Rabanal and Santiago'.

1993 was always going to a pilgrim year *par excellence,* both in Spain and closer to home. Holy Year walkers took courage and inspiration from two 1992 pilgrimages: Laurie Dennett's third major walk, this time from London to Jerusalem (after Santiago in 1986 and Rome in 1989), and Frank Taylor's pilgrimage to Santiago from his home in Hampshire. Once again Laurie was fund-raising for research into multiple sclerosis and met up with MS Society members in the countries she walked through, France, Italy, Greece and Israel. Frank Taylor walked to Santiago in memory of his son Guy, who had died of cancer. On hearing the reason for Frank's pilgrimage the Cathedral authorities awarded him two *compostelas,* one for him and one for Guy. Frank raised over £22,000 for the Imperial Cancer Research Fund and the Royal Marsden Hospital where Guy was cared for.

Encouraged by these examples of fortitude and determination, some 40 members ventured on to the roads and trackways of southern England in May 1993, for the Confraternity's pilgrimage to Canterbury. The cyclists, led by Terence Morris, started from Winchester and the walkers from Reading Abbey, led by Stephen Badger. Both groups began with a service of blessing, the cyclists at St Peter's Winchester, one of the oldest Catholic parishes in southern England, and the walkers at St James Reading, the neo-Romanesque Catholic church hard by the ruins of Reading Abbey. Both cyclists and walkers endured various pilgrim trials and tribulations en route.

Terence Morris wrote afterwards that he felt 'like a destroyer shepherding a convoy' as he 'endeavoured not so much to keep everyone together as to try and remember where everyone was'. A tandem rear chain broke in Alresford and Robert Ivens suffered two punctures in one day, the second at Runfold near a half life-size statute of the Virgin Mary, encased in a glass-fronted box. The band of walkers had little trouble from traffic, enjoyed much idyllic countryside on Stephen's carefully chosen route (some North Downs Way, some Pilgrims' Way) but suffered from what came to be called 'Badger miles', a new terrestrial unit of some 2000 yards which prolonged already lengthy days. In the end everyone survived and the two groups met at the Friars in Aylesford on the Friday evening. The pilgrimages culminated in Canterbury where, on Sunday evening, William Griffiths led a small ceremony of arrival and greeting to St Thomas. On Monday morning cycling and walking pilgrims and other members came together for a moving ecumenical pilgrim service. Held in the Norman crypt chapel of the Cathedral, it was led by David Stancliffe, then Provost of Portsmouth and Bishop-elect of Salisbury who, with his wife Sarah, had walked to Santiago in 1991. A small Confraternity choir had assembled, with Mary Remnant playing the organ and her organistrum. Present too was a silver statue of St James brought from the church in Spanish Place, London, and censed by David Stancliffe during the service.

Three months on, in late August, 14 Confraternity walkers and two car drivers met up in La Coruña for the short (75-kilometre) pilgrimage to Santiago along the way known as the *Camino Inglés*. We were possibly the first group of pilgrims from the British Isles and France (represented by Yves and Edith Saint-Léger), to walk the route since the early sixteenth century. That the pilgrimage happened at all was due in very large part to Joaquín Vilas, a local CSJ member, and to Rafael Arias, Holy Year press officer for the Archbishop of Santiago. Joaquín provided us with a special *Camino Inglés* pilgrim record and arranged a Mass and pilgrim blessing in the church of Santiago in La Coruña, while Rafael had reserved all our accommodation along the way. Press releases sent from London had alerted TV Galicia and local papers to our presence and the former caught up with us on day 1, in pouring rain, just before the town of O Burgo. A few kilometres further on we squelched into the bar in the hamlet of A Xira, where we were instantly recognized by the proprietor who showed us a photograph and article about the group on the back page of the *Voz de Galicia*.

By lunchtime the following day we had reached the historic village of Hospital de Bruma. As its name indicates, a pilgrim hospital next to the tiny church of San Lourenzo (St Laurence) is attested from the twelfth century, its remains now incorporated into a house on the same site. By happy chance – or Camino coincidence – the hospital house is owned by the elderly aunt of a friend of Coruña member, Magdalena Stork de Yepes. The church key is also held by her family who kindly opened San Lourenzo for us, the only rural church whose interior we managed to see. By now a watery sun had appeared and we pressed on to the town of Órdenes through a series of villages and groves of oak trees. Órdenes, explained the mayor, D. Teodosio Martino Martino, as he stamped our pilgrim records in the council chamber, had taken the lead on the waymarking of the *Camino Inglés,* and indeed we had noticed that the intermittent arrows of day 1 had given way to neat blue and white Camino de Santiago signposts. Sadly these ran out on day 3 as we entered the Sigüeiro district, some 13 kilometres from Santiago, but by good fortune we managed not to get lost. The only mishap of the pilgrimage occurred on the outskirts of the city when Gosia Brykczynska twisted her ankle within sight of our first Santiago de Compostela sign. Fortunately she was able to continue after being bandaged up by William Griffiths. Once in the old town Hilary Shaw unfurled her impressive Bredereth Sen Jago banner and with James Hatts (now 12), led us in procession to the Plaza del Obradoiro and our destination, the shrine of St James.

Pilgrim activities continued the next day when Jeannine Warcollier, in Santiago with a group of Société des Amis de Saint-Jacques members, invited us to take part in the European Associations' Day which she had organized. After Mass in the Cathedral, which included readings and prayers by representatives from different countries, we enjoyed a sunny boat trip on the Ria de Arosa up to the town of Padrón. Here we climbed the long hill at the back of the town to the spot where St James may have preached in the first century AD, from a natural altar made of huge boulders. The day ended back in Santiago with a celebratory dinner at the monastery of San Martín Pinario where we were all staying, followed by a spectacular *queimada* demonstrated and set alight by María Barcena, a Santiago resident and friend to many pilgrims.

St James's Day itself – Sunday 25 July – was joyfully celebrated in 1993, and reported on in detail in Bulletin 47 (September 1993), with articles by members in Santiago on the day, in Rabanal, in south-west France and with the Confraternity in Gloucestershire. The late Fr John Rogers had been acting as English-language confessor at Santiago Cathedral for the month of July, and was invited to concelebrate the main Mass on the 25th, in the presence of King Juan Carlos and Queen Sofía. He wrote: 'The end of the Mass was memorable; the priests were sitting on benches placed along the sides of the transept that happens also to be the path of the *botafumeiro.* As the great silver censer made its first pass 12 inches from my head I sat down. A few of those next to me

The Mayor of Ordenes stamps the Pilgrim Passport of Paul Newman, Camino Inglés, 1993

Exmo. D Alberto Aza Arias with carved staue of St James, made by Peter FitzGerald. St Etheldreda's, Ely Place, London 1993

almost fainted and the King started to laugh…One of the canons told me that the pilgrimage had been asleep but was now wideawake.'

St James's Day in rural Gloucestershire could not have been in greater contrast to the crowded royal ceremonies in Santiago. A morning walk took us from St Mary the Virgin at Syde to Daglingworth (Holy Rood) and on by car or minibus to Seven Springs. The highlight of the day was the special 3.30 p.m. pilgrim service held at the tiny Norman church of St James Stoke Orchard with its wall-paintings depicting the life of St James in 28 continuous scenes. We were given a warm welcome by the vicar, the Revd John Homfray, before the Confraternity choir, led by Mary Remnant, swept into the now familiar '*Ad honorem Regis summi*'. The service itself was divided into three parts: Departing on Pilgrimage, The Journey, and The Arrival, with pilgrim hymns, prayers and readings. Members particularly appreciated a prayer which mentioned the work for pilgrims at Rabanal and that of two prominent deceased members, Mrs Constance Storrs and Professor Derek Lomax.

The third Confraternity pilgrimage of the Holy Year took place in October when a 16-strong group managed to visit (by plane and mini-bus) many of the most significant monuments in northern Spain between Oviedo and Finisterre, including the village of Rabanal del Camino. Here the October warden at Gaucelmo, Eric Talbot, had arranged a late lunch for us at Antonio's Bar/Mesón, before the main ceremony of the day, the presentation to the *refugio* of a very fine photo of part of a twelfth-century document exempting the hermit Gaucelmo of Foncebadón from the need to pay taxes. The photograph, in its maroon leather frame, was the gift of D. Bernardo Velado Graña, director of the diocesan museum of Astorga, as a thank-you for the translation of a museum leaflet into English. In the presence of the El Bierzo Association Committee and our good neighbours, Charo and Asumpta, Pat Quaife received the photograph on behalf of the Refugio Gaucelmo, to the accompaniment of brief speeches in Spanish and English, a prayer said by D. Bernardo and *Ad honorem* … sung under the direction of Mary Pryer. That night we took up every available non-*refugio* bed in the village, with one group at Chonina's, one at Antonio's and two members invited to the home of the village postman, Julio and his wife Quica.

In Santiago the ever-welcoming Hostal Suso provided a base for four nights. The city was now relatively tranquil after the intensive celebrations round St James's Day although crowds still flocked to the Cathedral for Mass, especially the 12 noon Pilgrims' Mass when the *botafumeiro* was swung. Further west, a trip to Finisterre was enhanced for everyone by the presence of Magdalena Stork de Yepes and her husband Valeriano. In her account of the day she wrote: 'the first thing to do when you arrive [at Finisterre] is to go immediately to the lighthouse or *faro*. We were   very lucky with the weather and the sun was shining brightly. There was yet an hour or more for it to sink into the ocean, but already it shed its golden pathway on the water. I thought myself in the [Roman] Ara-Solis, to which all kinds of pilgrims and adventurers used to come ... to contemplate this same sun, setting at the end of the world'.[2]

During this October visit sad news was received by telephone from London. The caller was Mary Remnant, ringing to tell us that her mother, Joan, had died peacefully in hospital at the age of 91. That her death should have happened in a Holy Year, and on 25 October – the second anniversary of the inauguration of the Refugio Gaucelmo and of the Rabanal party in her and Mary's home on that same date in 1991 – somehow made it easier to bear. Many of the group had happy memories of Joan Remnant at her home in Chelsea, always smiling and hospitable and interested in everything that the Confraternity did.

The calendar Holy Year in London concluded with the seventh and last lecture in the Wednesday series: *Camino de Santiago - Camino de Europa,* given (in English) by Pat Quaife. In fact the Confraternity's own Holy Year programme came to a close on 19 March 1994 with a postponed concert of twelfth-century music entitled 'The Field of Stars, a galaxy of music in honour of St James of Compostella' by the Schola Gregoriana of Cambridge, directed by Dr Mary Berry, and generously sponsored by the Spanish Ministry of Culture. The Romanesque Priory Church of St Bartholomew the Great in the City of London provided a perfect setting for the liturgical music sung so mellifluously by the gentlemen of the Schola. This was Mary Berry's first Schola performance in London for some years – an event the Confraternity felt privileged to be associated with.

★ ★ ★ ★ ★

If the Confraternity's Holy Year ended in March 1994, on the publications side it started in the summer of 1992 with the launch of the first ever full translation into English of Book V, *The Pilgrim's Guide,* of the twelfth-century *Liber Sancti Jacobi.* The translator was James Hogarth of Edinburgh, whose scholarly efforts were complemented by Mollie Coviello's frontispiece drawing of a pilgrim and by the desk-top publishing (not to mention dispatch) undertaken by Barry Humpidge.

Later, in 1993 itself, an American member, William Melczer, Professor of Medieval and Renaissance Studies at Syracuse University, New York, published his translation of Book V which was preceded by a very full introduction to the cult of St James and followed by a series of notes, bibliography, gazeteer and hagiographical register. St James continued to be well served in the early Nineties as the eagerly awaited new *guía*³, *The Pilgrim's Guide to the Camino de Santiago* by the late Elías Valiña Sampedro appeared late in 1992 in five languages, the English version translated by Laurie Dennett, the French by Odile Lutard and the German by Herbert Simon. Its diagrammatic maps were to be complemented a year later by Elías Valiña's final posthumous publication, *The Way of Saint James: the Cartography of the Camino Francés*, beautifully drawn, to scale, on which he had been working before his death. Thanks to the hard work and determination of Laurie Dennett, Joe May and publisher Roger Lascelles, it finally saw the light of day in late 1993 and was an immediate success with pilgrims. Indeed, seven years later, the present writer held it in her left hand from Saint-Jean-Pied-de-Port to Santiago, and gave thanks each day for its existence.

Two other Holy Year publications were contributed by John Durant and Phinella Henderson. The former's *The Pilgrimage and Path to Saint James by Hermann Künig von Vach* consisted of an annotated English prose translation of the original rhyming version of 1495/6 and was published as the Confraternity's Occasional Paper no.3. Phinella spent much of 1993 collecting pieces, both published and unpublished, for her *Pilgrim Anthology*, which was launched at the 1994 AGM. Divided into six sections, the anthology consists of contributions ranging from Chaucer, Dante and Erasmus to a modern 12-year-old's uninhibited diary of his pilgrim experiences. Indeed, the index of authors reads like 'the great and the good' of the Camino over the last 800 years, including the three well-known Walters: Raleigh, Starkie and Ivens in the respective fields of poetry, prose and twentieth-century pilgrim reflections.

A different kind of contribution to Holy Year was made over the winter of 1992/3 by a team of five Confraternity translators, led by Janet Richardson. The Spanish Diocesan Commission for Holy Year had earlier published a short and well-illustrated book entitled *El Apóstol Santiago y su proyección en la historia: 10 temas didacticos*, which was designed as an introduction to the subject for school and parish groups. D. Jaime García Rodríguez, the cathedral canon responsible for the Pilgrim Office, had persuaded several Jacobean associations, including the Confraternity, to translate the book into their mother-tongue. The original (Spanish) authors were all experts on their particular topic which included 'St James, biblical roots', 'The New Testament tradition', 'The martyrdom and burial of St James', 'The rise of the Cathedral', 'The pilgrimage and its spirituality' among others.

Members were busy writing their own books in 1993 and 1994, notably Bettina Selby and Alison Raju, long-distance cyclist and walker respectively. Bettina's *Pilgrims' Road, a Journey to Santiago de Compostela,* published by Little, Brown, starts at Vézelay, the first Santiago travel book in English to do so. Alison Raju, a valued Confraternity guide-writer (and now, in 2003, a Vice-Chairman) produced for the Cicerone Press, a detailed walkers' guide, *The Way of St James, Spain,* including an outline of the Vía de la Plata from Seville to Astorga.

Alison, with Confraternity colleagues, continued to work on our own pocket guides and late March 1993 saw the publication of five of the six guides planned for the Holy Year, including the perennial *Pilgrim Guide to Spain* (eleventh edition, Pat Quaife) and *Le Puy to the Pyrenees* (third edition, Alison Raju). A new and ground-breaking guide to the Vézelay route was produced by John Hatfield, assisted by Joe May, after wide consultation with fellow cyclists and walkers in France and other European countries, It was hoped that its appearance would encourage feedback from those following the Vézelay route as well as spur the development of a pilgrim infrastructure for walkers, particularly low-cost *gite d'étape*-style accommodation. A second new route guide, written by Alison Raju, was *The Camino Mozárabe or Vía de la Plata,* a contribution to the propagation of routes other than the traditional Camino Francés. She also revised her *Finisterre: hints for walkers,* which takes intrepid walkers across country from Santiago to Finisterre. *Notes for Walkers and Notes for Cyclists,* prepared by various people for practical pilgrim days, featured practical advice and were aimed at people embarking on their first pilgrimage.

Two enormously important books on the pilgrimage appeared in 1994, both landmarks in Camino scholarship. Maryjane Dunn's and Linda Kay Davidson's massive bibliography, *The Pilgrimage to Santiago de Compostela* (Garland Publishing, New York), includes nearly 3000 detailed entries, covering books and articles in nine different languages and in fields such as art, architecture, anthropology, history, literature, geography, sociology and music. On this side of the Atlantic, Constance Storrs's University of London thesis, *Jacobean Pilgrims from England to St James of Compostella from the Early Twelfth to the Late Fifteenth Century* was published in December 1994 by the Xunta de Galicia, 30 years after it was first written for her MA thesis and seven years after she had been 'found' by the Confraternity. Its appearance was due to the efforts of Professor David Mackenzie of the University of Birmingham who arranged the painstaking transfer of the text on to a floppy disk and of Professor Brian Tate who contributed a foreword which summed up the importance of Constance Storrs's labours in sifting through the official records found in the Public Record Office and elsewhere.

★ ★ ★ ★ ★

In the history of the Refugio Gaucelmo at Rabanal, 1992 will be remembered as the first year of full (April to November) operation, and by Timothy Wotherspoon and Maurice Fox as the spring when they dismantled the barn roof. On the fund-raising side, a colour postcard, showing some of the improvements made to date, was published with an appeal in verse by Laurie Dennett, with the aim of raising a further £20,000 that was needed for the barn:

We're just steps from the end of the road,
(Thank you for sharing the load!)
We've rebuilt our Hostal (sic)
And we've made Rabanal
A much happier place, so we're told ...

But there's still that old barn left to do?
(Did you all really think we were through?)
Crumbling walls, broken floor,
Leaky roof and no door –
Fixing those is all part of Phase Two!...

A welcome boost to the Appeal came in early March in the form of generous donations from the United States, thanks to the efforts of Ronald R. Atkins, a New York lawyer and keen CSJ member, working in conjunction with the International Center of Medieval Art.

As well as dismantling the barn roof, Timothy was also the first warden for 1992. He had promised to arrive on 31 March in order to open the refuge to pilgrims on 1 April, but snowstorms in northern Spain threatened to delay his journey. Arriving at 4 a.m. at León station, with his heavily-laden bicycle, Timothy set off for Astorga, stopping to thaw his fingers at regular intervals. A lesser character might have taken shelter at Castrillo de los Polvazares as the rain turned to sleet and then snow. In Bulletin 43 (August 1992) Timothy recounted his journey from Castrillo to Rabanal: 'By El Ganso the snow was too thick for me to be able to continue riding. The blizzard became extremely painful as I pushed my bicycle against the gale, because deforestation has exposed the road to the full force of the gale. Hailstones pelted my face like gunshot. You can imagine my relief on wiping the ice from my glasses to read 'Rabanal del Camino' on a signboard just before noon.' Life hardly got any easier once Timothy was installed in the refuge. 'The place was filthy! Workmen reroofing the side wing had thrown all the loam from the top of the building to the ground, coating everywhere with a thick layer of fine mud. The kitchen was empty in readiness for laying a new floor.'

Two days later Pat Quaife arrived for the weekend and helped Timothy to sort out a large box of papers – 30-year-old magazines, circulars and ephemera – that had been moved out of the barn. As well as a number of religious journals sent to the earlier priests of Rabanal, they also found some of the first issues of *La Ruta Jacobea*, the journal of the Estella Amigos whose President, D. Francisco Beruete, had founded the association in 1962. The most interesting discovery was an undated sheet headed 'El Pueblo de Rabanal del Camino', appealing for funds to restore the churches of the village, the cemetery and the parish house, the latter 'a total ruin and therefore uninhabitable'. The priest of the time, whose name was not given, himself started the Appeal with a donation of 100 pesetas and called on the sons and daughters of the village 'scattered throughout Spain and across the seas, to respond in similar fashion'. How strange, we thought, that 30 years on it was the Confraternity appealing to the pilgrims of Europe to contribute to the rebuilding of the parish house and indirectly to the well-being of the village.

The Confraternity Spring Working Party, led by Stephen Badger, reached Rabanal a few days later. More cleaning and removing rotten timber from the barn took place, interspersed with some more pleasurable tasks. One of these was to spend £300 on a piece of furniture for the refuge, the money donated by Joanne Land in memory of her late brother, John Halliday. A visit to a local carpenter proved fruitless but eventually the perfect solution was found - an antique Maragato settle *(un escaño)* carved with traditional motifs in oak. It fitted exactly against a side wall in the entrance, under the noticeboard, and proved to be an excellent resting-place for weary pilgrims.

In May, Maurice Fox spent ten days in Rabanal working with

Timothy on removing tiles from the roof of the barn and debris of all kinds from the interior. Initially they had no tools nor was there any equipment to get up on to the roof. Timothy improvised with some pieces of wood which he extended into a walkway along the roof as tiles were taken down. On his first full day, Maurice's legs went through rotted boards on the roof and Chonina's son Miguel-Ángel, brought a ladder to help. Most of the tiles had been removed by the end of the third day, and as anticipated, a section of wall collapsed. Several items found in the barn were of interest to people in the village: including a makeshift wooden chicken feeder fitted with spindly legs. This had been made by the grandfather of one of the villagers.

Throughout 1992 pilgrims continued to flock to the Refugio Gaucelmo, writing kind remarks in the pilgrim book and, with a few exceptions, making a generous donation for their night's stay. In total 2677 people slept in the dormitory or the smaller rooms, some of them in September when a special Barn Working Group, led by Ken Thomas, spent nearly two weeks reroofing the barn and helping to rebuild its walls. The team included Barry Aston, Paddy and Tony Marris and Ted Dickinson, then aged 72, who had promised his wife he would keep his feet firmly on the ground. Using ancient oak timbers, boards and over 2000 traditional, baked clay tiles, Ken 'did everything requiring experience and skill ... and inspired everyone. Tony and I [Barry Aston] did whatever we were told and soon progressed from teetering along the roof on all fours to using the power-saw on the apex', wrote Barry in his report of the visit.

In the meantime, back in London, Paul Graham had had one of his most brilliant fundraising ideas for 1993. The Refugio Gaucelmo Sub-Committee as the Appeal Sub-Committee was now called, had been aware for some time of the need to build up a maintenance fund for the refuge, to be drawn on in later years. While pilgrim donations in the peak period of June to September were largely covering day-to-day outgoings, this was not the case in the quieter months. Paul's idea, known as 'Sponsor-a-Week', would enable members to make a special donation of £50 to 'sponsor' a week of their choice perhaps marking an anniversary or birthday – between April and October. In return the warden/s for the week would write to the sponsor telling him or her what had happened in the village, the number of pilgrims who had stayed and any other interesting news.

The village post-box would be mentioned in letters to sponsors from time to time, as it was periodically threatened with removal. 1992 pilgrims were encouraged by the wardens to use the yellow box affixed to the wall of Julio's house, situated on the main road going west, just beyond Chonina's bar. Janet Richardson, a Spanish philatelic specialist, had heard from Julio that if the volume of mail did not increase the village was in danger of losing the post-box, along with the 'Rabanal del Camino' postmark on letters. A striking postcard of the statue of St James in his niche on the front of Gaucelmo published by the Confraternity, proved popular with pilgrims, and helped – we heard in 1993 – to reprieve the postbox for another year or two.

At the end of 1992 the Confraternity was saddened to hear of the resignation of Alberto Morán from the El Bierzo Committee, after several years of close collaboration with Walter Ivens and others on the Refugio Gaucelmo. Conversely, we were pleased for Alberto as he had been appointed to a parish of his own in the Bierzo area: the town of Dehesas, not far from Ponferrada where he would be able to exercise his gifts more widely. Early in 1993 he was replaced on the El Bierzo Committee by Antolín de Cela, rector of the Basilica of Nuestra Señora de la Encina, and Alberto's erstwhile 'boss' – a change that heralded the replacement of that Committee en bloc.

For Gaucelmo, the 1993 Holy Year started well with the Sponsor-a-Week campaign launched at the AGM proving to be a great success. A seven-strong Spring working party, led by Walter Ivens and Joe May, arrived in Rabanal on 29 March for a hard-working week spent cleaning, painting, sawing wood and gardening, as well as meeting with Antolín and the new El Bierzo president, Domíngo Sánchez. Among other tasks, Joe May had made an impressive donations box from English oak which he fixed securely to the wall of the entrance.

Roger Cocks, the April warden, coped stoically with the banging, sawing and drilling that went on around him and by the end of his first week had welcomed – and provided breakfast for – some 80 pilgrims. As Mary Ivens recorded in the 1993 Spring Newsletter, the pilgrims 'were mainly Spanish but included a Brazilian, two English, a Belgian, four Germans and an Argentinian with a large blister which was expertly dealt with by Pat May. On the coldest night we found "wall-to-wall" pilgrims sleeping on the *salón* floor in front of the fire.'

A tidal wave of pilgrims was expected for 1993, following the massive promotion of the Holy Year throughout Europe and beyond; after the 401 received by Roger in April, the wave rolled in as predicted, bringing no fewer than 1657 pilgrims in the peak month of July. For the first time the wardens were having to turn pilgrims away through lack of space, once the 70 or so (double the number for whom beds were available) who could be accommodated had registered and claimed a bed or floor-space. In her article 'Heads Above Water in Rabanal'[4] Caroline Crossley, one of the July wardens, describes turning away 'groups of 20 priests and hordes of Scouts. Large groups could be directed to the municipal refuge in the main square, but that too filled up rapidly.' It was particularly unfortunate that our own pilgrim President, D. Alberto Aza Arias and his family group, arrived too late to stay in the refuge in early August. The high-season 1993 wardens, Caroline, Veronica Santorum, Stuart Goldie, Richard Hankinson and some Spanish assistants deserved special thanks for their efforts.

'It'll be quieter in September', was David Wesson's optimistic forecast to his wife Diane as they prepared to set off for Rabanal to act as wardens. This proved to be correct for the first week, with some 30 arrivals a night, including Helmut a church organist from Düsseldorf, who walks to Santiago every year, and a Madrid chef who one evening prepared a splendid dinner for pilgrims and wardens out of seemingly minimal ingredients.

After that, even though the weather worsened, a second tidal wave of pilgrims started arriving, many of them cyclists, many of whom had started 'only' at León or Astorga. 'The reason?', David asked in Bulletin 48, providing the answer himself: '1993 was the year of the mountain bike explosion ... This year several hundred [cyclists] passed through Rabanal every day. As a result Gaucelmo was full to overflowing every night. Walkers were given priority over cyclists and by 6.30 p.m. at the latest the 'Full' notice would go up outside the front entrance.' Altogether David and Diane served 1142 breakfasts to pilgrims during September alone, while David's 1993 statistics showed a total of 6437 pilgrims from 34 different countries, 5116 on foot, 1315 cyclists and six horse-riders.

THE AFTERMATH – 1994

By early 1994 the Rabanal Appeal Fund had reached nearly £74,000, much helped by the success of Sponsor-a-Week, which was again promoted at the AGM. Walter Ivens, the Gaucelmo 'supremo', welcomed Joe May in his new role as coordinator of wardens, and an attractive new postcard was produced: Emma Poë's watercolour of the Rabanal church tower and village, seen from Gaucelmo's meadow.

The now traditional Spring working party laboured as hard as ever at the refuge, moving 35 tons of stone, using 120 litres of paint and cutting and stowing one and a half cubic metres of firewood. They also set up in the hallway a wooden statue of St James, carved by Peter FitzGerald, which was blessed by Padre Julián, the last priest of Rabanal to live in the parish house, from 1952 to 1958.

Two deaths overshadowed that spring and summer. The first was that of Ted Dickinson in April, at the age of 73, as he was cutting down trees in his garden. He contributed generously to the Appeal fund, had a deep love of Rabanal, and worked there on several occasions. To honour his memory the Confraternity, in agreement with his family, set up the Ted Dickinson Fund, with the objective of raising a capital sum of £3000. The purpose of the fund was to help people in exceptional circumstances who could benefit the Camino or the refuge but were unable to afford the travel costs. In June we learned of the death of D. Antonio Briva Mirabent, the genial, chain-smoking Bishop of Astorga. It was he who had inaugurated the Refugio Gaucelmo in October 1991 and who had always been very supportive of the project.

As expected, pilgrim numbers in 1994 (4000) were well down on those of 1993 but above the 2677 recorded for 1992. Even with pilgrims present every day in the season, important jobs were carried out by the builder, Amando. He relaid and tiled the floor in the storeroom and passage, laid a new floor in the barn and did considerable work in the meadow and on the well. All this was due to the generosity of donors to the Appeal which reached £79,000 by the end of the year, including £1900 for the Ted Dickinson Fund.

One of the most popular events of the year was a talk, in February, on his Holy Year pilgrimage by D. Alberto Aza Arias, the Spanish Ambassador appointed in December 1992 and Confraternity President. It was the first time the Confraternity had enjoyed a talk on the pilgrimage from a Spanish viewpoint. His pilgrim group of ten consisted of family and friends, including his wife Lalla and youngest son Miguel. As a native of Oviedo, D. Alberto had always been aware of the Camino de Santiago which he evoked with a mixture of erudition, personal reminiscence and practicalities.

D. Alberto and his wife did not confine their pilgrimage activities to Spain. In early May 1994 they were enthusiastic participants in the inaugural, 13-mile St Michael's Way pilgrimage in Cornwall, from Lelant (church of St Uny) to Marazion and St Michael's Mount, organized by Rod Pascoe and Hilary Shaw of the Bredereth Sen Jago. A Council of Europe representative at the blessing of St Michael's Way put it into its European context: 'a stretch of the Camino de Santiago walked by Irish and Welsh pilgrims wishing to avoid the hazards of the seas around Land's End.' Outside the church the Ambassador and Lord St Levan, President of the Bredereth, jointly unveiled a St Michael's Way plaque, before the 100 or so walkers were led by Rod Pascoe to the Cornish coastal path.

St James's Day falling on a Monday in 1994, it was decided to celebrate on Saturday the 23rd, with a Library Open Day in Dulwich at the home of Stephen and Katharine Badger. They generously invited members to Burbage Road from 10 a.m. to peruse or borrow books, to play CDs and videos, followed by a lunch-time barbecue. Visitors also had the chance to inspect their modern stained glass St James in the dining-room window, to play croquet and to visit the nearby Dulwich Picture Gallery. Nobody knew at that point that three months later the Confraternity would be transferring the Library to the new office, so with hindsight the Library Open Day was a particularly appropriate celebration.

The Basque Country was the setting for a week-long August walk from Bayonne to Pamplona, following an alternative, western pilgrim route through the Baztan valley. Twenty-three CSJ members, invited by the Amis de Saint-Jacques des Pyrénées-Atlantiques, joined a similar number of Amis to cover some 110 kilometres in six stages and in great summer heat. The logistics and the walking were masterminded by Jacques Rouyre and Yves Saint-Léger respectively. The picturesque landscape with its massive Basque farmhouses and towns such as Ainhoa and Elizondo more than compensated for any daytime discomforts, and in the evenings and on rest days we were splendidly entertained, notably in Olite by Maribel Roncal and Jesús Tanco of the Amigos de Santiago de Navarra. Anglo-French (and Spanish) friendship flourished all week.

Back home again, Liz Keay was the organizer of a well-attended 'St James in London' walk, based as far as possible on the London a medieval pilgrim group would have seen and walked through, much of it in the original medieval streets near the River Thames. Medieval and later churches were visited en route: All Hallows by the Tower, St Olave's, Hart Street and St James Garlickhythe, where we learned that it was Spanish sailors unloading garlic, who first began the devotion to St James there.

A long weekend in Paris, arranged by Hilary Hugh-Jones in late October, tempted a number of members to cross the Channel to spend three nights in a Left-Bank hotel. The success of the visit also owed much to Humbert Jacomet, a long-standing member of the Amis de Saint- Jacques, Conservateur du Patrimoine and a leading authority on St James and the pilgrimage in France. As well as guiding two walks in search of Jacobean vestiges in Paris, one on the Right Bank and one on the Ile de la Cité and south of the Seine[5], Humbert also generously invited the group to his roof-top flat (cum library) on the Friday evening. There he gave a fascinating talk on the topography of medieval Paris and was presented with a bottle of whisky by Hilary and renderings of *'Ad honorem Regis summi'* and *'Dum Paterfamilias'*, led by Mary Remnant. Following Humbert's Right-Bank walk Jeannine Warcollier took the group to the church of St Gervais and St Protais, the base for the Monastic Fraternity of Jerusalem, and on Saturday accepted an invitation to the farewell dinner in the *6e arrondissement*.

The last event of 1994, on 24 November, followed on seamlessly from the Paris experience: an evening at St Etheldreda's in London on the French pilgrim routes, with a variety of speakers on the Arles, Vézelay, Paris and le Puy routes. Jocelyn Rix's account of her 'back-to-front' walk from Puente la Reina to Vézelay was perhaps the most striking, as she described her ad-hoc sleeping arrangements, which included one night spent on carpet tiles laid out on the desk of a village mayor.

★ ★ ★ ★ ★

Just as 1992/4 was a period of great Confraternity activity in Britain, so it was elsewhere in Europe. New Jacobean associations were set up, international conferences organized and new refuges, inspired by the Rabanal model, opened their doors to pilgrims.

November 1992 saw the foundation in Dublin of the Irish Society of the Friends of St James, with Patricia Kennedy, a long-standing CSJ member, as Secretary and Don Heenihan as President. Throughout the 1990s they were to organize a series of group fund-raising pilgrimages to Santiago, in aid of the MS Society, mainly led by Bert Slader, a former Deputy Director of the Sports Council for Northern Ireland and author of *Pilgrims' Footsteps* (1989), an account of his own 1985 pilgrimage. Another organization with Camino links was founded in 1993, in La Coruña, La Coruña en Bici, with CSJ member Joaquín Vilas as Secretary. Although primarily a cycling group, its leading members were pilgrim- and Camino-orientated and encouraged the authorities to protect the Camino Inglés from motorway and other developments.

As well as being a Holy Year, 1993 also seemed to be the year of 'the

105

conference' whether under the title of 'colloquium', 'congress', 'forum' or *'encuentro'*. The conference year started in Toulouse in February, with an International University Colloquium on *Le Pendu Dépendu: Miracles et Légendes sur les Chemins de Saint-Jacques,* organized jointly by the University of Toulouse-Le Mirail, the Centre Européen d'Etudes Compostellanes and the Association de Coopération Inter-Régionale 'Les Chemins de St-Jacques de Compostelle'. Confraternity attendance, at seven members, was high for a conference abroad, and Pat Quaife gave a short paper in French on 'The Miracles of St James at Reading Abbey', paying due tribute to the work of Professor Brian Kemp who had translated the Miracles from the Latin original held at Worcester Cathedral Library. Pat also attended the inaugural Forum of Jacobean Associations held in Burgos in July 1993, organized by Ángel Luis Barreda, president of the Spanish Federation of Jacobean Associations. The purpose of this Forum was to bring together representatives of all Jacobean associations in Europe so that a common position could be agreed on topics of mutual interest such as the form of the pilgrim record (*credencial*), the problem of cheap tourism along the Camino, and the coordination of events organized by different associations to avoid clashes in the European diary. A second Forum was held in Tongerlo in Belgium in February 1994, attended by Laurie Dennett and Marion Marples, which further strengthened European links.

In November 1993 both the Xunta de Galicia and the Council of Europe organized conferences, held in Santiago and Strasbourg respectively, Laurie Dennett and Brian Tate attended the Xunta's *Congreso de Estudios Jacobeos,* with the latter presenting a paper on the maritime route from Britain to Santiago: 'A Vía Maritima dende as Illas Brittanicas a Compostela durante a Idade Media'. Later in the month Brian, together with Joe May, travelled to Strasbourg to represent the Confraternity at a meeting, called at short notice, on the physical integrity of the Camino.

1994 was a quieter year – the 'quieter' forecast for once proving correct, at least with respect to conferences. In September, under the guiding hand of Dr Lucia Gai and Professor Paolo Caucci von Saucken, the Centro Italiano di Studi Compostellani invited sister associations to a conference held in Pistoia, that looked back on ten years of Jacobean studies: 'Peregrinatio Studiorum Iacopea' *in Europa nell'Ultimo Decennio.* Brian Tate and Pat Quaife represented the Confraternity on this occasion, with Brian giving an excellent paper, in Spanish, on Jacobean studies in the UK, for which he provided a full bibliography.

Pat's contribution, in French, was a short account of the founding and activities of the Confraternity, given, along with similar presentations by other associations, in the medieval Hospital of the Tau in Altopascio, where the conference ended with a three-hour medieval banquet in the courtyard.

In late November Laurie Dennett attended the first international meeting of Confraternities of St James, at the invitation of the Archicofradía del Glorioso Apóstol Santiago. As Laurie wrote in Bulletin 52 (Feb.1995) 'The *archicofradía* was founded in the fifteenth century and exists to promote devotion to St James and pilgrimage to his shrine. ... Emphasis in the working sessions ... was on the anthropological, religious and psychological dimensions of the pilgrimage ... Further sessions focused on the history of confraternities [and] the situation of the pilgrimage at the end of the second millennium.'

★ ★ ★ ★ ★

The importance of pilgrim refuges along the Camino featured in both these 1994 conferences, with the Refugio Gaucelmo at Rabanal mentioned as an example of a foreign confraternity working in conjunction with the local Spanish association and with the people of the village or town concerned. At Azofra, a small village in La Rioja six kilometres west of Nájera, the work of Herbert and Liliana Simon and other members of the Cologne/Düsseldorf Association in setting up a small refuge next to the church came to fruition in May 1992 with its formal inauguration by the Bishop of Calahorra as one of the chain of *albergues* on the Camino Francés. The honour of being the first pilgrims to sleep in the Azofra refuge fell to Confraternity members David (now Bishop of Salisbury) and Sarah Stancliffe on their 1991 pilgrimage to Santiago. Similarly, Herbert Simon was an early visitor to Rabanal (see Appendix 3). In 1993 a number of refuges were opened in Galicia by the Xunta to provide much needed accommodation for the tidal wave of pilgrims mentioned earlier. Further east on the Camino work had been under way throughout 1993 on what is possibly the most atmospheric of all the refuges in Spain: the 13th-century chapel of the Hospital de San Nicolás de Puente Fitero at Itero del Castillo. This tiny building, which in mid-1993 stood roofless in a cornfield, had a year later been converted by the Italian association, under the energetic leadership of Paolo Caucci, into a charming small refuge sleeping 12 pilgrims. Inaugurated formally on 20 July 1994, the Hospital de San Nicolás makes a notable contribution to the architectural variety of Camino refuges.

★ ★ ★ ★ ★

The Committee had long been considering how it might pay permanent tribute to the memory of Constance Storrs, whose work on pilgrimage to Santiago had been largely unrecognized during her own lifetime. After much discussion, it was agreed in mid-1994 to institute an annual Constance Storrs Memorial Lecture to be delivered by distinguished scholars, alternating between British and foreign speakers. Mary Remnant was able to convey this news to Constance Storrs's widower, Francis, and his new wife Susan, née Tracey, both of whom were delighted with the idea. The first lecture was to take place early in 1995 (see Chapter 6).

Official recognition of the Confraternity's work, both at home and abroad, came in October 1994, when the Spanish authorities awarded Walter Ivens the *Cruz de Oficial* and Pat Quaife the *Lazo de Dama* of the Order of Isabel la Católica. A letter from the Confraternity's Honorary President, H.E. the Spanish Ambassador, D. Alberto Aza Arias, had informed them of the granting of the honour by H.M. the King of Spain and the ceremony took place in the drawing-room of the Embassy on Spanish National Day, 12 October, before the start of the annual reception. The Ambassador read a page-long citation about the activities of each recipient before pinning the insignia to their lapel or dress. Walter's citation referred to the conception of the Rabanal *refugio* project and his tireless work in making it a reality, while Pat's referred to her 12 years service as Secretary and latterly Chairman of the Confraternity, plus production of Camino guides and 50 issues of the Bulletin. Both Walter and Pat felt that their awards were in large measure those of the Confraternity as a whole, and a mark of confidence in its future.

NOTES

1   At one earlier AGM supper the food disappeared so rapidly that there was little left for members who delayed their visit to the tables. A food coordinator was appointed for the following AGM with the task of judiciously holding back some dishes until later in the evening.

2   Bulletin 50, July 1994, page 50.

3   Elías Valiña's pioneering route guide, under the title *El Camino de Santiago: Guía del Peregrino,* was first published in large format in 1982 and again, spiral-bound, in 1985. Known affectionately as 'the *guía*' or 'the big red book' it was the first full-length guide to the Camino in Spanish.

4   Bulletin 47 (September 1993), pp. 29-31.

5   For more information about traces of St James in Paris, see *Paris Pilgrim,* by Hilary Hugh-Jones and Mark Hassall, published by the Confraternity in 1998.

Chapter 6
Change and Consolidation
1995 to 1998

The period 1995 to December 1998 was marked by a number of changes which were to have a profound long-term effect on the Confraternity and its activities. Notable among these were the development of the office, acquired in October 1994 and which moved to new premises early in 1996, and a change of status for the Honorary Secretary, Marion Marples, to that of paid administrator. The purchase of a Dell computer system, researched and installed by Howard Nelson, also had a major impact on the work of the Secretary and volunteers, and on the Library, run by Howard alone since late 1994.

Early in 1995 Laurie Dennett was elected Chairman, following Pat Quaife's standing-down from the Committee at the end of 1994, and it was she who would steer the Confraternity through the next eight years and into the twenty-first century, supported by Vice-Chairmen William Griffiths and Howard Nelson. Timothy Wotherspoon had already taken over the Treasurership from Stephen Badger and, with Peter Tompkins, would be largely responsible for reforming and reshaping many aspects of the Confraternity's status, finances and accounts. With 1995 being the Confraternity's thirteenth year, other long-standing officers felt it was time to move on and were duly replaced, the Membership Secretary and the Pilgrim Records Secretary among them. A considerable effort was made to attract younger members into the organization, the most important initiative being the setting-up of the Confraternity Bursary in late 1996, an annual grant of up to £1000 awarded to one or more university students aged 18 to 25 who put forward the best research proposal on a topic linked to the pilgrimage. Confraternity events, which included a memorable lecture-recital by Mary Remnant at 11 Downing Street, continued undiminished at home and abroad and were on several occasions enhanced by the presence of members of the Belgian (Flemish) Vlaams Genootschap and the Amis de Saint-Jacques des Pyrénées-Atlantiques. The annual Constance Storrs Memorial Lecture, the first of which took place early in 1995, also widened members' European horizons and knowledge.

In Rabanal the Refugio Gaucelmo thrived during these years and at the end of 1996 the Confraternity was delighted to learn that it had been awarded the inaugural Premio Elías Valiña of a million pesetas, then worth nearly £6000, by the Xunta de Galicia.

While all these very positive developments were taking place, the years 1996, 1997 and 1998 were marked by a number of deaths – some sudden and unexpected – among both Confraternity members and foreign colleagues. The latter included an elderly Frenchman and – tragically – a young Spaniard, whose outstanding contributions, to pilgrimage studies and to the physical well-being of pilgrims respectively, were to be much missed.

★ ★ ★ ★ ★

In her first Chairman's report, Laurie Dennett characterized 1995 as 'a watershed year and year of transition, not due to a change of personnel so much as a recognition that we had outgrown some of the ways in which we functioned and with how we have responded to the challenges of size and relative prosperity'. In terms of size, membership had by the end of that year reached 1300 people, living in 23 different countries. Partly because of this and thanks to careful stewardship by successive Treasurers, the Confraternity's bank balance was almost embarrasingly healthy which gave the Committee the opportunity to consider how some of the surplus should best be spent, in keeping with our charitable objectives. Two major items would be the rent for the office and the employment of Marion Marples as administrator.

Early in 1996 Marion lived through one of the more hectic weeks of her life. Two days after the thirteenth AGM held on 20 January, the office, set up only 15 months earlier at 3 Stamford Street (which was now being redeveloped), moved to two first-floor rooms at 1 Talbot Yard, Borough High Street, London SE1. The extra space allowed for Committee meetings and Bulletin mailings which until October 1994 had taken place in members' homes. Other benefits included easier access to the Library and to publications and the chance once a week for enquirers to call in for advice about the pilgrimage either from Marion or from a volunteer. There could be no more appropriate place for a pilgrim office than Talbot Yard, for it was from here, formerly Tabard Yard, that Chaucer's pilgrims set off for Canterbury some 700 years earlier.

Not every Committee meeting took place in the office however. With agendas becoming longer and time for reflection and discussion of longer-term strategic issues reduced, Howard Nelson proposed that a less formal meeting take place, in June 1995 in his garden at London

SE15, weather permitting. The success of this initial gathering assured it of a regular place in the Committee's diary in later years.

Whether at Stamford Street or Talbot Yard, the chief office volunteer John Davies, a member since 1988, was always a quiet and competent presence who not only trained new volunteers but took over responsiblity for Bulletin mailings – no small task – and improved a number of office routines. It was therefore a great shock to Marion and to the membership to learn in late May 1997 that John, aged 65, had died of a massive heart attack in his flat a few days earlier. His passing left a gap in the volunteer ranks for a considerable time, although other regulars, Alan Hooton, Alison Pinkerton and John Pickering were soon joined by Bernard Masson and Charles Francis. The Confraternity owes a great debt to John Davies and to all the volunteers, without whom the office could not function the way it has done since late 1994.

To the English (and French) volunteers was added in autumn 1998 a young Galician, Arturo Lezcano, a media studies graduate of Santiago University. Arturo won a bursary from the Xunta de Galicia to work and study in London for a year, his main work placement being with the Confraternity. Friendly and with good English, Arturo assisted the more experienced volunteers, particularly during Marion Marples's absence on pilgrimage (see below) and proved his worth for the six months he spent in London.[1]

Another vital voluntary role, that of Membership Secretary, was nobly fulfilled by Walter Ivens for a number of years. Using old-style 5" x 3" index cards (which, unlike computers, are never 'down'), Walter had worked since 1987 with successive Secretaries and more recently with John Hatfield, seeing membership rise from a few hundred to 1300 by December 1995. Not surprisingly, he felt it was time for a change and early in 1996 handed over to Committee member Doreen Hansen. She, with John, oversaw the computerisation of membership data and the issuing of membership numbers for the first time. After two very full years as Membership Secretary and with a full-time post at the Diocese of London's Board of Education, Doreen in turn handed over to Vincent and Roisin Cowley at the 1998 AGM.

Another important change of personnel took place in mid-1996 when Alan Hooton became Pilgrim Records Secretary in succession to Rosemary Clarke. Rosemary had put in countless hours of work over many years during which the number of pilgrims and pilgrim records issued had doubled and tripled, including last-minute applications from very new members. Since 1995 a 'feedback' form devised by John Hatfield was also dispatched to departing pilgrims, with their pilgrim record, to make it easier for them to record changes they encountered that did not appear in the relevant CSJ guide.

For the Treasurer, Timothy Wotherspoon, the period was marked by the coming into force of the Charities Act 1993, which introduced considerable changes in the presentation of the annual accounts to conform with the Charities (Accounts and Reports) Regulations of 1995. The CSJ accounting records were transferred from a manuscript book to a computer-based accounting package. Sven Tester, who had performed exhaustive audits up to and including 1995/6, was succeeded by David Taylor in the slightly less demanding role of Independent Examiner.

The most significant change of all during the period in question was undoubtedly that undergone by Marion Marples in her role as Confraternity Secretary. As Honorary Secretary since 1989 and, as a Trustee, no longer eligible under new Charity Commission rules to receive an honorarium, Marion's commitment went well beyond the call of duty: attendance at the office at least two days a week, organising and attending Committee and Sub-Committee meetings, production of minutes, overseeing the production of guides, supervising volunteers … the list could go on and on. Late in 1997 the Committee decided it was time to recognize her selfless devotion to the Confraternity and to offer her some remuneration. A proposal was therefore put to the 1998 AGM that the Constitution be altered to allow the new Committee to appoint a Secretary who could be remunerated. This was duly agreed by members present at the AGM and Marion resigned as Honorary Secretary on 31 January 1998 with the new arrangement taking effect on 1 February 1998. The letter of appointment from the Committee included a particular remit for the Secretary to further the work of the Confraternity through the office volunteers and the voluntary effort of all its members.

Marion's work and that of the volunteers had already been simplified and speeded up thanks to the purchase of the Dell computer system in 1995. The first event effectively organized by means of computers was Le Walk (the Anglo-French pilgrimage from Southampton to Reading Abbey described below), when most of the organizers were on e-mail, using it also to make the editing of the guide a rapid and collective effort.

The age profile of members, including pilgrims, remained high and to attract students and younger people generally to the study of the pilgrimage, the Confraternity Bursary was launched in late 1996 with a mailing to a number of universities. The Bursary subCommittee, chaired by James Maple, interviewed five candidates for the inaugural bursary in 1997, awarding it to Joel Burden, a York University post-graduate student. He planned to extend the scope of his D.Phil thesis to investigate the royal tombs at Burgos and León. A smaller grant of £250 was made to stained-glass artist Rachel Thomas to work on a project of creating glass sculptures connected with the pilgrimage. The 1998 Bursary winner was William Purkis of the University of Lancaster whose project was entitled 'Pilgrimage to Santiago: the Past as a Present'.

During 1998 it was impossible to be unaware of the 1999 Holy Year. Just as for 1993 the Cathedral at Santiago and the Xunta de Galicia promoted and publicized the Camino and the pilgrimage on a world-wide scale. For its part, the Confraternity started preparations for 1999 by setting up a Holy Year planning group to develop a programme of activities, although with less intensity than in 1993.

★ ★ ★ ★ ★

Plans, programmes and events continued to be reported in the Bulletin, produced three or four times a year, supplemented from time to time by a shorter newsletter. Like the Confraternity, the Bulletin grew in size and scope between 1994 and late 1998, often reaching 60 pages. The substantial editorial effort required needed to be fitted in around part-time professional work and absences abroad; so Pat Quaife who had been editor since issue no.1, was therefore happy to be joined in September 1997 by Anthony Brunning as production editor. Appropriately, Anthony's input started with Bulletin 60, the improvement in presentation being obvious thanks to his skilful use of desk-top publishing software.

The contents of the Bulletin also evolved, with more emphasis on scholarly articles, particularly spiritual aspects of the Camino, and fewer pieces on members' own pilgrimages. (The latter continued to be placed in the Pilgrim Archive, kept in the Library and available for members to consult.) This trend was exemplified in Bulletin nos.55 and 56 with the publication of a long and thoughtful two-part article by Barbara Haab, a Swiss anthropologist. Translated from German by Howard Nelson, 'The Way as an Inward Journey: an anthropological enquiry into the spirituality of present-day pilgrims to Santiago' provided a background of reflection for those who had already been on pilgrimage and preparation for those anticipating pilgrimage. This article led to an editorial, also in Bulletin 57, on the difficulties of the return and reintegration into normal life. A number of interesting responses was received from members, some short, some long, which were also published in later Bulletins. Perhaps the most noteworthy contribution on that theme came from Nancy Frey, a U.S. member, veteran pilgrim, warden and also an anthropologist, whose article, 'The Return, when the Yellow Arrows no longer Mark the Way', was based partly on her 1996 doctoral thesis on the effect of the Camino on modern-day pilgrims. A more general reflective piece on the physical integrity of the Camino and the quality of the pilgrim's experience, 'To be a Pilgrim ...' was contributed by the Chairman, Laurie Dennett in Bulletin 59 (May 1997). It arose directly from the second garden Committee meeting of June 1996, held to consider fears raised by the popularisation of the Camino de Santiago.

The Bulletin did not ignore the historical and personal aspects of the pilgrimage. Christabel Watson's scholarly article on 'The Western Parts of the Cathedral of Santiago de Compostela: a reassessment', (no.62, June 1998. pp.19-31), challenges the traditional view of the construction of the cathedral and will have caused members to look more closely at it when in Santiago. Among individual pilgrims one of the most original on the Camino was Desmond Herring of Suffolk. Desmond, the (Morris) dancing pilgrim, cycled and danced his way along the Camino and joyously related his experience in Bulletin 56 (May 1996).

Desmond no doubt carried a copy of the Confraternity's *Camino Francés* guide for 1996, its fourteenth edition which included some notes for winter pilgrims by Alison Raju. The 1997 edition was dedicated to the memory of George Grant, the Confraternity's first pilgrim, who died in March 1997. His passing marked 15 years of the guide and its long-standing editor, Pat Quaife, produced a final 96-page (sixteenth) edition in spring 1998 before handing her pilgrim baton on to David Wesson, a cycling and walking pilgrim and dedicated warden at Rabanal.

The French guides series was enhanced in 1996 by the publication of a detailed walkers' guide to the Arles route (to Puente la Reina) by Marigold and Maurice Fox. Alison Raju spent the winter months producing an edition (or updating sheet) of the le Puy guide each year as well as, in 1997, a substantially revised guide to the *Camino Mozárabe, Vía de la Plata,* a route becoming more popular with experienced pilgrim walkers as accommodation became more plentiful. That same year also saw the publication of the first guide to the *Camino Portugués* by Cornish members Francis Davey and Rod Pascoe. The north coast routes were not neglected either and the fruits of Eric Walker's researches were made available to members in spring 1997: a general booklet entitled *Los Caminos del Norte*. Readers were invited to let Eric know which particular route interested them, whereupon he would dispatch the latest detailed version to them. Tired pilgrims in the north would have been pleased to have a copy of James Hatts's revised guide to *FEVE and ET: narrow gauge rail in Northern Spain*, 28 pages of information on rail travel from Hendaye on the French border to Ferrol in the west.

The 1995 to 1998 publishing programme was completed by several important pamphlets and catalogues on a variety of topics. The first of these was the long-awaited county guide to *Leicestershire and the Pilgrimage to Santiago de Compostela*, by Ted and Peggy Harper, using the format developed by the Research Working Party: churches dedicated to St James or with artefacts related to St James and the pilgrimage, details of access, and possible pilgrim routes across the county. 1996 saw the publication of a full Library catalogue by Howard Nelson, using a bibliographic software package and consisting of more than 1000 items listed by both author and title. The Library continued to grow rapidly and a second edition, with almost 1500 entries, appeared in January 1998. On a far smaller scale, Pat Quaife compiled an eight-page annotated bibliography of books in English on the pilgrimage which, from early 1998, has been sent free of charge to members and enquirers. Two occasional papers were published: Phinella Henderson's *Pre-Reformation Pilgrims from Scotland to Santiago de Compostela* and the text of Robert Plötz's inaugural Constance Storrs Memorial Lecture given in March 1995 (see below). And finally, Constance Storrs's own invaluable work on English medieval pilgrims was reprinted by the Confraternity as a facsimile edition. (Copies are available from the office.)

The Slide Library, overseen by John Hatfield, also flourished, with the slide catalogue updated annually to reflect new donations, and with an increasing number of members borrowing slides to use in lectures. Periodically, John and knowledgeable photographer members would review the whole collection, rationalising it to prevent it from becoming too unwieldy to manage.

Three significant external publications – all scholarly translations of earlier texts – appeared in 1995, 1996 and 1997: the first was Brian Tate's and Thorlac Turville Petre's *Two Pilgrim Itineraries of the Later Middle Ages* (those of the early fifteenth-century Purchas' Pilgrim and of Robert Langton) published by the Xunta de Galicia; secondly, a first translation into English of *The Miracles of Saint James* by an American trio, Thomas F. Coffey, Linda Kay Davidson and Maryjane Dunn[2] and thirdly, a year later, CSJ member, Jim Hall's translation of the seventeenth-century Italian pilgrim Domenico Laffi's diary of his pilgrimage from Bologna to Santiago de Compostela, *A Journey to the West*.[3] 1998 saw further important works, all by American scholars. The first of these, a major reference source on the twelfth-century manscript tradition, *The Pilgrim Guide to Santiago de Compostela, critical edition in two volumes* by Annie Shaver-Crandell, Paula Gerson and Alison Stones, consists of an illustrated catalogue of manuscripts (vol. 1) and an extensively annotated translation of Book V of the *Codex Calixtinus* manuscript, with an analysis of other extant copies and a detailed bibliography (vol. 2). Completely different, and of the late twentieth century, was Nancy Frey's engaging book, *Pilgrim Stories: on and off the Camino de Santiago*, published by the University of California Press, based on fieldwork done largely in Spain on the motivations and experiences of modern pilgrims. Late in 1998 Howard Nelson published *Trust and Tears: Poems of Pilgrimage*, one of which he read at the service of thanksgiving for the life of Stephen Badger (see below).

★ ★ ★ ★ ★

Over a busy four-year period, the number of events: lectures, Practical Pilgrim sessions, visits at home and abroad, organized and attended by a wide spectrum of members, was such that it is not easy to select just a few for special comment.

Perhaps the event that stands out the most, due in part to the number of participants from the UK and France, was *Le Walk* of July 1996, an English counter-point to the 1994 Bayonne to Pamplona walk. Twenty-five members of the Amis du Chemin de Saint-Jacques des Pyrénées Atlantiques, including their president Jacques Rouyre and two of his grandchildren, joined a similar number of Confraternity members to walk the 120 kms from the port of Southampton to Reading Abbey, in fact the St James's Way in reverse. As Laurie Dennett said in her Chairman's report for 1996: 'Route planning was done well in advance by Stephen Badger and Howard Nelson[4] but the logistics of providing shelter, food, medical standby, transport and entertainment for a group of more than 50 people involved literally dozens of Confraternity members in an event that brought great pleasure to everyone.' Four birthdays (two English and two French) were celebrated en route, as was St James's Day when a relaxing boat trip was organized on the Thames from Reading to Marlow – 'a stroke of genius' said one tired walker after several very hot walking days in a row. Marlow was also the setting for a special St James's Day Mass in the Church of St Peter when the Hand of St James was on display to possibly its biggest assembly of pilgrims since the twelfth century when it headed the list of relics venerated in Reading Abbey. In the Bulletin account of Le Walk,[5] no fewer than 35 different people are thanked for their efforts, with a special mention of Doreen Hansen and John Hatfield who provided some 55 participants with breakfasts and picnic lunches on six consecutive days. 'Would we ever do it again, if asked?' was Doreen's rhetorical question in her Bulletin article on feeding the pilgrims, 'Yes, but not this year!'

Doreen Hansen and Stephen Badger had also taken a particular interest in St James, Stoke Orchard, whose wall-paintings of St James make it the most important jacobean monument in Britain. Both joined the Friends of Tredington and Stoke Orchard Churches in the mid 1990s, with Doreen writing a five-page history of the church in 1995. This document was later used to prepare funding submissions for surveys and conservation work (see below).

A couple of months later 19 members took part in a historic visit: to Rabanal and the surrounding Maragatería area where a Confraternity study visit had been arranged for late October. The week had been billed as a mix of lectures, walking and exploring the area, which attracted a slightly different group from other Spanish trips, including a number of Spanish speakers. Some people stayed in the Refugio Gaucelmo, where the October warden Howard Hilton hospitably coped with the 'special' pilgrims, while others stayed in Antonio's Mesón Hostería on the other side of the church square. Evening meals were carefully divided between the two bars, Chonina's and Antonio's, while Howard provided a pilgrim breakfast for us at the refuge. Foreigners, especially on foot, are a rare sight in Maragato villages off the pilgrim route and we met a number of friendly local people including a lady who offered everybody walnuts to eat. On the Camino, near Foncebadón, where we had heard the yellow arrows were not very plentiful, Roger Cocks remedied matters with a tin of yellow paint he had brought from home. On the way back Mary Remnant had a brief entanglement with some Maragato cows as she tried (successfully) to photograph their bells. Music, as always, was in the air, especially on the afternoon of 25 October, the fifth anniversary of the inauguration of the Refugio Gaucelmo when a special celebration was organized and the whole village invited. At 4.45 the bells of Santa María were rung in staccato fashion by Ublines, the village sacristan, to summon everyone to Gaucelmo. We were particularly glad to see our good neighbours, Charo and Asumpta, who had just returned to Rabanal from Madrid, while guests from Ponferrada and the El Bierzo association included Alberto Morán who arrived with his beloved guitar. From the balcony, William Griffiths welcomed everyone in impeccable Spanish. Alberto's music and that of Maximiliano, Rabanal's Maragato piper/drummer, encouraged young and old alike to dance on the patio. Mary Remnant's singers, who had been practising for some days, then took over and performed a number of well-known pieces, including 'Ad honorem ...'.

The following day a special procession and Mass took place in Rabanal at 6 p.m. At 5.30 the Confraternity group, on its last mini-bus excursion, was still in the shadow of Monte Teleno, some miles away, so our driver, Santiago, put his foot on the accelerator to speed us through landscape and villages as fast as safety allowed. To our delight, we arrived 'home' just in time to take part in the procession from the chapel of the Bendito Cristo on the outskirts of the village to Santa María, where Mass was celebrated in an overflowing church. The week ended with a copious dinner at Chonina's where Howard Hilton unexpectedly entertained us with a skilful display of juggling.[6]

Other trips abroad included a memorable visit to the Dingle Peninsula in County Kerry, Ireland, organized by Aileen O'Sullivan (a 1983 member) who lives in the small town of Killorglin.[7] As well as exploring Dingle, Ballyferriter and Killorglin on foot, we also enjoyed a number of special lectures on early Christians in Dingle, on medieval Irish literature and Spanish connections with the Dingle Peninsula. In return, to give local people the chance to learn more of the pilgrimage to Santiago, Marion Marples and Pat Quaife gave two slide lectures on the French routes and the Camino Francés. Stormy weather meant we were unable to visit the Blasket Islands but this was the only disappointment of the week. In Killorglin, it was a special pleasure to visit Aileen's house, unmissable as the door was covered with scallop shells, and her own church of St James, where her framed Santiago exhibition is prominently displayed in the church. If the pilgrimage to Santiago is now well known in Ireland, this is largely due to Aileen, who over the years, has been publicizing the Confraternity and its activities at every opportunity.

Earlier and later visits to Spain also took place: in October 1995 when we visited Navarre and Aragón, and 1998 when we went to Galicia, staying in La Coruña, Finisterre and Santiago. They were both organized by Pat Quaife, who was very grateful to Maribel Roncal (well known to pilgrims for her refuge at Cizur Menor, outside Pamplona) for all her help with accommodation in Navarre. Another 'helper', this time in La Coruña, was Australian, Barry McGinley Jones, known as Mac, who accompanied us around the city by bus and on foot. And at Finisterre, the mayor kindly opened the church of Santa María das Areas for us and arranged for the famous lighthouse or *faro* to be unlocked in the afternoon.

At home, four Constance Storrs Memorial Lectures were delivered between 1995 and 1998, the first being given by Dr Robert Plötz, Chairman of the Sanktjakobus-Gesellschaft, based in Aachen. Mary Remnant opened the meeting by explaining the significance of Constance Storrs and her work, both for pilgrimage scholarship generally and for the Confraternity in particular. It was a great pleasure that the Storrs's son, Dr John Storrs, and his wife were able to be present and to learn that, after many delays, the Xunta de Galicia had published Constance Storrs's important work. Dr Plötz then took the floor to deliver his lecture on '*Ad limina Beati Iacobi* - the origins and early development of the cult of St James in the German-speaking world', later to be published by the Confraternity as an Occasional Paper. Subsequent Storrs lecturers included Professor George Zarnecki in 1996 on 'Romanesque Sculpture of the Welsh Marches', Professor Fernando Lopez Alsina of the University of Santiago on 'The Early History of Santiago: written sources and archaeological evidence' and Dr Dagmar O'Rhiain-Raedel of the National University of Ireland, Cork, on 'In the Footsteps of the Saints: the Irish Pilgrimage to the Continent' (1998).

It is not every day that members are entertained in Downing Street, SW1, but this was indeed the case on 3 October 1995. Gillian Clarke, a 1984 member and wife of the then Chancellor of the Exchequer, had invited Mary Remnant to give her lecture-recital 'The Musical Road to Santiago de Compostela' in the State Room at 11 Downing Street, in aid of the Rabanal Appeal. The visitors enjoyed seeing Gillian's colourful quilted pilgrimage scenes, based on a medieval manuscript, which were displayed in the State Room. After collecting her drums

Gillian Clarke and Mary Remnant at 11 Downing Street

Prof Robert Plötz gives the first Constance Storrs Memorial Lecture, St Etheldreda's Ely Place, London 1995

from the no.11 airing-cupboard, Mary recreated the recent musical pilgrimage to Santiago made by Associates of the Schola Gregoriana of Cambridge in which she had participated. The Confraternity Choir assisted her in a number of pieces, and the President D. Alberto Aza Arias and his wife won applause for their competent playing of the organistrum. Gillian Clarke's generous hospitality included interval refreshments and the lecture-recital, in a unique setting, raised over £1300 towards the Appeal.

The Confraternity amply fulfilled its educational remit by organising eight further lectures in this four-year period, given by a variety of distinguished speakers. No one theme stands out although two were connected with hospitals, medicine and hospitality on the Camino de Santiago: Gosia Brykczynska's 1997 AGM address on 'Pilgrim Medicine and Hospitals of the Camino' and Hilary Hugh-Jones's and Pat Quaife's 'Hospitality on the Way of St James and the Refugio Gaucelmo' given in late 1996. Another memorable AGM lecture was given by the CSJ President, D. Alberto Aza Arias, on his 1995 family pilgrimage on the Camino Portugués. History and art history were not neglected either, with lectures by the American scholar, Dr Marilyn Stokstad on 'The Pilgrimage and Legends of the Road, illustrated by the Altarpiece in the Indianapolis Museum of Art', and archaeologist Helen Lubin speaking on the discovery of the Worcester Pilgrim, given at a Practical Pilgrim session in Warwick. Dr Diana Webb of King's College, London, set the Santiago pilgrimage in its wider medieval context in her 1997 lecture on 'A Choice of Destinations: the three Great Pilgrimages of the Middle Ages'. In many ways the last lecture of 1998, Marion Marples's 'The Return of the Vicarious Pilgrim' struck the deepest chord with members. She first set off from Poitiers in her student days in 1972, quite unprepared, getting only as far as Pamplona before funds ran out and she returned home. After marriage to Leigh Hatts in 1976 and the birth of their son James in 1981, there followed 15 years on the Confraternity Committee, ten of them as Secretary when she dispensed advice and information to innumerable members regarding their pilgrimages. Finally, in 1998, with James aged 17, it was the moment to stop being a vicarious pilgrim and take up her staff on her own account.

Marion has probably organized and attended more Practical Pilgrim sessions than anyone else, and in the period 1995 to 1998, with help from local members, she arranged days or weekends in towns as far apart as Durham and Salisbury (1995), Warwick and Chester (1996),

Ripon and St Albans (1997) and Liverpool and Dorchester-on-Thames (1998). In early years the events were often held outdoors in April and May. By the mid-Nineties, with increasing numbers of pilgrims leaving ever earlier in the year, the sessions took place mainly indoors in churches or church halls, using a well-tried formula: an introductory general session with a panel of experienced pilgrims, followed by separate walkers' and cyclists' meetings under the guidance of one or two 'veterans' (though not necessarily in age). Faced with a barrage of earnest advice on what to do, when to do it and what to take, prospective pilgrims often voiced their anxieties about the journey. To make people feel better, an anonymous member would sometimes remind them of Jocelyn Rix's pilgrimage from Canterbury in 1982. She did nearly everything 'wrong' but still arrived in Santiago in one piece and in time for St James's Day (see Appendix 5).

St James's Day too was a regular diary date, with London, the River Thames and Marlow, Norfolk and Cottenham (Cambridgeshire) being the respective venues for 1995, 1996, 1997 and 1998. The delights of a boat trip on the Thames have already been mentioned as part of Le Walk and Gosia Brykczynska wrote a detailed account in Bulletin 61 (December 1997) of a well-attended weekend at King's Lynn and Castle Acre, with much walking, singing and celebration of two birthdays (her own and Marion's). St James's Day proved to be equally popular in 1998 when Timothy Wotherspoon and Peter Tompkins opened their home, the historic Three Horse Shoes, in the village of Cottenham, to the Confraternity and friends for a garden-party and guided tour of the house. One of the highlights of the day was a pilgrim hat competition, suggested by Jocelyn Rix and won by cycling pilgrim, Shirley Snell of Sherborne (Dorset). The afternoon provided a musical treat: a visit to All Saints, Cottenham for the first performance of the newly discovered 'Vespers of St James' from the *Codex Calixtinus* given by the Schola Gregoriana of Cambridge, directed by Dr Mary Berry. On the Sunday a small group of walkers met at Waterbeach station to walk along the banks of the River Cam to Ely. For once the walk had not been 'piloted' and for the first time ever the Confraternity managed to be on the wrong side of the river for the two pubs passed on the way. Luckily, Joe Cheer had acquired two enormous chocolate birthday cakes which he managed to hide in his rucksack until they were eagerly consumed at lunch-time. The group arrived at Ely Cathedral in the middle of a lengthy sermon, delivered in a sonorous voice, which caused one or two tired walkers to nod off in their chairs.

'Welcoming groups of pilgrims from Europe is an excellent way of recreating the atmosphere and fellowship of the Camino here at home', wrote Marion Marples in Bulletin 60 (September 1997). She was referring specifically to a group of Flemish Vlaams Genootschap members, led by Berte-Marie Reichardt Bosch, who visited Kent, Sussex and Somerset in 1997/8 and a Belgian and Dutch group who visited London in late 1998. Sussex members Peter FitzGerald, Ben Burrows, Rosie Slough and Joe Cheer organized a joint Vlaams Genootschap/Confraternity weekend based in Chichester, at which members were able to walk round the Roman walls, along the Chichester Canal to Birdham, and its a church of St James, and travel by ferry to the Saxon church of Bosham.

Herefordshire remained a popular county for Confraternity visits, with that of 1998 being the third since 1984. Organized by Liz Keay and Marion Marples, the group enjoyed talks by local historians on the Shobdon Arches, the church of St James at Wigmore and a special visit to Wigmore Abbey, now a private house and seldom open to the public. Sadly, the Shobdon Arches were still in a very poor state, although a long-awaited rescue plan seemed to be coming to fruition. Ten churches in Herefordshire and Shropshire were visited as well as Hereford Cathedral. The cathedral city of Lincoln was the object of a visit organized by Rosie Slough in the autumn of 1997. Here the Saturday was devoted entirely to the Cathedral, with highlights being a roof tour and a lecture by Carol Bennett in the Cathedral Library on 'The Pilgrimage of Master Robert Langton, Clerke, and other Lincolnshire pilgrim connections'. Brian Tate was a welcome guest at the lecture, having 'discovered' Robert Langton's account of his early sixteenth-century pilgrimage in the cathedral Library at Lincoln some ten years earlier.[8]

★ ★ ★ ★ ★

Pilgrims continued to beat a path to Santiago, via Rabanal del Camino where the Refugio Gaucelmo received another four years' worth of walkers and cyclists. Steady improvements were made to Gaucelmo's facilities, thanks to the members of the annual Spring Working Groups, the wardens, Asumpta and Charo next door and of course members of the El Bierzo association. Fundraising too prospered, with donations arriving regularly.

By spring 1995, the 'famously cold showers'[9] of Gaucelmo had been replaced by more pilgrim-friendly hot showers and the *salón* fitted with an efficient wood-burning stove, which also fed warm air into the dormitory above. The floor of the barn had been tiled throughout, providing space for 12 extra bunk beds in the peak month. Perhaps the biggest improvement of all was the installation of a bathroom, complete with washing machine, next door to the warden's room, the operation organized and directed by the Madrileñas using trustworthy builders in Astorga, and paid for by the Confraternity. It was intended not only for the wardens, but also for old or ill pilgrims sleeping in the adjoining small bedrooms.

The news in mid-1996 was not so good, with confirmation that the beams in the barn had been infected with dry rot. As Joe May wrote in 'Refugio Gaucelmo News' in Bulletin 57 (August 1996): 'a consultation with our neighbours, the Madrileñas, proved helpful and they had a preliminary discussion with a local architect, D. Juan M. Múgica Aguinago, who offered his professional services free'. A firm of specialists was commissioned to undertake the remedial work which included reroofing the barn, an expensive project for which a Sponsor-a-Tile Appeal (for £3 each) was launched in mid-November.

Two weeks later a miracle of St James took place: the Confraternity heard that it had won the first Premio Elías Valiña awarded by the Xunta de Galicia for a practical project undertaken in the spirit of the Camino. The prize was one million pesetas (worth around £5000 when finally received) − a vital addition to the Appeal account at an opportune moment. In fact the prize was due less to any miracle than to the skill and linguistic ability of the Chairman, Laurie Dennett, who singlehandedly prepared the Confraternity submission within a very short timescale. She wrote in Bulletin 58 (December 1996):

> 'The Confraternity entered the Refugio Gaucelmo for the Premio Elias Valiña considering that the project that has united us all for so many years was an outstanding example of 'the spirit of the Camino' in action. ... It clearly seemed so to the 43 judges, drawn from the Spanish and European associations who met in Santiago de Compostela on the weekend of 30 November 1996 ...'

Buoyed up by this news, members responded generously to the Sponsor-a-Tile Appeal with the list of donors taking up almost a page of Bulletin 59 in May 1997. The figure of £3600 included a special donation of 1000 francs from the Association Rhone-Alpes des Amis de Saint-Jacques. Their Secretary, Jacques Cambet, wrote:

'These few square metres of tiles represent our gratitude for the warmth of the welcome at Rabanal and for the high quality of its facilities, and are in the old tradition of helping others on the Camino ...'

Another major piece of work carried out in spring/summer 1997 was the levelling of the meadow, with the laying of new drainage pipes and manholes. The contractors took their time, but landscaping was finally completed and the trees donated by Aileen O'Sullivan planted, under the supervision of Asumpta and Charo. A large and energetic Spring Working Group spent many hours in the upstairs *servicios* cleaning and improving the shower facilities amongst other jobs. Howard Nelson made good use of the barn where he built new doors for the showers and WCs, under lighting rigged up by John Snell.

In October 1997 the new kitchen was fitted out during the wardenship of Alison Pinkerton and Ginny Lighton, one of their many achievements being to coordinate the arrival of the supplier of units and the plumber. Fortunately, the kitchen was out of bounds for pilgrims for one day only, and Alison and Ginny were able to provide breakfasts throughout the month.

The 1998 Spring Working Group enjoyed the new kitchen in between refurbishing, painting and varnishing the first floor of the *refugio*, and eliminating a large area of damp on one of the kitchen walls. In the meadow, the well was also refurbished by Damián from the village, which meant that the 30 or so new trees could be watered by hose-pipe rather than by endless buckets of water. By now it was clear that the barn, on which so much time, attention and money had been lavished, needed a new door. Howard Nelson offered to make one and, pausing at Rabanal for a couple of days during a pilgrimage, took a number of photographs of nail-studded doors in the village, on the basis of which Walter Ivens and Joe May chose a design. Howard and Etienne, the current warden, ordered 45 four-inch long, hand-crafted nails from the blacksmith in Rabanal Viejo (the next village). The nails then went on a circuitous journey via Buckinghamshire, the CSJ office in London, East Finchley and the Charente-Maritime before reaching their initial destination, Howard's workshop at La Marteille (Dordogne) where the door was made that summer – the first nail being ceremonially banged in by Pat Quaife.[10]

However, all news from Rabanal was overshadowed in autumn 1997 by the tragic death of Miguel-Ángel, Chonina's beloved youngest son (aged 28) and husband of Pili, in a shooting accident on Saturday

Howard Nelson making the new Barn door with the 'Rabanal nails', 1998 (photo: Patricia Quaife)

Icon of Santiago Peregrino by Sr Petra Clare, commissioned in memory of Stephen Badger, with Katherine Crosten, 10th Anniversary of Gaucelmo, October 2001

18 October. 'Many of our members', wrote Walter Ivens and Joe May in Bulletin 61 (December 1997), 'have known Miguel-Ángel since the opening of the Refugio Gaucelmo and back to the time when Chonina handed over the daily running of the bar to him.' With a permanent population of only 28 and Miguel-Ángel and Pili the only young couple in Rabanal, the whole village was deeply affected by his death. Wardens Alison and Ginny represented the Confraternity at the funeral and the Confraternity sent a telegram of condolence to Chonina from London.

Miguel-Ángel had supplied countless meals to tired and hungry pilgrims (and wardens) over the years, helping Chonina when she was still in charge of their Bar Santiago de Compostela. On his death, the bar was closed leaving Antonio's Bar/Mesón El Refugio the only place in the village where pilgrims could buy a hot meal, although a small food shop opened in 1998. Chonina also used to let two rooms to pilgrims who wanted more privacy than a refuge could provide. Fortunately, in 1995, Antonio had opened a traditionally built hotel *(hostal)* with 16 en-suite rooms able to accommodate 25 people – an impressive addition to the facilities in Rabanal. Another welcome addition to the village had opened in August 1996, a new private *refugio* on the main square, in the *corral* or yard of Serafín's and Esperanza's house, run mainly by their daughter Isabel. This *refugio*, of Nuestra Señora del Pilar, is an attractively designed building with some 24 beds plus the usual amenities. Turning pilgrims away when Gaucelmo was full had always been difficult and the wardens were pleased to have somewhere to refer groups of pilgrims, or indeed individuals, in the peak summer months.

Janet Richardson's account of the 1998 Spring Working Group 'Spring-cleaning in the Maragatería'[11] makes special mention of links between the participants and the villagers: Damián the handyman, ex-postman Julio and his wife Quica, Serafín and Esperanza and their son José-Ricardo, and, of course, Chonina, who was still in mourning for Miguel-Ángel. 'A visit by five of us to Chonina', wrote Janet, 'proved an emotional experience, and perhaps cathartic too. At all events, Chonina invited us all to a superb meal in her bar on the last night, a giant step in her fight against despair.'

The numbers offered hospitality at Gaucelmo between 1995 and the end of 1998 totalled 21,046: 5,047 in 1995, 4,812 in 1996, 5,192 in 1997 and a peak of 5,995 in 1998, although the latter figure was still less than the 6,447 of the 1993 Holy Year.

Among the 1995 pilgrims received by David Wesson, who was also instrumental in drawing up the wardens' handbook, were John (75) and Audrey (69) Timmins from Derbyshire, who achieved their ambition of reaching Santiago on foot by 16 June in order to celebrate their golden wedding anniversary. Credit for the longest pilgrimage of all must go to Richard Spence, a New Zealand member from Napier in the North Island. He began his journey by visiting the exact antipodes of Santiago de Compostela, in the Southern Alps of the South Island. Passing through Rabanal in late August, when water was very short, Richard's claim to fame was washing his socks in drinking water kindly given to him by a village resident – real *sopa de peregrino* - as a fellow pilgrim remarked.

The July 1996 pilgrims included a group of eight from the new Czech Republic who told the warden, Annie Shaver-Crandell, that more would be coming as Czechs were no longer discouraged from visiting the West. A few days later, on St James's Day, Gaucelmo received its 1000th pilgrim of the month, Enrique from Seville, on whom Annie bestowed a diploma and a small crown of flowers. By October pilgrim numbers were declining, which meant more space for the Confraternity study group, whose visit was described earlier.

Of the 5192 pilgrims of 1997, one, Nekane Carballo Gutierrez from Pamplona, received a special welcome. The reason? She was the 30,000th pilgrim to spend a night at Gaucelmo since its opening in June 1991. To mark the occasion she was given a silver Confraternity brooch by the October wardens, Alison and Ginny, who had also been intending to celebrate the event with a fiesta to which the whole village would have been invited. Very sadly the tragic death of Miguel-Ángel intervened and the fiesta had to be cancelled.

While the village remained subdued during 1998 the number of pilgrims soared, almost to 1993 levels. Alison Raju spent six weeks as warden at Gaucelmo in the summer of 1998 and reported: 'Fifty to 60 pilgrims every evening nearly all on foot, night in, night out, with at least that number, and often more, in the other two *refugios* in the village. ... Not to mention the (often huge) groups who camped in the field by the road ... and the innumerable others who used us as a place to rest up a while before continuing on to Manjarín or El Acebo.' Were the pilgrims different from those of previous years? Alison and the other summer wardens often felt that 'many of them were not really *peregrinos* but only *turigrinos* or *perituristas,* very definitely on holiday rather than on a pilgrimage as such, interested primarily in whether our showers had hot or cold water and seeing *refugios* in general as youth hostels or cheaper options than a hotel ...'[12] One small boy for whom these were academic considerations arrived smiling in his scallop-adorned pushchair in mid-September. At six months old he holds the Gaucelmo record as the youngest pilgrim to stay, accompanied by his twenty-something parents.

The wardens had a strenuous year in 1998 and Joe May, Wardens' Coordinator, warned of a similar year in 1999, the forthcoming Holy Year. He was well prepared however, with almost a full complement of wardens registered by December 1998.

Joe, along with Walter and Mary Ivens and James Maple had played a full part in the Gaucelmo project from its earliest days, all four being involved in administration, working groups and meetings with El Bierzo members, contractors and others. By December 1998 they were looking for successors to carry on their work and indicated they hoped to retire at the end of 1999, once the demands of the Holy Year had been met.

★ ★ ★ ★ ★

Many Confraternity members like to add an element to their pilgrimage by raising funds for a particular cause or charity. One of the biggest groups that went to Santiago in 1995, 'Relay St James 1995', consisted of more than 80 wheelchair participants from England and a large contingent from Spain, with the appropriate back-up. While most completed stages of the journey, which started from Paris, two, Bill Thornton from Sennen (Cornwall) and an experienced wheelchair marathon athlete, together with a Spaniard, made the complete journey. The whole enterprise raised money for the International Spinal Research Trust which works in 15 different countries to end spinal paralysis.[13] On a different scale, Joel Burden and Christian Turner walked from le Puy to Santiago in the summer of 1997 and raised over £7000 for Shelter. The following year Howard Nelson walked from Périgueux to Santiago in aid of l'Arche (an ecumenical Christian charity which runs residential communities for people with learning disabilities), arriving in May and raising over £6000 for the organization. Interestingly, especially in the light of the Confraternity's growing interest in pilgrimage for people with a disability, Howard later accompanied members of the l'Arche Lambeth community, in stages, from le Puy to Santiago. Vincent Kelly of Reading also took to the road for a second time in May 1997 and was sponsored to help the Berkshire Multiple Sclerosis Therapy Centre. En route he met up with

John Revell, who was being sponsored in both the UK and his native Australia for the Refugio Gaucelmo for which he raised over £800.

Despite grave disabilities, Tim O'Neill McCoy of Totnes (Devon) made no fewer than four pilgrimages between 1997 and 2001 – alone, on foot, unable to walk on footpaths, so constantly at risk from passing cars. 'Through the pilgrimage', he wrote in a much later Bulletin (no. 83, September 2003), 'I have now come to terms with my problems – to recognize and to accept my disabilities. Now enough is enough. Or is it?'

Other people have to wait many years before they are free to make their pilgrimage to Santiago. Marion Marples was one and her story has been told earlier in this chapter. Another was Mary Ivens, a 1986 member who, as part of an all-woman team, cycled to Santiago in June 1998. Similarly, Cornish members Hilary Shaw and Jill Pascoe gained their *compostelas* the same year, walking together from Hospital de la Condesa. A few members, notably Alison Raju and Marigold and Maurice Fox, have walked countless times using different routes. The latter pair walked the Vía de la Plata, from Cádiz to Santiago for the third time in 1998, a long and taxing route at the best of times. The Confraternity has profited immensely from their walks through the many guides the three have written over the years.

Three Confraternity supporters accepted honorary membership in 1997 and 1998: Herbert and Liliana Simon of Cologne who had worked with young people on the Camino for many years and who had set up the *refugios* in Azofra and Hospital de Orbigo; and Dr John Storrs, son of Constance and Francis Storrs, on the publication of the Confraternity's facsimile edition of his mother's work.

Other members received an official honour of one kind or another in the period 1995 to 1998. In mid-1996 Patric Emerson (a 1983 member) was awarded the OBE in the Birthday Honours List for services to ex-service men and women. 1996 also saw the election of Jinty Nelson, Professor of Medieval History at King's College London, as a Fellow of the British Academy. A year later came the exciting news that Professor George Zarnecki CBE, an honorary CSJ member, was to receive the honour of membership of the Spanish *Orden de Isabel la Católica*, 36 years after the award was first announced in 1961, for his work as Chairman of the British Committee of a major international exhibition of Romanesque art held in Barcelona and Santiago de Compostela. For various reasons he was not able to be presented with the insignia of the Order at that time, but the current Spanish

Ambassador, D. Alberto Aza Arias, investigated and confirmed Professor Zarnecki's membership of the Order and a special ceremony took place at a reception at the Spanish Embassy on 28 May 1997. To mark the occasion Professor Zarnecki presented the Library with a copy of the rare 650-page catalogue of the 1961 exhibition, which has since been rebound. A further Santiago-linked award went to Christabel Watson in late 1998 when she gained her MA at the University of Warwick for her thesis on the origins of the western end of Santiago Cathedral.

Mention has already been made of the number of deaths in this period. The first of these was that of the distinguished American scholar Dr William Melczer, Professor of Medieval and Renaissance Studies at Syracuse University, at the age of 70 in early 1995. Laurie Dennett's obituary which appeared in the Spring Newsletter of May 1995 refers to Willy Melczer's immense erudition (acquired relatively late in life) and the way the Travelling Seminars he organized 'introduced many American students to the fascinations of the Camino de Santiago'. To commemorate his old friend, New York member Ronald R. Atkins gave the Confraternity an annual subscription to the International Center of Medieval Art, which he has generously maintained over the years.

Another foreign scholar whose passing was greatly mourned was Dr René de la Coste- Messelière at the age of 77 in May 1996. René de la Coste-Messelière had been arguably the most important scholarly influence on pilgrimage studies in France and Europe for over 40 years. An early honorary CSJ member he was not only an archivist, palaeographer and author of numerous books and articles on the pilgrimage, but an authentic pilgrim, riding to Santiago in the Holy Year of 1965, walking in later years and providing help and hospitality to Paris-route pilgrims in his splendid Chateau des Ouches near Melle. Members who attended the 1990 Hengrave Hall conference will remember his lively contributions to the round-table discussion and to the conference as a whole. At a memorial weekend meeting held by the Société des Amis de Saint-Jacques de Compostelle at Saint-Jean d'Angély, the Confraternity was represented by Mary Remnant who subsequently wrote a Bulletin article on the weekend.[14] In it she describes a moving ceremony at the nineteenth-century Gothic mausoleum in the grounds of the Chateau des Ouches: 'There where the Marquis had been laid to rest with his ancestors, wreaths were laid, a recording of his voice was played and prayers and hymns were led by Père Pierre Kieffer and Don Javier Navarro.'

February 1997 brought news of the death of another European CSJ member, Bernard Schweers from Bremen in Germany. In his late seventies, Bernard was an Anglophile who became known to many of us at the Hengrave Hall conference, where he presented the Confraternity with a copy of a medieval document from Bremen on the time the Hand of St James spent in his home city. He was a cyclist and until the last year or so would make an annual cycling pilgrimage, alone, to Santiago. A 'gentle man' of the old school who spoke knowledgeably about Jacobean matters, especially the Hand of St James and its history, Bernard was our longest-standing German member and someone who enhanced the international nature of the Confraternity.

A fellow cyclist and well known to all early members as the Confraternity's first pilgrim was George Grant. He died of lung cancer on 2 March 1997 just before his 79th birthday, having been a cycling champion in his time and a triallist for the Berlin Olympics of 1936. George always received a particular welcome at Confraternity AGMs and it was his absence at the 1997 meeting that alerted people to the fact that not all was well. The 1997 *Camino Francés* guide was dedicated to George's memory.

However, no death in 1997 was more sudden and unexpected than that of Stephen Badger, aged only 57, the Confraternity's Treasurer and former Librarian, on 14 November. 'Typically', wrote Marion Marples in Bulletin 61 (December 1997) 'he had been loading his car for a complicated journey north to play croquet and to accomplish Confraternity book business when he felt unwell and died very shortly afterwards.' Stephen had been a member since mid-1983 and had always played a full part in all activities, enlivening meetings with generous doses of red wine and laughter. His logistical talents came to the fore when he organized the 1993 Holy Year walk from Reading Abbey to Canterbury Cathedral (the origin of the notorious 'Badger-mile') and masterminded Le Walk of 1996 which has already been described. A crowded thanksgiving service for his life and work was held in Christ's Chapel, Dulwich and a number of members and friends paid glowing tribute to him. His wife Katharine asked that, instead of flowers, people make a donation to a memorial fund, which would be given to the Friends of Stoke Orchard to help save the St James wall-paintings. In the event, £4769 was collected, a sum which covered over 90% of the cost of a very full survey of the wall-paintings carried out by Tobit Curteis in 1998/9. Subsequently the Confraternity Library, which Stephen did so much to develop, was renamed the Stephen Badger

Library of Pilgrimage. Katharine felt that amassing the library gave Stephen more pleasure than any of his other Confraternity activities. A further tribute in late 1998 took the form of a commission to an icon painter, Sister Petra Clare, to produce a commemorative icon which would combine the traditional eastern representation of St James with emblems of his cult and pilgrimage in the West. At the top of the icon a family of pilgrims would be painted, father, mother, son and daughter, representing the Badger family's own pilgrimage to Santiago. Katherine gave the icon to the Confraternity and it was blessed twice at Masses in 2001 (see Chapter 7).

Two more Confraternity deaths took place in April and July 1998, those of Hispanophile Jim Wilson of Nottinghamshire and cyclist Alfred Peacock of Suffolk. Jim Wilson had taken part in the 1994 Bayonne to Pamplona walk and the Maragatería study visit of October 1996; during a late Spanish dinner in Olite he had come to the linguistic rescue of the CSJ group putting into English a complex description of a wine-making process. Alf Peacock, a keen mountaineer and cyclist and connoisseur of Suffolk churches, had completed his pilgrimage from le Puy to Santiago in three stages. He later produced the cyclists' notes for the le Puy route guide, contributed to Practical Pilgrim cycling sessions and to the Bulletin on several occasions. The families of both men asked that donations should be made to the Confraternity at the services of thanksgiving for their lives. In Jim's case a new table and benches were bought for the Refugio Gaucelmo as a lasting memorial in a place he loved.

On a happier note, members were delighted to hear of the birth of Helena and Paul Graham's son, Lawrie, on 5 May 1998. With a Spanish-speaking pilgrim father, young Lawrie too seems destined to 'take the scallop' in due course.

★ ★ ★ ★ ★

1995 to 1998 provided many opportunities for members to attend meetings on the pilgrimage in Spain (and Switzerland) even if the conference scene was less crowded than in the earlier Nineties.

Lausanne was the venue for the General Assembly of the Swiss Association in late March 1995. Their AGM covers a whole weekend, with lectures on this occasion on topics as varied as medicine and pilgrimage, tourism and pilgrimage, St James in Majesty and Black Virgins. The Confraternity was represented by Pat Quaife, who answered a number of questions about the history and running of the Refugio Gaucelmo.

A year later five members gathered in Pamplona for the annual conference of the Navarre Association, chaired by D. Jesús Tanco, on the theme 'Anden los que Saben, Sapen los que Andan' – a nice play on the use of the subjunctive mood in Spanish. Held in the handsome Pamplona Planetarium, the conference covered the physical, cultural and spiritual aspects of pilgrimage. On Day 3, devoted to 'The role of Amigos and Associations of the Camino', Pat Quaife spoke on the way Confraternity members, especially returned pilgrims, contribute to assisting new pilgrims and to the ethos of the organization. At their 1997 conference, entitled 'Paso a Paso' Laurie Dennett gave an appreciation of the life and achievements of Elías Valiña.

Five months later the Xunta de Galicia's conference on 'Atlantic Pilgrimage Routes to Santiago de Compostela' held in Ferrol also saw a good representation of Confraternity members. The theme of the conference attracted historians from Scandinavian countries who spoke, in English, on maritime pilgrimage and boat building, amongst other topics. The Camino Inglés was not neglected and one of the highlights of the conference was a visit to an exhibition 'Rutas Atlanticas de Peregrinación a Santiago – maritima e terrestre.' The fifteenth-century English alabaster depicting scenes from the life of St James, known as the Goodyear Retable, featured in the exhibition and on the accompanying poster. The nearby town of Neda saw a tree-planting ceremony one afternoon, organized by a Galician CSJ member Francisca Shaw, now based in Cambridgeshire. The Mayor of Neda provided Marion Marples and Pat Quaife with a shovel and two small yew trees which they duly planted just outside a former pilgrim hospital on Neda's *Camino Real*.

Two days later numerous Ferrol delegates travelled east to Carrión de los Condes to attend the Federation of Spanish Associations' fourth international conference entitled 'Peregrinos a Santiago ... mil años de historia, ante un nuevo milenio', a theme broad enough to encompass the myriad subjects proposed by speakers in lectures, communications (short papers) and round tables. On the Saturday Laurie Dennett, one of the few foreign speakers at the conference, contributed to a round-table on the return of pilgrims. Intellectual stimulation, an outstanding venue, the restored monastery of San Zoilo, generous hospitality and well-thought out cultural visits all combined to make this a memorable event, organized with his usual panache by Ángel Luis Barreda, president of the Spanish Federation.

Santiago de Compostela became the conference centre for 1997, with the third International Conference of Jacobean Studies, organized by the Xunta de Galicia on 'Santiago, Rome, Jerusalem' and held in the Hotel de los Reyes Católicos. Brian Tate's Bulletin account of it mentioned the two British speakers, both from the University of Nottingham, one of whom was Dee Dyas, a research student, who spoke on the main strands of the debate in fifteenth-century England for and against the physical pilgrimage to holy places.

With the Holy Year of 1999 imminent, a number of new organizations to promote and/or protect the Camino de Santiago were founded between 1996 and 1998, two in Spain itself and three in countries as distant as Australia, Austria and Norway.

Formed in February 1996 on the initiative of Confraternity Chairman Laurie Dennett, the Fundación del Santo Milagro de O Cebreiro aimed to protect the character of O Cebreiro, to augment the attention offered to pilgrims there and to promote the locality in educational and cultural terms. The Xunta de Galicia had earlier ceded the use of one of the vacant *pallozas* and over the next couple of years it was restored as a meeting place for pilgrims. The Fundación sponsored the presence of three young Franciscans from La Coruña who celebrated early-morning Lauds for pilgrims, and held get-togethers for them in the church of Santa María before and after the evening Mass. Even in these early years the gatherings attracted up to 150 pilgrims, whose reactions were overwhelmingly positive. In addition, each was given a bookmark containing a resumé of the history of O Cebreiro and a small booklet of readings and prayers. The Fransicans moved in 2002 to Vega del Valcarce, where they offer the same warm welcome to pilgrims.

In Galicia the Cofradía del Apóstol Santiago de La Coruña was set up in mid-1998, following a decree signed by the Archbishop of Santiago. Its founders included Confraternity member, Joaquín Vilas de Escauriaza who was also Secretary of La Coruña en Bici, another local organization promoting the pilgrimage. Among the objectives of the new Cofradia were the promotion of the cult of St James and of pilgrimage, particularly on the Camino Inglés and to bring together all residents of La Coruña who had made the pilgrimage. Based in the church of Santiago in the old town, its first official event took place on 25 July in that church, with a special invocation to St James and the traditional hug for the Apostle behind the high altar.

In the meantime interesting pilgrim developments were taking place in Norway. At the Confraternity AGM of January 1996, Norwegian member Knud Robbertstadt spoke of the revival of the Norwegian pilgrimage to the shrine of St Olav at Trondheim, as part of the 1000th anniversary celebrations of the city. This led to the setting up on 28 September 1996 of the Norwegian Pilgrim Fellowship of St James, open to anyone interested in the two pilgrimages to Santiago and to Trondheim. The following year, 1997, saw the foundation of both the Austrian Association, known as the St Jakobs Brüderschaft, and – on the other side of the world – of the Amigos del Camino of Melbourne, set up by Laura and Bill Hannan.

While new associations were being formed, the older ones continued to flourish, the Walloon Association des Amis de Saint-Jacques de Compostelle being a case in point. They met at the Abbey of Floreffe, near Namur, in April 1996 to celebrate their tenth anniversary. John Hatfield represented the Confraternity and took the opportunity to have some useful discussions on the pilgrim 'feedback project'. Guided visits round the Abbey and Namur, a special Mass at the church of St Jacques, performances by two groups of Galician bag-pipers and an ebullient presidential speech by Dr Armand Jacquemin contributed to a memorable weekend.

From Belgium to the French border town of Saint-Jean-Pied-de-Port, where pilgrims from every European Jacobean Association – and none – pass through on their way to Roncesvalles. For some 40 years they were welcomed, and occasionally scolded, by the redoubtable Madame Jeanne Debril, given advice and information and pointed in the direction of a bed for the night. With numbers increasing throughout the Nineties and to take some of the strain off Madame Debril, the Amis de St Jacques des Pyrénées Atlantiques opened the Accueil Saint-Jacques in mid-1996 at 39 rue de la Citadelle, where volunteers, mostly former pilgrims, staff the Centre for a week at a time. The Accueil has gone from strength to strength since its inception and many CSJ members have had reason to be grateful to it. Howard Nelson, Irmgard Churchill and John Irvine are frequent volunteers and all report that though the work is demanding, it is rewarding and often fun.

Nearly all those passing through St Jean also stay in Villafranca del Bierzo at the gateway of Galicia, most often at the friendly and hospitable refuge run by Jesús Jato and his wife next to the church of Santiago. For a number of years, both before and after a serious fire in 1993, the refuge 'looked more like a makeshift circus tent, made of dusty plastic sheeting and wooden beams...'[15] In mid-1996 came the good news that the plans for a permanent building on the same site had finally been approved and all building permits granted. Rising from the ashes (literally), the new building would be known as the Hospital de Peregrinos Ave Fenix, and would incorporate stones from the cathedrals of Cologne and Aachen brought to Villafranca in 1993 by two of the German associations.

Beyond Santiago, developments – good ones – were taking place on the route to Finisterre, traditional epilogue of medieval and modern pilgrimages. In August 1997, just before their inaugural group pilgrimage from Santiago to Finisterre and Muxía, the Asociación Galega de Amigos do Camiño de Santiago put the finishing touches to their waymarking of the route. A gruelling but rewarding group walk took place over four days and is now an annual event in the Galician pilgrim calendar.

★ ★ ★ ★ ★

With 1999 on the horizon, all the European associations, the Confraternity included, were making their plans to celebrate the last jubilee year of the millennium. The administrative and other changes made between 1995 and 1998, would, it was hoped, stand the Confraternity in good stead for the busy Holy Year to come.

NOTES

1 Halfway through his time in London, Arturo was successful in gaining a full-time sports broadcasting post with the Spanish TV station, Antenna 3.

2 The full title of the book is *The Miracles of Saint James: translations from the* Liber Sancti Jacobi: *first translation of the Introductory Letter, the sermon Veneranda Dies and the 22 miracles of Book 2,* published in New York by the Ithaca Press.

3 Domenico Laffi, *The Diary of a Seventeenth-Century Pilgrim from Bologna to Santiago de Compostela,* translated, with a commentary by James Hall. Leiden, Primavera Press and Xunta de Galicia.

4 Other members of the planning team included William Griffiths, Hilary Hugh-Jones and Marion Marples.

5 See Bulletin 58 (December 1996), pp.46-51, for two accounts of Le Walk.

6 For accounts of the study visit, see Bulletin 60 (September 1997), 'CSJ Study Visit to the Maragatería' by Pat Quaife and Leslie Smith, and 'Sounds and Silences of the *Camino*' by John Revell.

7 The visit to Ireland was described by Marion Marples in her article 'Ireland - a Personal View of the CSJ visit' in Bulletin 57 (August 1996), pp.47-53.

8 See Bulletin 45 (January 1993), pp.19-32, for Brian Tate's detailed article 'Robert Langton, Pilgrim (1470-1524)'

9 David Wesson, 'Spring News (1995) from Rabanal', Bulletin 53 (July 1995), pp.10-14.

10 Bulletin 63 (Sept. 1998), pp.13-15, 'A Year in the Life of the Rabanal Nails'.

11 Bulletin 62 (June 1998), pp-15-18.

12 Bulletin 64 (December 1998), pp.9-12.

13 An 80-minute video of Relay St James '95 can be borrowed from the Library.

14 Mary Remnant, 'In the Steps of the Marquis', Bulletin 58 (December 1996), pp.36-37.

15 Ann Kruyer, 'The Jato Experience' in Bulletin 57 (Aug 1996) pp.23-27.

Chapter 7
Into the New Millennium
1999 to 2002

A number of key events, challenges and changes took place in these last four years, both at home and in Spain. On the domestic side, concern about trustees' open-ended liability was translated into the setting up of a parallel limited company, also registered as a charity, while the volume and complexity of the work carried out by the Hon. Treasurer had become such that a Finance and Systems Manager was appointed in May 2002. A second international conference, on pilgrim hospitality, was organized at the University of Kent at Canterbury and the Confraternity office moved for a third time, still within the London SE1 area. New technology was fully utilized with a web-site and on-line bookshop set up, which greatly increased the Confraternity's public profile. A Rabanal Church Tower Appeal early in 1999 made a major contribution to the repair of the tower of Santa María and, as expected, the Refugio Gaucelmo came under enormous pressure during the peak months of the Holy Year. Gaucelmo's wonderful neighbours, Asumpta and Charo, moved away from Rabanal, their house being donated to a small community of Benedictine monks who became responsible for Santa María and its services for villagers and pilgrims. In 2001 the tenth anniversary of the inauguration of the Refugio was joyfully celebrated and the 60,000th pilgrim welcomed for the night.

The period opened with only the second Holy Year (1999) that the Confraternity had experienced. And as Holy Years have a distinctive ethos and special programme, a monthly diary format has been adopted here to give an impression of its sequence of events.

January 1999 At the sixteenth AGM, held on 23 January, the Rabanal Church Tower Appeal was launched, with a target of £8000. The tower had become so dangerous that the sacristan could not safely ascend it to ring the church bells. The Appeal was conceived as a way of thanking the village for all it does for pilgrims, and the Diocese of Astorga for ceding the parish house in 1989 to become the Refugio Gaucelmo. An attractive explanatory appeal leaflet seemed to strike a chord with members as the sum of £6500 came in remarkably quickly including the proceeds from the sale of the Confraternity's first calendar. A further £1500 was later released by the El Bierzo Association from the joint *refugio* account.

At the same meeting, the creation of the Pat Quaife Study Grant was announced, an annual award to be made from 2000, open to any member pursuing research into the pilgrimage. Preference would be given to applicants whose topics had a British dimension and to those with a good grasp of the language of the country they proposed to visit.

February A heart-warming piece of news got February off to a good start: the birth of a son, Jacob, to CSJ member Nancy Frey and José Placer in Galicia. At about the same time we were also pleased to hear that member Dr Charles Burnett of the Warburg Institute had recently been promoted to Professor of the History of Islamic Influences in Europe.

The first event of the Confraternity's Holy Year programme – wide-ranging but less ambitious than that of 1993 – took place at The Friars, Aylesford at the end of the month: a weekend school on Holy Years and Souvenirs, attended by 44 people. Chaired by Mark Hassall and Laurie Dennett, the school's speakers included Dr Geoff Egan of the Museum of London on Pilgrim Badges, Laurie herself on 'The Origin of Holy Years and the Compostela', Francis Davey on 'William Wey's Holy Year Pilgrimage to Santiago in 1456', Pat Quaife on 'Holy Year Curiosities' and, as guest of honour, Mademoiselle Thérèse Franque, Archivist of Lourdes who introduced a historic and nostalgic film made in black and white in 1951 by Monseigneur Henri Branthomme recording his pilgrimage to Compostela.[1] After breakfast and Mass on Sunday morning, participants were able to watch a two-hour video of the ceremony of the opening of the Holy Door of Santiago Cathedral on 31 December 1998.

March Late in 1998 we had learned, to our dismay, that the Confraternity's pilgrim President for the past six years, D. Alberto Aza Arias, would be recalled to Madrid early in 1999. A farewell reception organized in the St Alban's Centre on 5 March enabled members to pay tribute to him and his wife Eulalia, an occasion on which William Griffiths sang a special ode he had composed, in the style of 'Domus Venerabilis' (a twelfth-century song from Roncesvalles). The climax of the ode was reached in the last stanza:

> Don Alberto Adios,
> Doña Eulalia, hasta luego!
> Wherever you may be posted next,

Iceland or Tierra del Fuego,
You will always be to us
El Presidente Peregrino
Don Alberto Aza Arias
Caballero del Camino.[2]

D. Alberto later accepted honorary membership of the Confraternity.

The Confraternity's long-planned web-site finally went 'live' in early March, following much development work by James Hatts and Howard Nelson. It initially replaced and expanded on the information pack sent out to enquirers from the office, but soon grew to become the most comprehensive English site devoted to the Santiago pilgrimage on the world-wide web. More than 5000 visits were recorded in the first nine months of the web-site's operation – and more than 20,000 in 2002.

Practical Pilgrim days had not yet reached Iceland but the first Scottish session, arranged by John Malden, took place in his home town of Paisley. Other 1999 venues included London and Ripley (Yorkshire). March 1999 also brought members Bulletin 65, the last to be edited by Pat Quaife after 16 years in the editor's chair. In her final issue she thanked the numerous Bulletin contributors as well as the office volunteers whose collating, folding, stuffing of envelopes and carting of heavy mail-bags to the Post Office ensured that the Bulletin reached members all around the world. The new editor was to be Anthony Brunning, current production editor, a pilgrim to Rome and Santiago and quondam editor of the De La Salle Order's newsletter.

In Rabanal the 1999 Spring Working Party met at the Refugio Gaucelmo on 21 March for a week of hard labour, with Peter and Eileen FitzGerald as acting wardens for early pilgrims. Important meetings took place with the Bishop in Astorga and with the El Bierzo Association in Ponferrada. The Bishop was delighted to receive a cheque for £6500 for the restoration of the church tower, on which work was due to start in April. Rain, snow and blizzards interrupted the working party's progress at the end of the week, but as recompense they were all invited to Chonina's for tea one afternoon, well wrapped up in double layers of clothes.[3]

April The Confraternity welcomed Professor Paolo Caucci von Saucken and his wife to London for the occasion of the fifth Constance Storrs Memorial Lecture. One of the best known scholars of the Camino, President of the Italian confraternity and University of Perugia Study Centre and Chairman of the Xunta de Galicia's Committee of experts, Paolo Caucci spoke in Spanish on 'Roma, Jerusalén y Santiago', with a written English translation made available to members thanks to Laurie Dennett. He set the Santiago pilgrimage within the wider context of Rome (celebrating a Jubilee Year in 2000) and Jerusalem and demonstrated how certain 'itineraries – in Italy and central Europe, at least - were frequently used by pilgrims to all of these three major destinations'.[4]

Across the Channel two new French regional associations were founded: les Amis de Saint-Jacques en Alsace and the Association Normande des Amis de Saint-Jacques based in Caen. Another Spanish regional association was also set up, based in Santander and covering the *Caminos del Norte.*

May Timothy Wotherspoon, the long-serving Treasurer, carried out a large-scale Holy Year mailing to all churches dedicated to St James within the Church of England. He posted 504 packages of eight items each, including a calendar, Bulletins and a book, the material being first transported by bicycle from the office to Holland Park, where a Royal Mail van collected them.

Down in Cornwall a remarkable land and sea pilgrimage was under way, from Padstow, on the north coast, to Santiago via Fowey and La Coruña, organized by Hilary Shaw of the Bredereth Sen Jago, with major Confraternity participation. The Cornish land section of the 'Pilgrim Sea Voyage '99', of which one of the patrons was D. Alberto Aza Arias, started at the church of St Petroc in Padstow with an ecumenical service, followed by a two-day, 27-mile walk to the port of Fowey on Cornwall's south coast. Over 50 people, led by Rod Pascoe, took part in the walk, including most of the 24 sea pilgrims and the 19 Ferrol group walkers (see below). Fowey Town Council gave the sea pilgrims a special welcome which included a buffet supper and a civic ceremony on the Town Quay before they embarked on their two chartered sailing ships (with a professional crew) the brig *Phoenix*, a medieval replica, and the smaller schooner, *Carrie*. Gale force winds prevented the two ships from leaving harbour and by the end of the week, after more bad weather and various misadventures, the ships were still in the Bay of Biscay on the day the sailors had planned to reach La Coruña and walk south on the Camino Inglés to Santiago.

The pilgrims acknowledged their disappointment, accepted their fate stoically and disembarked instead at Santander. Here they boarded a coach to take them to Órdenes, a town on the Camino Inglés in

Galicia. Why Órdenes? Because that was where they could meet up with the 19 Ferrol pilgrim walkers, led by Pat Quaife and Francis Davey, who had coped with a wet and difficult walk from Ferrol, via Neda, Pontedeume, Betanzos and Hospital de Bruma. Complex arrangements had to be made at Ordenes where the two original groups of sailors divided into three: those who were going to join the Ferrol walkers on the last, 29-kilometre, stretch into Santiago, those feeling battered and bruised who opted to get a bus to Santiago, and the heroic 'La Coruña Six' (as they became known) who chose to make the planned walk from La Coruña come what may. Briefed at 11 p.m., seen off on the 7.50 a.m. bus to La Coruña, they reappeared three days later in Santiago having endured horrific weather – to a round of applause from the rest of the group who had been relaxing in the city. The 'Six' deserve to be recorded for posterity: Desmond Herring (the dancing pilgrim), Jan Lelijveld, Frances Nieduszynska (who later wrote an article for *The Tablet* on the sea pilgrimage), Christine Pleasants, Gaby Wingfield (who died in 2002) and Anna Yandell (whose pilgrimage was sponsored in aid of a charity for the homeless).[5]

To say that communications were problematic between the different parties involved – at sea, on land, in La Coruña, elsewhere on the Camino Inglés – would be an understatement. In La Coruña Barry (Mac) McGinley Jones acted as a central point for telephone calls and liaison with the port authority while Marion Marples in London also fielded and relayed messages. Pat Quaife, in charge of walking and accommodation in Galicia, spent many hours on a borrowed mobile phone unmaking and remaking bookings for 43 people as the situation changed from day to day. Just when everyone had arrived safely and been provided with a hotel room, she heard early one morning that a sailing pilgrim was ill and being taken to Santiago Hospital for urgent neuro-surgery. Fortunately the patient, having survived her sailing pilgrimage, also survived her operation.

In France, efforts to revive the Vézelay route for walkers came to fruition with the publication of a 240-page walker's guide, *Guide du Pèlerin de Saint Jacques en Périgord sur la Voie Historique de Vézelay,* covering the stretch from Saint-Léonard de Noblat to La Réole, and published by the Association des Amis de Saint-Jacques et d'Etudes Compostellanes de Dordogne. Further east, the waymarking of the section of the German Jakobsweg from Nürnberg to Ulm meant there was now an unbroken route from Tillyschanz on the Czech border or from Würzburg to Santiago, via Konstanz, Einsiedeln and Le Puy.

A detailed guidebook on the route across Switzerland, *Les Chemins de Saint-Jacques à travers la Suisse,* edited by Jolanda Blum, was also published in 1999.

June A more domestic month, notable for the appearance of Bulletin 66, the first to be edited by Anthony Brunning. A good cover picture of work on the Rabanal church tower heralded some other changes, mainly a re-ordering of events, news and articles, the latter including a thoughtful piece by the 1998 bursary winner, William Purkis, on 'Pilgrimage to Santiago: the Past as a Present'. The 1999 Confraternity bursary winners were announced in the same issue: Ruth Holtham of Jesus College, Oxford and Ranji Guptara of Magdalen College, Oxford, who were each awarded grants of £500. The Committee's annual 'garden' meeting took place *chez* Howard Nelson where members considered the changes that needed to be made to the running of the Confraternity (see below).

The first of the three Holy Year Lectures took place in the crypt of St Etheldreda's Church, Ely Place, London EC1. Christabel Watson spoke on 'A Reassessment of the Western Parts of the Cathedral of Santiago de Compostela' and described the fresh evidence she had discovered on the origins of the west end of the cathedral.

Two days later walking members living in the south of England enjoyed an 11-mile walk in Kent to St James the Great, Elmstead, organized by Andrée Norman-Taylor, partly along the North Downs Way. Andrée's spring walks in Kent and Sussex were now an annual event.

July One of the two busiest months on the Camino and at Rabanal, with this Holy Year July exceeding all expectations and creating an unprecedented work load for the Gaucelmo wardens. The title of Alison Raju's article in Bulletin 68 (December 1999) says it all: 'Gaucelmo's 200-Seater Sardine Tin: Rabanal in July 1999'. She wrote: 'Over 2000 pilgrims slept in "our" *refugio* in July this year, a quantity that is normally spread over three to four months. ...The other two *refugios* in the village had the same problems too, as the vastly over-promoted Camino had nothing like the infrastructure necessary to provide sleeping places for the veritable avalanche of pilgrims unleashed by this year's *Año Santo* advertising campaign. Many seemed to be *excursionistas* rather than real pilgrims ... and many were extremely exigent, expecting (preferably free of charge) beds, sheets and hot water and were surprised to find they often had to sleep on the floor, even on mattresses.' Fortunately all the July wardens spoke fluent Spanish: Alison, Rosemary Scott and a relay of invaluable Spanish volunteers from a Salesian order near Bilbao, two at a time for ten days each. This meant that each warden could do all the jobs involved and each could deal with the complicated situations that inevitably arose when demand (for a bed) massively outstripped supply. Positive things happened too: for example the pilgrim prayers held in the church at 7 p.m. every evening when there was no Mass, organized by Enrique and the other Salesians.

A giant paella might seem more reminiscent of Spain than Birmingham but Colin Jones's vicarage at Perry Barr was indeed the venue for a pre-St James's Day (23 July) celebration for Midlands members, when he prepared a dish that any Camino chef would have been proud of. In the event around 80 people (not all CSJ members) were tempted by the paella and the chance of exchanging pilgrim news.

St James's Day itself was celebrated in different ways in Santiago, Exeter, Dublin and Périgueux. The ceremonies in the Cathedral in Santiago were even more elaborate than usual, with King Juan-Carlos and Queen Sofía heading the list of the 'great and the good'. They included Jeannine Warcollier from Paris who, in the afternoon of the 25th, was awarded the silver medal of the Xunta de Galicia for distinguished service to the Galician community. Jeannine was also a member of the Archbishop of Santiago's Holy Year Committee and richly deserved her award, following over 40 years as Secretary-General of the Société des Amis de Saint-Jacques de France, a record never likely to be matched.

Exeter was the venue for the Confraternity's own St James's Day weekend organized by Marion Marples and local member David Hughes. Tours of the city and of Exeter Cathedral (with a fine medieval St James carved on the west front) were followed by a four-mile, very hot walk along the towpath to the ancient pilgrim port of Topsham to visit the museum and a riverside pub for supper. Sunday, 25 July, opened with a Sung Mass for the patronal festival at the (Anglican) church of St James in north Exeter. Instead of a sermon talks on St James and the Confraternity were given by Marion Marples and Mark Hassall. A country fair in nearby Powderham Castle occupied the afternoon pleasantly.

In Dublin, Aileen O'Sullivan celebrated the feast day with members of the Irish Society of St James who had come from all over Ireland for the weekend. After Mass at the Carmelite church in the city centre, members went on an open-top bus tour of Dublin, the first stop being at St James's Gate, the headquarters of Guinness where free samples were enjoyed. Dinner and speeches in a Belgian restaurant brought the day to a close.

Meanwhile, Confraternity Vice-Chairman Howard Nelson was taking part in a memorable pilgrim day at the cathedral of Saint-Front in Périgueux (on the Vézelay route). 'The occasion', wrote Howard, 'initiated by the Association des Amis de Saint-Jacques et d'Etudes Compostellanes de Dordogne, was a solemn Mass for the dedication of a chapel (newly restored in one of the oldest parts of the building) to St James, and the blessing of a statue of the saint, carved in walnut by a local sculptor. The day ... was the culmination of many months of work by the local Association under the very active President Mme Monique Chassain ... The inauguration of the chapel not only revives Périgueux as a high point on the Vézelay route, it also gives us a new *monument jacquaire*.'[6]

The day after St James's Day, three members attended the funeral of Edna Clare (1925-1999) at Mortlake Crematorium. Edna was one of the great Confraternity Hispanophiles, a teacher of Spanish who had taken part in nearly every CSJ visit to Spain. Even when not well in October 1998 she came on the Galicia visit – her last trip – to see Santiago for one more time. She died on 13 July 1999.

August A quieter month in London, but an extremely busy one on the Camino, when 45,680 pilgrims received their *compostela* at Santiago, over 18,000 more than in August of the last Holy Year of 1993. At the Refugio Gaucelmo wardens Max and Ida Ritler, Lin Galea and Patricia De Gemmis coped with a flood of pilgrims, helped also by more Salesians from Bilbao.

One of the most significant events of the Confraternity's Rabanal year took place that month. Our friends and neighbours for ten years, Asumpta and Charo, had been spending increasing amounts of time away from the village and earlier in the year had decided to move to a tranquil part of Andalucía. So what would happen to their house? Would it be sold? Would it be let? How would it affect the Refugio Gaucelmo? By chance three young Benedictine monks had visited Rabanal in July while looking for somewhere on the Camino to set up a monastery and retreat-house. Asumpta and Charo had come to Rabanal for the 25th July celebrations and Alison Raju told them the monks' story. This inspired them to offer the monks their house on a permanent basis which, with the agreement of their Abbot, was accepted. With the consent of the Bishop of Astorga they became the parish priests of Rabanal and the surrounding villages and moved into their new home in mid-August. The church, so often locked before, was kept open with three services a day, including Vespers, attended by many pilgrims; they, the villagers and wardens were delighted with the new arrangement. The monks, led by English speaking Fray Juan Antonio, were willing to take over from Asumpta and Charo the tasks connected with the *refugio*, i.e. hold the keys, inspect it in winter, look after the *huerta* and arrange any necessary repairs.[7] All seemed to be set fair.

September London came to life again after the holidays and we were gratified to learn that the new Spanish Ambassador, H.E. the Marqués de Tamarón, one of whose Christian names was Santiago, had accepted our invitation to become Honorary President. A welcome new guidebook was received, *El Camino de Madrid a Santiago de Compostela* published by the Amigos de los Caminos de Santiago de Madrid, and an encouragement to pilgrims to try other routes, at least from Madrid to Sahagún in this case. On the 23rd the Very Revd Stephen Platten, Dean of Norwich Cathedral, delivered the second of the Holy Year Lectures at St Etheldreda's, on 'Patterns of Pilgrimage – Pilgrimage Today' in which he distinguished between pilgrimage, tourism and retreat, seeing pilgrimage as a rite of passage and source of reconciliation and healing.[8]

October The month not only of the Confraternity visit to Santiago but also of the inauguration of the Rabanal church tower, timed to coincide with the CSJ group's being in Galicia. Unpredictable weather, mainly wet, did not spoil the latter's enjoyment of Santiago, where the restored choir in the cathedral was a spectacular sight, and of other towns on the itinerary: Lugo, where Laurie Dennett provided a guided tour, Mondoñedo where James Hatts (now aged 18) translated the priest's commentary in the cathedral; Pontevedra, another fine provincial capital and Caldas de Reis with its church dedicated to St Thomas of Canterbury. On the day of the inauguration (27 October), despite the coach driver's best endeavours, the group arrived at Rabanal just after the Bishop of Astorga had begun the celebratory Mass for the church tower. The simple service was organized by the Benedictine monks, who had thoughtfully prepared an order of service in both Spanish and English. Afterwards at Gaucelmo the El Bierzo president, Domingo Sánchez presented the Confraternity with a handsome silver plaque to mark the occasion. He had also co-opted the Ponferrada hospital chef to prepare the celebratory *tapas* on the spot. The latter had arrived with gas cylinders, a huge gas burner and an even larger pan in which he made a vast and delicious paella which, along with *empanadas* and *tortillas,* was washed down with quantities of El Bierzo wine.

For the last wardens of the 1999 Holy Year, Howard Hilton and Mike and Anja Mannion, the inauguration brought more visitors to Gaucelmo than usual. Even in October they had had a full house of pilgrims every night, each of whom was offered a chocolate wafer on arrival, thanks to the enterprise of Mike and Anja and the generosity of Thomas Tunnock Ltd of Glasgow which sent 1500 bars to Gaucelmo, enough for the whole month.

As Joe May wrote in 'The Wardens' Year 1999' in Bulletin 68, 'An astonishing 9090 pilgrims from 47 different countries were sheltered at Refugio Gaucelmo. The number of pilgrims is almost 50% greater than in Holy Year 1993 and a significant proportion of the total since we opened in June 1991, which now stands at 45,210 pilgrims from a total of 78 different countries.' This was Joe's final 'Wardens' Year' report as he, James Maple (Chairman of the Refugio Gaucelmo Sub-Committee), Walter Ivens (Coordinator) and Mary Ivens (Secretary) formally stepped down at a meeting on 18 November. All had served on the Sub-Committee since its inception in 1988 and had been the mainstays of the Confraternity's efforts to serve pilgrims in Rabanal and to help bring life back to a dying village.

At home, work started on the Confraternity's 2000 calendar, using images of St James found in Britain.

November The Confraternity month opened on the 11th with Holy Year Lecture III, given by Laurie Dennett on 'Elías Valiña Sampedro and the Camino de Santiago: an Appreciation', shortly before the tenth anniversary of his death on 11 December 1989. Speaking from the heart, Laurie painted a vivid word-portrait of the life, character and achievements of the remarkable 'man with the gigantic soul who was the scholarly and tireless defender of the Camino de Santiago, the "friend and brother to all pilgrims" as the words on his grave attest.' Those to whom Elías Valiña is 'just a name' are recommended to read Laurie's lecture, published in full in Bulletin 69 (March 2000), to gain an idea of his immense achievements and the extent to which modern-day pilgrims are in his debt.

Later in November the Art and Antiques Fair took place at London's Olympia. Mary Ivens and a friend went to look round and to their astonishment they saw, on a corner stand of early carvings in wood, a familiar figure of St James as a pilgrim. He was about 14 inches high, wore a hat with a scallop shell affixed to the front and a cloak under which his scrip was slung across his chest; in his left hand he held a short staff. One bare foot was striding forward and his hair was long and curly, like his beard. His 'label' described him as: 'A North Netherlandish oak figure of St James of Compostella, late 15th century'. 'Perfect for the Confraternity in a Holy Year', thought Mary, who promptly contacted Timothy Wotherspoon in his capacity as Treasurer and Howard Nelson as Vice-Chairman regarding the proposed purchase. Timothy then had a lengthy discussion with the dealer, while Francis Davey, another Committee member, arranged an appointment with specialists at the Victoria and Albert Museum for verification of its period and origins. The V & A experts confirmed its fifteenth-century date, adding that it was likely to have been part of a larger North European altarpiece. The decision was made to buy this image of the patron saint of the pilgrimage, to be displayed at principal Confraternity events. To protect the new St James, Howard Nelson made a fine Gothic-style wooden case in which the statue now stands.

December The last month of the last Holy Year of the second millennium. Pilgrims were still making their way, in wintry conditions, to Santiago, in many cases for the ceremony of the closure of the Holy Door of the cathedral on 31 December. These included the former President, Alberto Aza Arias, his wife and family group, who had booked their accommodation in Santiago at least a year beforehand. In all, just over 150,000 pilgrims were awarded their *compostelas* in 1999.

The last Confraternity publication for 1999 appeared: Marigold and Maurice Fox's guide to the Madrid route, checked for accuracy by the Madrid Amigos, and available for members at the 2000 AGM.

Finally – an unexpected end-of-year surprise – the El Bierzo Association awarded the Confraternity their annual prize for the group which, in their view, had best expressed the spirit of the pilgrimage during the year.

2000-2001-2002

At the 2000 AGM Laurie Dennett referred to the challenges facing the Confraternity arising from the open-ended liability faced by its individual trustees. The question had first arisen during 1999 when the Committee was considering the future of Confraternity visits abroad. Much anxiety had been expressed by members that in the event, for example, of an accident involving a coach hired by the Confraternity and the resulting death or disablement of the victim(s), they as trustees would be liable to pay any damages awarded once insurance cover had been exhausted. An interim decision, pending members' agreement, was therefore taken to convert the Confraternity from a simple charity into a limited company with charitable status, in effect creating a new body, but with neither the objects, nature or name of the Confraternity changing. Howard Nelson took the lead in steering the changes through the different stages, completing legal forms and drafting the Memorandum and Articles of Association for the new body. A key stage in the process occurred on 30 September 2000, when an Extraordinary General Meeting was convened (coinciding with the 2000 Constance Storrs lecture) at which the two documents were adopted unanimously by members present. Two further steps remained: to have the incorporated Confraternity registered as a charity and to persuade members of the unincorporated association (the 'old' Confraternity) to become members of the company, each with liability limited to £1. To cut a complex story short, two AGMs took place on 20 January 2001, of the unincorporated association and of the company limited by guarantee, the former passing resolutions confirming the transfer of undertakings to the latter and enabling it to be wound up when the Trustees were satisfied that there was no further justification for keeping it in existence. The company proceeded to elect a full Committee, whose members would serve both as company directors and charity trustees.[9]

Much to the relief of the Trustees, membership of the company in its first year, 2000-2001, was two per cent higher than membership of the unincorporated association in 1999-2000, despite the slightly daunting nature of the forms that members had to complete. The 2001 AGM elected the first Committee where members had the new dual role; it consisted of Laurie Dennett (Chairman), William Griffiths and Howard Nelson (joint Vice-Chairmen), Timothy Wotherspoon (Company Secretary and Treasurer), Gosia Brykczynska, Hilary Hugh-Jones, Brian Mooney, Mary Moseley, Aileen O'Sullivan (Ireland), Alison Raju, Willy Slavin (Scotland), Eric Walker, Paul Graham (Chairman, Rabanal Sub-Committee) and Alison Pinkerton (Wardens' Coordinator). The Charity Commission finally issued the incorporated Confraternity with its registration number, 1091140, on 15 March 2002, with the 1983 organization still registered as a charity. For the time being the Committee decided to retain the two concurrently, for reasons connected with possible legacies and with the Library.

Membership statistics, provided at regular intervals by John Hatfield, the long-serving database manager, recorded 2068 members at the end of October 2000, rising to 2284 in early February 2002 and 2358 in mid-November 2002, just before this history ends. In between times, particularly at the beginning of a new financial year in October, numbers would drop as members resigned or failed to renew for a variety of reasons, and rise again as new members joined and existing members renewed late.

To return to January 2001 and the eighteenth AGM, Timothy Wotherspoon, having been Treasurer for seven very demanding years, invited expressions of interest from possible replacements for him. He outlined the tasks and commitment involved in 'A Year in the Life of the Treasurer', 18 tasks spread over the year and seven day-to-day jobs. In some ways it was not surprising that no-one came forward to replace Timothy as Hon. Treasurer, not to mention Peter Tompkins (who often referred to himself as Under-Treasurer) and who kept the accounts on computer. The two of them bowed out at the 2002 AGM with an animated "Power Point" presentation, illustrating how the financial performance of the Confraternity had improved over the years from 1994 onwards. Following 19 months advertising for a new Treasurer the Committee came to the conclusion early in 2002 'that the job had simply grown too big for anyone to be expected to continue doing it on voluntary basis.' In May 2002 therefore a Finance and Systems Manager was appointed on a two-year, part-time contract, working for 16 hours a week. The appointee, Alison Thorp (sister of volunteer Pat Watson) was a certified accountant working part-time for a number of organizations and took over responsibility for three of the five main work divisions identified by Timothy. He remained as Company Secretary for the time being, with a vacancy remaining for an Honorary Treasurer. The scale of Timothy's achievement for the Confraternity was partly reflected in the fact that it took six hours to describe the contents of the files he handed over to Alison.

Alison soon found her feet, reviewed the way the office worked, improved the filing system, reviewed the membership arrangements and speeded up processing of publications orders with a faster printer and a franking machine, all of which helped Marion Marples and the volunteers in their work.

The years 2000 and 2001 also gave rise to another major anxiety: the Confraternity office, which had been functioning well on the first floor at Talbot Yard, above the friendly Copyprints shop/office on the ground floor. In mid-2000 we learned that the whole building, and others nearby, had been sold by the Special Trustees of Guy's Hospital to a development company. There seemed to be no imminent danger of demolition, but with the Confraternity lease expiring in November 2001, the new landlord was bound to increase the rent, possibly even doubling or trebling it. The problem was put to the AGM in January 2001, in order to obtain an in-principle agreement from the membership to raise the subscription by up to £10, with effect from 1 October 2001, if it became necessary. A Sub-Committee was set up to examine all the issues related to the office, and in the event Marion Marples found new premises, at Blackfriars (still in SE1) within the Christ Church complex of offices at 27 Blackfriars Road. The move took place just two weeks before the lease on Talbot Yard expired and although Marion and the Committee and volunteers were sad to leave they found the new office lighter, more attractive and obtained at a very reasonable rent. However, the rooms at Talbot Yard still had to be painted and repaired to comply with the terms of the lease, a mammoth and thankless task willingly carried out by Peter Tompkins and Timothy Wotherspoon.

While Laurie Dennett continued as Chairman until January 2003, supported by William Griffiths and Howard Nelson, changes occurred among other office holders, whose work was becoming increasingly demanding as membership grew. Doreen Hansen became Membership Secretary for the second time in 1999, taking over from Vincent and Roisin Cowley. In April 2001 she was succeeded by a recent member, Tim Siney, who responded to an appeal made at the 2000 AGM. Between March and October the Pilgrim Record Secretary is kept almost as busy as the Membership Secretary. Alan Hooton, who started as an office volunteer at Talbot Yard, had undertaken the job for several years and issued thousands of pilgrim records in that time, including 584 sent out in 2000 alone. In May/June 2002 he handed over to Eric Walker, who also maintained his interest in the North Coast routes. Office volunteers keep the non-stop administrative work moving and Marion Marples was pleased to recruit some new volunteers in 2001: Maggie Sweeney, Mary Ivens, Ken Mann and William King, who joined the established team of Alison Pinkerton, Charles Francis, Bernard Masson, John Revell and Pat Watson; Christine Pleasants joined them in 2002.

2001 also saw the setting-up of the on-line bookshop, operated by Marion and office volunteers. Its introduction brought about a four-fold increase in sales, which meant that in the first six months of operation it more than covered the cost (£400) of the software package. Members could also use the on-line facility to renew their subscriptions.

The Bulletin editorship also changed in the spring of 2001. After more than two years in the post and having produced eight excellent issues. Anthony Brunning resigned in April, due to pressure of work. He was warmly thanked in Bulletin 74 (July 2001), a joint effort by Gosia Brykczynska (soon to be appointed editor), James Hatts, Marion Marples and Pat Quaife. Gosia soon found her feet as editor, contributions came flowing in from members and James Hatts, by now a student at Royal Holloway, University of London, continued his role as production editor.

Timothy Wotherspoon, whose many and energetic contributions to the Confraternity have already been documented, relinquished his post as Company Secretary at the 2003 AGM. His work, and that of Peter Tompkins, had been central to the Confraternity over the past nine years, particularly their management and presentation of financial affairs. David Wesson, who edited the annual *Camino Francés* guide to the route with much devotion for five years, also stepped down.

The announcement of these last two departures was made at the 2003 AGM, held on 18 January 2003, 20 years and five days after the Confraternity came into being, and the last event to be included in this history. The meeting was especially noteworthy for being the last to be chaired by Laurie Dennett. Having been Chairman for eight years and Vice-Chairman and Committee member before that, Laurie's contribution to the Confraternity and the pilgrimage to Santiago has been inestimable. In particular she has always striven to protect the Camino, to work with European colleagues and to be true to the spirit of pilgrimage. Her last Chairman's report and AGM talk entitled 'Gifts and Reflections' fully mirrored these qualities and were a fitting climax to her many years of service. Her 'leaving' presents included a silk scarf inspired by the windows of León Cathedral, a dozen bottles of wine each from a different place on the pilgrim routes in France and Spain, and a cheque to which the membership had contributed generously. Typically, Laurie did not intend to spend money on herself. Instead, provided the Bishop of Lugo consented, she was going to commission a bronze plaque for the church or *hospedería of* O Cebreiro, to commemorate the Benedictine monks who ministered to pilgrims for over a thousand years (from c. 836 to 1858) and yet who had been largely forgotten.

Founder members cut the 20th Anniversary cake: Jocelyn Rix, Patricia Quaife, Mary Remnant, January 2003 (photo: Marion Marples)

Farewell presentation to Laurie Dennett by William Griffiths, AGM January 2003

The Confraternity's own charitable activities continued to bear fruit. Bursaries of varying amounts were awarded between 2000 and 2002 to students from the Courtauld Institute, Oxford University and King's College, London and it was gratifying to learn that William Purkis, an earlier Bursary winner, had enrolled for an MA on the medieval pilgrimage to Santiago, which he hoped would lead to doctoral research. The first Pat Quaife Study Grant was awarded to Katherine Lack of Whitbourne, near Worcester. It enabled her to continue her researches into the life of Robert Sutton – who may have been 'the Worcester pilgrim' – and to recreate Sutton's possible journey on foot across fifteenth century France and Spain. Katherine was awarded a second grant in 2001, with a view to publication of her work in 2003.

A different kind of award, the St Christopher Fund, was set up late in 2002 on the initiative of James Maple. It was established to provide support in the form of a payment of up to £500 for a companion for an elderly, frail or disabled person to make the pilgrimage to Santiago who would otherwise be unable to contemplate such a journey. It was hoped that any money which members might wish to give in memory of relatives, friends or fellow pilgrims would be made into this Fund.

★ ★ ★ ★ ★

The most important Confraternity event in the UK between 1999 and 2002 was undoubtedly the second international conference, 'Body and Soul: Hospitality through the Ages on the Roads to Compostela', held in mid-April 2001 at the University of Kent at Canterbury. Organized by Mary Moseley and Marion Marples, the conference – fruit of over two years' planning – approached the subject of hospitality from different angles and at different points in time, modern as well as medieval. As well as a sizeable home contingent, delegates came from France (including Jeannine Warcollier and Thérèse Franque), Germany (Dr Robert Plötz), Spain (José Ignacio Díaz and Juan Antonio Torres, the prior at Rabanal), the USA and Ireland (including Aileen O'Sullivan). Papers ranged from CSJ member Colin Jones's thoughtful 'The Needs of Strangers' through 'When a Pilgrim Dies' by archaeologist Barney Sloane, 'The Benedictine Tradition' by Dom Aidan Bellinger and 'Modern Hospitality' by José Ignacio Diaz to Naomi Turner's 'Food for Pilgrims', an entertaining live cookery demonstration in which Naomi shared her medieval recipes. Specific pilgrim destinations examined included Rabanal ('A Monastery on the Way of St James') by Fray Juan Antonio Torres Prieto of Rabanal, 'Hospitalité Saint-Jacques at

Estaing', by Marie-Claude Piton, assisted by William Griffiths, Aachen by Robert Plötz, Hospital de Bruma by Pat Quaife and St Mary Rouncival, Charing Cross by Marion Marples.

The lectures were complemented by films, music exhibitions, and visits. Everyone enjoyed the two French films shown, the historic *Chemin de Compostelle* (1951) introduced by Jeannine Warcollier, and *Une Couronne de Sanctuaires Pyrénéens sur les Pas des Hospitaliers,* presented by Thérèse Franque of the shrine at Lourdes. Mary Remnant's latest lecture-recital 'Music in the Life of St Thomas Becket' paid due tribute to Canterbury's own special saint, with a wonderful mix of twelfth-century Goliard songs, plainsong and others from a variety of sources. Three exhibitions also contributed to the richness of the conference: the Horniman Museum's 'Santiago Trek' of 1993, 'Pilgrim Welcome Sites in Palencia' and 'The Work of the *Hospitaleros'* prepared by Laurie Dennett. On the Saturday afternoon delegates all visited the pilgrim church of St Nicholas at Harbledown before splitting into groups for a city walk in Canterbury or a coach visit to the Romanesque churches of Patrixbourne and Barfreston. At the closing banquet they themselves provided the evening entertainment, reflecting on hospitality received along the Camino, with a general consensus that the University of Kent too scored high marks in this field.

As in earlier years, a wide-ranging programme of lectures was arranged, including the AGM and Constance Storrs Memorial Lectures. Topics presented at the former included 'The Development of the *Camino Inglés*' (Pat Quaife, 2000), 'William Wey' (Francis Davey, 2001) and 'Pilgrim Snail' (Ben Nimmo, a young pilgrim with his trombone, 2002). Constance Storrs was commemorated by Dr Alexandra Kennedy in 2000, speaking on 'Cluny in the Development of the Pilgrimage to Santiago' and by Professor Caroline Barron in 2002 on the more personal subject of 'The Pilgrimages of Margery Kempe'. The 2001 Storrs lecturer, the French scholar Humbert Jacomet, was prevented by illness from coming to London. His lecture on pilgrim iconography was translated at short notice by Miranda Jones of Oxford and presented by William Griffiths. A fascinating glimpse of the Camino in the last 26 years of the twentieth century was provided in June 2001 by Linda Davidson and David Gitlitz from the US Friends of the Road to Santiago. They first went on pilgrimage in 1974 and documented for us the amazing changes that have occurred since then. An equally personal pilgrim occasion took place on 12 October 2002, Spanish National Day, when an afternoon session entitled 'At Your Own

Pace: Special Pilgrims on the Way to Santiago' featured two disabled pilgrims, Paul Darke, a wheelchair user and a Winston Churchill Travelling Fellow[10], and Major Tim O'Neill McCoy, a walker who had been injured in a vicious mugging at Euston Station. Andrée Norman-Taylor rounded off the afternoon speaking on making the pilgrimage as an older person. It was on this occasion that the St Christopher Fund, mentioned above, was formally launched.

Two events linked with the Refugio Gaucelmo proved to be particularly successful. The first of these, a Wardens' Workshop, took place in November 2000, organized by Alison Pinkerton, the new Wardens' Coordinator. Rather along the lines of Practical Pilgrim, both new and experienced wardens attended, to introduce the former to the work done at Rabanal and to gain the benefit of the latter's experiences – all with the aim of enhancing the quality of service given to pilgrims throughout the season. The second event, 18 months later, was quite different: neither a lecture, not a presentation, but an evocation, on 20 June 2002, of Rabanal and the ideals behind the creation of the Refugio Gaucelmo. A panel of speakers, all closely connected with the project from its inception, answered the 'why?', 'how?' and 'when?' questions of the *refugio*, mainly with newer members in mind. James Hatts made an edited recording of the evening, which now exists as a CD in the Library. Another of those present was John Revell, pilgrim, Bulletin contributor and proof-reader, who wrote a moving account of the evening and of an earlier visit to Rabanal, which is reproduced in Appendix 6.

Weekend or St James's Day visits, with a mixture of walking, searching for St James and local sightseeing, sustained members' interest in Shropshire, Dorset, Hampshire and Hertfordshire in 2000 and 2001. The Hertfordshire highlight was undoubtedly the pilgrim procession at St Alban's Abbey on 17 June 2000 (St Alban's day) when the new Confraternity banner, created by Moya Jolley, made its first public appearance. Moya, a friend of Gosia Brykczynska, had been commissioned by her to make the embroidered banner in 1998, on the theme of pilgrimage.[11] The design, incorporating 58 different stitch types and 100 different colour combinations, represents three aspects of pilgrimage: the physical, the psycho-spiritual and the developing mystic awareness of the journey from death to life. Moya generously made no charge for the hours of work she had put into making the banner, but did accept honorary membership of the Confraternity.

Later, on St James's Day, at a patronal Mass at St James, Spanish Place, the banner, the medieval statue of St James and the icon in memory of Stephen Badger (see below) all received a special blessing. As he had done for the statue, Howard Nelson made a special box to house the banner.

Visits were also made abroad, to Belgium (2000), Spain (2001) and France (2002). In Mechelen (Malines) north of Brussels, the Confraternity group was amazed to find themselves climbing the 536 steps of the tower of the cathedral, the tallest in Belgium. Also on their pilgrim itinerary were Antwerp, Brussels and Le Roeulx, a village south of Brussels with a well-preserved hospital of St James. Dirk Aerts, Secretary of the Vlaams Genootschap (Flemish association), and Berthe-Marie Reichardt Bosch organized walking tours while a dinner with members of both the Belgian associations at the Gallego Centre in Brussels cemented friendship in good Camino style.[12]

The visit to Spain in October 2001 was of special significance, including as it did the tenth anniversary celebrations of the Refugio Gaucelmo in Rabanal. Led by Marion Marples and William Griffiths, with Janet Richardson as interpreter, the group first stayed at Carrión de los Condes, one of the few Camino towns not visited on earlier Confraternity trips. The restored monastery of San Zoilo, now a hotel, provided luxurious accommodation right on the Camino, on the western outskirts of Carrión. The historic buildings of the monastery had been ceded by the hotel group to the Palencia Amigos who had set up an impressive study centre, the Centro de Estudios y Documentación del Camino de Santiago. Ángel Luis Barreda, ex-Federation president, acted as guide to San Zoilo, the cloisters, church and study centre, which he runs and which is open in the morning between 10 and 2. Other Camino visits included the Roman villas of Quintanilla and La Olmeda, the towns of Palencia, Villalcázar de Sirga (and lunch at Pablo Payo's legendary *Mesón de Villasirga*), Sahagún and the Abbey of Sandoval. Marion Clegg described their arrival at Sandoval in her account of the visit, 'Carrion to Rabanal, 2001' in Bulletin 77 (March 2002): 'We waited while Marion and Janet sought the key-holder. A small, frail-looking woman hobbled towards us, balancing on wooden pattens, holding a stick and wrapped in a black shawl, through the abbey where restoration work was in progress. She was Munda, was 92 years old and had lived there all her life. She pointed out architectural features, asked questions and spoke in a strong clear voice, saying she was just an amateur, unlike the learned professors from Madrid. As she guided us around it became clear that she was an authority on the place. In the church, still a place of worship, she was delighted by the singing of the 'Salve Regina'. We left Sandoval glad to have met this extraordinary woman.'

Moving on to Rabanal for three nights, the group was divided between Antonio's Mesón El Refugio and the new hotel at the end of the Camino Real, La Posada de Gaspar. Other members had also made the long journey to Rabanal for the tenth anniversary celebration of Saturday 27 October. Prominent among them was James Maple, travelling by car from the Charente-Maritime with Maurice and Marigold Fox – and a precious cargo: the Confraternity icon made in memory of Stephen Badger[13] and which was to be blessed at the anniversary Mass in Santa María. The day dawned, the rain held off and the Mass of Thanksgiving for ten years of the Refugio Gaucelmo, celebrated by the Bishop of Astorga, assisted by Alberto Morán, Antolín de Cela and the Benedictines of Rabanal, proved to be a moving occasion. During the service, the icon rested on a wrought-iron stand, borrowed from Gaspar, until the blessing when Katharine Badger Croston, Stephen's widow, held it in her hands. After the Mass and photographs it was whisked away to be installed in its new frame, in the Gaucelmo library.

A fiesta followed in the meadow, with *tapas* and *vino* generously provided by the El Bierzo Association. The *tapas* were accompanied by speeches with the Confraternity and El Bierzo Chairmen (Laurie Dennett and Domíngo Sánchez) first at the microphone expressing their thanks in eloquent Spanish to all who had made the *refugio* a reality and looking back to the 1991 inauguration and the parish house as it was in the late 1980s. Laurie made particular reference to Walter Ivens as 'the Father of Refugio Gaucelmo' who, from the first inspiration some 13 years ago until very recently, and supported wholeheartedly by his wife Mary 'has dedicated himself completely to realising his dream *of giving something back to the Camino of the much that he had received.*[14] Very sadly Walter and Mary were unable to be present, for health reasons, and were much missed. Also missed were our former neighbours, Asumpta and Charo, as well as Joe and Pat May. Another speaker, and supporter of the Confraternity and Gaucelmo, was Joaquín Vilas de Escauriaza of La Coruña who presented Laurie with a plaque to commemorate the occasion. Ángel Luis Barreda was there, handing out leaflets and bibliographies from his new study centre, as were Herbert and Liliana Simon who had made the long journey from Cologne. So many pilgrims, wardens, colleagues and friends, not to mention the Rabanal villagers who contributed to an afternoon full of happiness and reminiscence.

A year later and a different country: France and specifically the Poitou-Charentes region were the focus of a Confraternity visit, organized by Marion Marples, to the Romanesque churches of the area. Starting at St Hilaire in Poitiers, the group went on to Parthenay-le-Vieux, Melle and the incomparable church at Aulnay before reaching James Maple's Charentais house in the village of Les Nouillers. At Le Pèlerin, James provided a magnificent spread, washed down with plenty of local wine, which in turn prompted a rendering of the Goliard song *'Bache bene venies'* after lunch. The town of Saintes, so important for the pilgrimage route, provided a good base for visits to a number of eleventh and twelfth-century churches as well as the pilgrim hospital of Pons, now well restored and its medieval graffiti still visible. Talmont, the picturesque crossing point over the Gironde, was the scene of a great picnic on the river bank, where people tasted the local aperitif Pineau des Charentes.[15]

★ ★ ★ ★ ★

A number of references have been made above to articles published in the Bulletin, which continued to flourish under the editorships of Anthony Brunning and, currently, Gosia Brykczynska. One of its strengths is the encouragement it has offered over the years to members to write for publication, a mixture of the personal and the scholarly characterising issues produced between 1999 and 2002. For the first time, Bulletin 75 (September 2001) was devoted to just one topic: the Proceedings of the Canterbury conference, 'Body and Soul: Hospitality through the Ages on the Roads to Compostela', held five months earlier in April of that year. Speed was of the essence in terms of production as a generous grant from the Xunta de Galicia's Consellería de Cultura, Comunicación Social e Turismo, Xerencia de Promoción do Camiño de Santiago was conditional on publication by the end of September. It was a difficult challenge to meet but the four-person production team of Gosia, Pat Quaife, James Hatts and Marion Marples burned the midnight oil to produce a 92-page special issue. (Copies are still available from the office.)

2002 saw the start of a new and streamlined Bulletin production process, with James Hatts becoming production editor and John Revell responsible for proof-reading. The editor, Gosia Brykczynska, prepares the copy supplied by members, which is then checked and proof-read before being e-mailed (to Madrid in 2002/3) to James, who formats the material. For two issues a CD-ROM was then sent to Colourworks (the printer) in London's Docklands. Latterly text has been sent in by e-mail. A proof copy is then delivered to the CSJ office for final checking before the arrival of the 2000-plus copies for mailing. Volunteers still stuff the envelopes but no longer have to drag heavy sacks to the Post Office, as these are now collected by the Royal Mail.

The Confraternity's most ambitious publication to date appeared in December 2000 and was launched at the 2001 AGM: Francis Davey's *William Wey: an English Pilgrim to Compostella in 1456.* The author, a West Country classical scholar and a CSJ member since 1992, had spent over five years exploring the world of William Wey – and his companions – and the original sources and locations. This was no easy task as Wey, a priest and native of Devon, wrote his *Itineraries,* an account of his extensive travels, mainly in medieval Latin, and which are found only in his own manuscript in the Bodleian Library, Oxford and in a nineteenth-century transcription published by the Roxburghe Club. Francis Davey's book consists of a new translation of the *Itineraries,* facing the Latin text, followed by a series of essays on topics raised by the text. The last of these solves a minor medieval mystery: the identity of the 'four English gentlemen' who were with William Wey in the cathedral at Santiago at Mass on Holy Trinity in 1456.[16]

Francis was also the author, with Pat Quaife, of the Confraternity's first and long-awaited guide to the Camino Inglés, published in May 2000. Other new guides that appeared in 2000-2002 included Bernhard Münzenmayer's second edition of the *Guide to the Camino Mozárabe, part B, Zamora to Santiago,* a route waymarked by the Galician Amigos, and Eric Walker's comprehensive 2001 guide to the northern Gijón to Arzua route, following the coast to Ribadeo and then inland to Mondoñedo and Villalba.

Three significant external publications were warmly received by both active and armchair pilgrims. Edwin Mullins's (a 1983 member) readable *The Pilgrimage to Santiago* of 1974, and long out of print, was reissued in the autumn of 2000 by Signal Books; Jonathan Sumption's classic general study *Pilgrimage* also reappeared in late 2002 after a gap of 27 years. *The Pilgrimage Road to Santiago: the complete cultural handbook* was the ambitiously titled 'fat book' – as Marion Marples called it in her Bulletin review – by David Gitlitz and Linda Kay Davidson (the Secretary of the U.S. Friends of the Road to Santiago) published in 2000. Its 440 pages contain a wealth of information on the Camino Francés – churches, landscape, history and customs – interspersed with personal anecdotes of pilgrimage which bring the story to life.

★ ★ ★ ★ ★

Early in 2000 a new Refugio Gaucelmo Sub-Committee was elected, with Paul Graham as Chairman and Alison Pinkerton, an experienced warden, as Wardens' Coordinator. They became responsible for the running of the *refugio*, recruiting wardens and encouraging newer members to join the annual Spring working parties.

One of the Sub-Committee's early tasks, working in conjunction with the El Bierzo Association, was to safeguard the work of the CSJ at Gaucelmo. Just as had happened on a lesser scale in 1989, Gaucelmo was being eyed enviously and needed to be defended vigorously. After some anxious moments on the part of the two associations, the Bishop of Astorga renewed his commitment to El Bierzo and the Confraternity, whose Committees learned the need for continual vigilance.

Pilgrim numbers at Gaucelmo went down in 2000, if one can call the figure of 7590 for 2000 'down', which it was only in relation to the 9000-plus of the Holy Year. On 12 October 2001, Spanish National Day and the Feast of Nuestra Señora del Pilar, wardens Alison Pinkerton and Ginny Lighton welcomed the 59,999th and 60,000th pilgrims to Gaucelmo. Luis Franco, an architect from Zaragoza, and his friend were delighted to be treated to dinner at Gaspar's to commemorate the event. After the pair had arrived safely in Santiago they sent a letter of congratulations to the wardens for the tenth anniversary (described above). As Laurie Dennett said at the end of her speech on 27 October: 'May the next 60,000 pilgrims find themselves similarly at home in Refugio Gaucelmo'. By the end of 2002, a total of 67,449 pilgrims had stayed since June 1991.

2001 was notable earlier for the installation of new showers and WCs in the barn – for use between mid-May and mid-September. Gaucelmo's plumber Señor Puente also succeeded in turning round the drainage system to travel downhill through the *huerta* (meadow) instead of uphill into the square by our front door. The Spring working group, led by Paul and Alison, found part of the *huerta* wall next to Chonina's vegetable patch had fallen down, due to high winds catching the vegetation on top of the wall. So they rebuilt the wall and severely trimmed the excess vegetation – and all the walls were done in this way. They also discussed with Gonzalo, the stone-mason, the building of a pergola as a tribute to the pioneers of the *refugio*. (It hasn't happened yet, but it will.)

The following year the Working Party, which included French member Blandine de Beaufort-Sanières from Paris, achieved so much that Alan Howard needed two bites of the cherry in terms of Bulletin articles (no.78, June 2002 and no.79, September 2002) to record all that had been done. The most troublesome problem, due partly to changes in regulations regarding water heaters, was the pilot lights, which had remained stubbornly uncooperative throughout 2001. The Rabanal Sub-Committee decided that a permanent solution was needed and by the end of March 2002 a fully insulated, 290-litre gas hot-water cumulator boiler was installed and an older model in the kitchen replaced by a heater with an automatic pilot light. No fewer than 51 separate tasks were listed by Alan in the first part of his report, which left Gaucelmo in sparkling condition and ready to receive the year's pilgrims. In part 2 he mentioned the 18 new double bunks for the dormitory, as well as numerous outside jobs in which villagers were or would be involved. The working party also welcomed Walter and Mary Ivens for a brief visit, as well as Alberto Morán and Asumpta and Charo, all except Alberto having been absent from the tenth anniversary celebration.

Wardens, like pilgrims, come in all shapes and sizes and from a variety of backgrounds, but it is not often that a bishop is numbered among them. This occurred in July 2002 when the wardens were the Bishop of Ramsbury (in the diocese of Salisbury), the Rt Revd Peter Hullah, and his wife Hilary. Writing in *The Sarum Link* of September 2002 Bishop Peter described living in Rabanal as 'not an easy task ... There is always work to be done, places to clean, food to prepare and stories to hear. However there are many compensations – dancing in the street on St James's Day, countless heart-searching encounters with an international, ecumenical community of religious pilgrims and the daily possibility that the road to Santiago leads first through Emmaus'.

2001 and 2002 saw over 7000 pilgrims received a year at Gaucelmo, with the once quieter months becoming more popular, although numbers were still greatest in July and August. This meant that wardens are under pressure throughout the season and finding that normally a two-week stint is enough. The Wardens' Workshop, introduced in November 2000, is now an annual event at which wardens can express their views candidly, discuss improvements and at the same time pass on their enthusiasm to new and prospective wardens. The ideas that come up are fed into the plans for the development of Gaucelmo and into the Wardens' guide, first prepared by David Wesson and which is updated every year.[17]

★ ★ ★ ★ ★

Just as pilgrims arrive at Santiago in life, so their – and our – earthly pilgrimage comes to an end sooner or later. Maybe members felt uplifted by the 1999 Holy Year but only two (to the best of my knowledge) – Madge Kong and Edna Clare (see above) – passed away in that year. In contrast no fewer than 18 deaths were recorded in the following three years, including a number of people who had contributed in varied ways to the life of the Confraternity.

Anne O'Donnell of Fife, despite being very ill, attended the Practical Pilgrim day in St Andrew's in March 2000 and died only two months later, while preparing for a Scottish pilgrimage. At her Requiem Mass on 27 May, attended by more than 800 people, the Camino was mentioned several times, including her own pilgrimage to Compostella in 1998 with her husband and teenage children.

Connie Burnas, wife of Robert van der Poorten, died on 10 April 2000, less than a year after walking from Ferrol to Santiago in May 1999. Tony Bambridge from Tring had been a member, with his wife Diana, since 1989 and contributed generously to the Refugio Gaucelmo. Tony and Diana were members of the group visits to León and Burgos in the early Nineties. Tony, who was devoted to St James, died peacefully after a short illness in August 2000.

The last pilgrim death of 2000 was that of John Durant of Bristol on 2 December. John, a pilgrim on many occasions, contributor to the Bulletin, a member of Rabanal working parties and translator of the fifteenth-century German poem by Hermann Künig von Vach, had a great love of Spain, the Spanish language and the Camino de Santiago. He first walked to Santiago in 1989, after which he explored a variety of routes, including the formidable tunnel of San Adrián in the Basque Country. John regularly supplied information about the northern routes to Eric Walker who remembered him with affection in Bulletin 73 (March 2001). At the funeral in Bristol the order of service followed the themes of pilgrimage and exploration. Six members were present, including Maurice and Sue Morgan, the latter writing an obituary in the same Bulletin.

Peggy Harper from Leicester, born in 1919, was one of the Confraternity's older members in both senses of the word. With her husband Ted she was a founder member of the Research Working Party and in 1995 they jointly produced the first county guide to St James's churches. They also organized a memorable Practical Pilgrim weekend in Leicester in 1991. After becoming increasingly frail, Peggy died in early 2001.

For her friends, Gabrielle (Gabi) Wingfield's name will always be associated with guts and courage. Even though not well in May 1999, she was one of the 'La Coruña Six' who walked to Santiago after participating in the Pilgrim Sea Voyage '99 (see above). March 2000 found her energetically working at Rabanal with the Spring working party. Later, even as she was undergoing unpleasant treatment for cancer, she came to the office to help stuff the July 2001 Bulletin. Gabi died in November 2001, thus missing the opportunity of a pilgrimage in 2002 with David Snelling and his mule Henry (see below).

Another older and much respected member, George F. Tull (1920-2002), died a few months later. Like Peggy he sat on the Research Working Party from the beginning, collecting information not only on 'his' counties of Surrey and Sussex but useful snippets for other county coordinators. A quiet, scholarly Francophile – and cat lover – George published a number of pamphlets on historical/religious topics and more recently *Traces of the Templars,* a gazetteer of Templar sites in England.

Late in May 2002 we heard of the death of John (Ian) Tweedie who, before joining the Confraternity in 1988, advised Fr Gerry Hughes in 1975 on the latter's walk to Rome. Ian had already walked to Rome, pulling his rucksack on a trolley with pram wheels, and was a source of knowledge and inspiration to other members making that pilgrimage. A contributor to the Bulletin on Scottish topics and a Research Working Party member who amassed a thick file of information on St James in Scotland, Ian joined the 1991 León group and was a great hit with the ladies of the Maragatería as he danced a Scottish jig, wearing his kilt, outside the Refugio Gaucelmo on inauguration day. Ill-health blighted his later years and his last pilgrimage took place in 1992 when he walked from Conques to Moissac on the le Puy route, with a private group.

Of Confraternity members living in Spain, Alison Shrubsole who died suddenly at the age of 76 in the autumn of 2002, was probably the most active. She joined the CSJ in 1989 and walked to Santiago from León that year, becoming an early supporter of the Refugio Gaucelmo. Before her marriage to George Hilton-Brown in 1983 Alison had had a distinguished career in education and teacher-training, both in the UK and Africa. She was appointed CBE for services to education in 1982. Her life changed radically on retirement with residence in southern Spain where her husband, who died earlier in 2002, farmed in the Alpujarras area of Andalucía. After her 1989 pilgrimage Alison helped with Confraternity membership matters in Spain and contributed to the Refugio Gaucelmo on several occasions.

At the same time we were sorry to learn of the untimely death from a heart attack of artist member Edmund Blood, aged 55. His pilgrimages to Santiago in 1999 and 2000 were punctuated with stops for sketching, the results forming an exhibition of drawings and paintings shown at the Upfront Gallery near Penrith in the summer of 2002. Edmund provided the cover illustration for Bulletin 74 and his widow Mary presented the Confraternity with an annotated drawing of his journey along the Camino, for use in the office.

The last 2002 death occurred shortly before Christmas, that of David Charlesworth of East Anglia and an enthusiastic pilgrim, walking pioneer and devoted grandfather. He and Marion Marples went on pilgrimage at the same time in 1998 but never actually met. David had already piloted a walk for St James's Day 1997 at Castle Acre, waymarking the route with yellow arrows and serving refreshments to weary members half-way round. Typically, even though on borrowed time, he reconnoitred the way from Bury St Edmunds to Walsingham for the 2003 twentieth-anniversary pilgrimage, making complex arrangements for accommodation. (In the event his large family, including his wife Valerie and son Seth, helped with the catering, and the Walsingham pilgrimage was dedicated to David's memory.)

To this litany of deaths must be added the names of Gordon Haller, John Stutter, Bryan Williams, W. Fortune, Dr R.J. Walker, the Revd A. Horne, Lorna Newton and Rachel de Araoz, the latter two members since 1983 and regular attenders at Confraternity events in earlier years.

★ ★ ★ ★ ★

Throughout 2000 to 2002 Alan Hooton and later Eric Walker were kept busy issuing over 1000 pilgrim records and pilgrim register forms to Confraternity walkers and cyclists, and – in far fewer numbers – to horse-riders or pilgrims walking with a pack animal. Some members succeeded in raising thousands of pounds in sponsorship for good causes. There were too many to record them all here but they often featured in recent Bulletins. Two special pilgrimages deserve a mention, as their protagonists demonstrated both originality and determination.

Over the summer of 2002 regular reports were coming to the CSJ office from David Snelling of Ivybridge (Devon) who was on his way from le Puy to Santiago with an unusual companion – his mule Henry. The Operation Henry Trust had been set up by David and supporters back in 2000, to raise funds for Macmillan Cancer Relief. Unfortunately a stroke (and the outbreak of foot-and-mouth disease) prevented his departure at that time. Gabi Wingfield had been the first of 12 people who volunteered to accompany David but her own illness made this impossible. David and Henry finally set out on 2 April 2002, had many adventures on the way and made numerous friends. Sponsorship contributions came flocking in, some of them in memory of Gabi Wingfield, and David and Henry arrived triumphantly at Santiago on 2 August.

Six days after David left le Puy, two sisters from Kent, Susie Gray and Mefo Phillips, left on horseback from Canterbury. Their mounts, Leo and Apollo, were no ordinary horses, but leopard-spotted Appaloosas, which attracted much attention on the Camino. Leo and Apollo's forebears went to South America with the Conquistadors and the breed is known for its stamina and gentle temperament. In Lourdes Mefo and Susie met up with their other three sisters, who joined them for part of the journey. They too were raising funds through sponsorship, for the Pilgrim Hospices in East Kent.

Two unusual pilgrimages, but it should not be forgotten that all pilgrim journeys are unique and special to those make them. Despite improved facilities along the Way, pilgrims on the Camino Francés in the twenty-first century have to cope with problems of crowding and accommodation that those travelling in the Eighties, for example, could not have dreamed of. Hopefully, the fellowship of the Road and the welcome extended by wardens are mitigating factors.

One of the regular office volunteers, Bernard Masson, did not go on pilgrimage in 2001 but was awarded the Légion d'honneur, France's highest decoration, for his services to exports, specifically in the textile industry. Five long-standing members completed degrees in 2000-2001 after several years of study. Gosia Brykczynska, the Bulletin editor, was awarded her Ph.D. from the University of London for her thesis on the nature of wisdom, while Canon Robert Llewelyn of Gloucester gained his from the Cheltenham and Gloucester College of Higher Education for his work on the anthropology of pilgrimage. Sue Morgan became a BA (from the Open University), Alison Raju a BA (Hons) in Hispanic Studies from the University of Nottingham, and Robin Neillands, the first CSJ Chairman, was awarded a BA (Hons) in history from the University of Reading. And in 2000 Jinty Nelson became the first woman President of the Royal Historical Society.

The Confraternity's only honorary institutional member is the

P.C.C. of St James, Stoke Orchard, mentioned in Chapter 6. After the initial survey of the wall-paintings carried out by Tobit Curteis in 1998/9, he negotiated with the Council for the Care of Churches to fund an environmental study of the moisture in the church in winter months. This was completed in mid-2001 as part of a long-term project to conserve the paintings, for which further major funding was being sought.

★ ★ ★ ★ ★

The Société des Amis de-Saint-Jacques de France (formerly 'de Compostelle') and its Secretary-General Jeannine Warcollier were mentioned early in Chapter 1 as a source of inspiration for some of the early members of the Confraternity. Seventeen years later, the Société celebrated the fiftieth anniversary of its founding, with a number of special events in Paris held in late November 2000. Among the highlights of the weekend were an anniversary dinner and a Memorial Mass at the church of Saint-Jacques du Haut Pas, in the rue Saint-Jacques, to remember both the founders of the Société and pilgrim members who had died during the past 50 years.

In Spain, the year 2000 saw Ángel Luis Barreda Ferrer retiring as president of the Federation of Spanish Association of Amigos del Camino, after 13 years of tireless work in that position. Earlier CSJ members will remember him at the 1990 Hengrave Hall conference, newer members met him at Carrión de los Condes on the 2001 visit, and we must all be grateful for his facilitating role in bringing the Refugio Gaucelmo project to fruition. He was succeeded as President in May 2000 by Fernando Imaz Marroquín, President of the Guipúzcoa Association of Amigos, a lawyer known already for his dedication to the Camino and to the legal protection of the routes. During the period 1999-2002 the Federation, through the Galician and La Rioja regional associations, organized two successful international conferences in Camino towns, the first at Cée near Finisterre in October 1999, under the heading *Fin de Seculo, Fin de Milenio, Finisterre* with the theme of 'Jacobean Pilgrimage and the Camino de Santiago in the Past 100 Years'. The second conference took place in November 2002 in Logroño supported by a Confraternity contingent of Laurie Dennett (who contributed to a Round Table), William Griffiths and Pat Quaife. Entitled 'Cuatro Pilares Para un Camino' the conference examined the four elements which support pilgrims on the Camino: local government, the Church, *refugio* wardens and the Jacobean associations in Spain and the rest of Europe. Laurie, in her talk, put forward "the fifth pillar": the people who live on the Camino, which was greeted with acclamation.

Two other European associations celebrated anniversaries in 2002. In May the Centro Italiano di Studi Compostellani, founded just a few months before the Confraternity, held an international twentieth anniversary conference on 'Santiago e Italia' in Perugia, to provide as complete a picture as possible of Jacobean connections in Italy, including confraternities, hospitality, local cults and devotions. Laurie also spoke at this event, her topic being 'Courtesía, Cultura y la Práctica de Peregrinación Hoy'. A couple of months later the Irish Society of St James marked its tenth anniversary with a special weekend in July in Kilkenny City, which was attended by Aileen O'Sullivan.

In Germany, the important development of pilgrim routes under the general title of Jakobusweg continued apace. In March-April 2000 the first group of 'guinea-pig pilgrims', led by Gerhilde Fleischer, author of four Jakobusweg guides, walked from Nürnberg to Konstanz. CSJ member Pamela Harris joined the international group, got over her initial alarm at being the only English person and soon enjoyed the singing that took place in churches, restaurants and the open air. Just under 60 churches were visited, with an average of three a day, and including Ulm Munster which has the world's tallest church tower at 528 feet.[18]

Peter Robins confirmed in Bulletin 68 (Dec. 1999) that waymarking was largely completed from the Czech-German border, through Germany, Switzerland and eastern France to le Puy. This was reiterated by John Hatfield in an article on 'Routes in South Germany and Switzerland' (Bulletin 69, March 2000) in which he encouraged pilgrims to follow the six routes from Tillyschanz to Konstanz, a total distance of 911 kilometres.

Alison Raju brought the situation up to date by joining Gerhilde Fleischer's Spring 2002 group to walk the route and check on the waymarking, commenting in Bulletin 80 on the iconography of St James in south German churches. Using the Via Gebennensis, set up by the Association Rhône-Alpes des Amis de Saint-Jacques in the mid-1990s, she walked on alone from Geneva to le Puy, gathering useful information on what she called a 'designer route' (compared with a historic route) bridging two points.[19]

Fifty years 'on the Camino' at Saint-Jean-Pied-de-Port came to an end for Madame Jeanne Debril on 12 May 2000, when she died after a short illness. Pilgrims' adviser and mentor, provider of the last *sello* in France, keeper for a few years of the first tiny refuge in the town, Madame Debril is remembered for her many kindnesses to true pilgrims, particularly people who had already walked or cycled through France. A familiar figure for decades, seemingly a fixture for pilgrims who encountered her on several occasions, Madame Debril was, in some way, St-Jean-Pied-de-Port. Her death certainly altered the pilgrim landscape of the town, already modified by the arrival of the Accueil St-Jacques a few years earlier. In an interview in 1990 she summed up her mission: 'To welcome pilgrims of all nationalities and of all ages and to give them all possible information for them to complete their pilgrimage beyond the Pyrenees. This is an increasingly difficult task, because how do you separate the wheat from the chaff ...? Abuses of the pilgrimage are a major concern. But I am here to serve, and I go on.'[20]

Another pilgrim pioneer who 'served' was Dom Willibrord (Jean-Marie) Mondelaers, the Benedictine founder and inspiration of the Flemish Vlaams Genootschap van Santiago de Compostela set up in 1985. He died in mid 2001 after ten years of ill-health and major operations. Earlier he had passed on the care of the Association to his nephew, Dirk Aerts, its long-standing Secretary whom the Confraternity welcomed to London in 1998. An impressive presence at the Bamberg conference held in 1988 and at the French fortieth anniversary celebrations in 1990, Fr Willi enlivened meetings with his bonhomie, generosity and pilgrim tales. John Hatfield recalls telling him in the early Nineties about an encounter, on the Vézelay route, with a Belgian pilgrim group of donkey, three-year-old boy, his parents and six young women. They had set off from Brussels at the end of March and by 18 July had arrived at Palas do Rei. Fr. Willi's eyes lit up and he said: 'I married the couple, I baptized the little boy and everyone is doing fine!'

It is not known if this ten-strong group went on from Santiago to Finisterre and Muxía, on Galicia's wild and windswept Costa da Morte, as many pilgrims did and still do. All the European associations, the Confraternity included, were very shocked to learn of the devastating oil-spill – the 'Prestige' disaster – off that coast in the autumn of 2002. The Galician Association took prompt action, contacting all its sister associations with a programme of bridge-building and cleaning up of the oil, in the hope that it would improve the Finisterre extension of the pilgrimage and thus encourage more pilgrims, whose presence would contribute to the threatened Galician economy.[21] The trustees of the Confraternity voted an initial contribution of 1000 (about £650) and in Bulletin 81 (March 2003) invited members to support the project. The Amigos recently published a special number of their journal *Libredón*, devoted to the Costa da Morte and the Finisterre/ Muxía extension of the pilgrimage.

★ ★ ★ ★ ★

This grant of £650 made early in 2003 to a Spanish association demonstrates just how much the Confraternity has developed since its beginnings 20 years ago, and equally how the European Jacobean movement itself has grown since that decisive Holy Year of 1982. Pilgrimage to Santiago, from being the preserve of the few who knew of it, has become available to the many and created international friendships on a scale unimaginable in the immediate post-war years of the twentieth century. As for the Confraternity, from six members to over 2000, from a small shelf of books to a serious Library of over 2000 volumes in a central London office, from meetings in early members' homes to international conferences in Suffolk and Kent, from a portable typewriter to the most up-to-date computer technology, from one individual's generous impulse to a thriving pilgrim *refugio* in Rabanal del Camino, its development has been quite literally phenomenal, particularly to those who joined in the early years of the 1980s. None of it would have happened without the dedicated work of its members, far too numerous to list again here, but whose names are sprinkled on the preceding pages of this history. Some of it would not have happened without the friendly cooperation of colleagues in our sister associations, whose names are also familiar to readers. In 2003, the Confraternity is in good heart and good hands – we can all look forward, in anticipation, to the next 20 years, firmly established among the Jacobean associations of Europe and beyond.

> 'And perhaps that is the most lasting value of the pilgrimage: men and women of all ages united in a marvellous confraternity. It was so in the Middle Ages, it is now.'
> David Charlesworth (2002)

Notes

1   René de la Coste-Messelière acted as adviser on historical aspects of the film, in which he is seen occasionally.

2   See Bulletin 65 (March 1999) for the full version of the ode which was sung to a tune composed by Mary Remnant for 'Domus Venerabilis'.

3   For a full account of the working party, see Shirley Snell's and Walter Ivens's article, 'The 1999 Working Party at Rabanal' in Bulletin 66 (June 1999), pp.9-12.

4   For a longer extract from his lecture, see Bulletin 66 (June 1999), p.19.

5   For fuller accounts of the sea pilgrimage, see Hilary Shaw's article in Bulletin 67 (Sept. 1999), 'Pilgrim Sea Voyage 1999', pp.3-7, and François Delauzun's 'When is a Pilgrimage not a Pilgrimage?' in Bulletin 71 (Sept.2000), pp.22-25. 'Ferrol to Santiago' by Pat Quaife can be found in Bulletin 68 (Dec.1999), pp.13-20.

6   See also Howard Nelson's article, 'St James's Day 1999 - in Périgueux', in Bulletin 67 (Sept. 1999), pp.12-13.

7   Mary Ivens's article, 'New Neighbours for Refugio Gaucelmo' in Bulletin 68 (Dec.1999), p.32, provides more details.

8   The text of part of Stephen Platten's lecture can be found in Bulletin 68, pp.3-12.

9   Author's note: I am very grateful to Timothy Wotherspoon who provided me with a lucid, four-page account of the whole complicated process, which required nearly three years to complete.

10 See Paul Darke's article, 'A Report and a Request' in Bulletin 81 (March 2003), pp.29-30.

11 Moya Jolley gives more details of the making of the banner in 'One Thousand Years of Pilgrimage' in Bulletin 70 (June 2000), pp.6-11.

12 Marion Marples's article, 'Visit to Belgium ...' in Bulletin 72 (Dec.2000) recommends Jacobean places to visit in Antwerp, Brussels and Mechelen.

13 'Santiago Peregrino', by Sister Petra Clare, Bulletin 76 (Dec.2001), pp.20-24.

14 'Chairman's Speech, delivered at Rabanal, 27 October, 2001' by Laurie Dennett in Bulletin 76 (Dec.2001), pp.25-27.

15 For more details see Rosalind Billingham's article, 'Confraternity Visit to Poitiers and Saintes', Bulletin 80, (Dec. 2002), pp.18-20.

16 Copies of *William Wey* ... are still available from the Confraternity office.

17 I am indebted to Alison Pinkerton for the information in this paragraph.

18 Pamela Harris's article on her walk, 'Jakobus Pilgerwanderung, Nürnberg to Konstanz' can be found in Bulletin 70 (June 2000), pp.30-33.

19 'From Nürnberg to Konstanz and through Geneva to le Puy' in Bulletin 80 (Dec.2002), pp. 11-15.

20 'Remembering Madame Debril' in Bulletin 74 (July 2001), pp.23-25.

21 As the Xunta de Galicia took responsibility for the bridge-building, the funds collected were destined for a new refugio at Corcubión.

Appendix 1
Accounts by founder and early members of their pre-1983 pilgrimage interests

Some of the following accounts have been shortened for reasons of space but in all cases the full version has been placed in the Confraternity History Archive which is available in the Confraternity Library.

IAN DODD, FOUNDER MEMBER

'Celia and I made our pilgrimage to Compostela over three weeks in the summer of 1978. Although I had previously explored part of the Canterbury Pilgrims' Way, I really only found out about Compostela through a book by a German author (*The Great Pilgrimage* by V. and H. Hell) which I found when a student in 1976. That was the inspiration and for two years we made our plans. Our interest lay primarily in the spirituality of the medieval churches along the routes, and initially we had wondered about taking several months over the endeavour. In the event we ended up with full-time jobs sooner than we expected, and a three-week break was all we could manage. ... We travelled by train because we travelled everywhere by train, and had the option been available I am sure that our medieval predecessors would have done the same!'

PETER JOHNSON, FOUNDER MEMBER

'I first became interested in the pilgrimage after having seen a TV programme which aroused my curiosity. I then tracked down Mlle Warcollier, who, of course, brought the other founding members in the UK together. I remember fondly our initial meetings and watched with amazement as the Confraternity hatched and then kept growing ... and growing. I did my own pilgrimage before the start of the Confraternity, so used some fairly rudimentary sources and maps to do my two-month walk from Vézelay to Santiago. I kept a pilgrim's journal and wrote an unpublished book. It was a wonderful passion in my life for several years and I still get a buzz of excitement when I meet people who are potential pilgrims to Santiago or those who have done all or part of the walk.'

ROBIN NEILLANDS, FOUNDER MEMBER

'Thinking back 20 years, I think my interest in the pilgrimage to Compostela was aroused by reading either Starkie's *The Road to Santiago,* or more likely, Jonathan Sumption's book on pilgrimage. This also coincided with the realisation that whatever it took to be a tycoon of industry, I didn't have it. So I sold my publishing company and looked around for a diversion ... I was then 46 years old, ready and willing for a mid-life crisis, and flogging across France and Spain in the full heat of summer struck me as both delightfully daft and just what I needed.

'My interest in the pilgrimage was not religious but I would not say that it is simply or entirely based on my long-standing love of travel and history either. Though the pilgrimage combines these two delights, it has something else, something no less attractive for being less tangible and harder to explain, especially to someone who has never done it. ... On the Road the other attraction was a familiar one: comradeship, something I had found and lost 20 years before in the Commandos and is best described as friendship forged in adversity. Those who have walked or cycled to Compostela will be very familiar with friendship and adversity.

'So I bought the bike and rode the Road and got extremely shattered on all the usual torments and had a simply wonderful time. I joined the French Amis de Saint-Jacques before the trip as I recall. They sent me an oblong metal badge with a pilgrim image on it to hang round my neck and the image washed off with sweat, much to my annoyance, a few days into the trip. I met a lot of nice people, including Jocelyn Rix, and one thing led to another, or in this case to Mary Remnant's house and the rest is history.'

PAT QUAIFE, FOUNDER MEMBER

'It was during a university lecture on the *Chanson de Roland* in the Sixties that I first heard the pilgrim route to Santiago mentioned. Even then, in my early twenties, I made a mental note that one day I would like to follow it from Roncevaux, the setting for a famous scene from the 'Roland'. Years passed, the thought of the Camino was still there but work and living in New Zealand until 1970 prevented me from doing anything about it. The Seventies found me back in London and also saw the publication in 1973/4 in a *Sunday Times* colour supplement of two articles by Edwin Mullins about the pilgrimage. These I read eagerly and subsequently bought Mullins's book, published in 1974,

The Pilgrimage to Santiago, which I suspect encouraged many readers to explore the routes for themselves. Other books appeared a few years later: T.A. Layton's *The Way of St James,* and the evocative *Priez Pour Nous à Compostelle,* by Barret and Gurgand. The latter brings the Camino to life through the accounts of pilgrims over the centuries, as well as containing the *carnet de route* of their own pilgrimage. *Priez Pour Nous* ... also has an excellent bibliography, contributed by none other than Jeannine Warcollier.

'In early December 1980 I noticed that a lecture-recital on the pilgrimage route was being given in the Purcell Room by Mary Remnant. I made a point of going, sitting in the front row, and enjoyed it enormously making some notes of places, particularly churches with a St James connection or dedication, that I could myself visit in England. The following year, a colleague from my University of Auckland days, Judy Grant, came to Europe on sabbatical leave and stayed with me in London. 'Why don't we cycle to Santiago this year?' I suddenly found myself saying to her one summer evening. 'Why don't we, in the autumn?', she replied, and that was it. If I could get leave from my work at Camden Council we would have time to follow the Vézelay route, which on the map looked very attractive for cyclists, longer than the Le Puy route and with fewer main roads than the Paris/Tours route.

'There followed three months of intense preparatory activity. One of the first things I did was to write to Jeannine Warcollier applying to become a member of the Amis de Saint-Jacques. Instead of sending me material by post she surprised me by telephoning one evening to say that she would be in London for the forthcoming royal wedding and perhaps we could meet. I agreed with alacrity and a couple of weeks later we met at Piccadilly Circus and had supper together in a nearby restaurant. She was very easy to talk to and as well as membership details she had brought a detailed itinerary of the Vézelay route and of the route in Spain, plus a pro-forma 'help' letter, confirming my membership of the Amis, that we could use in France and Spain if we got into difficulties on the way. She also gave me the name and address of a young Englishman, Peter Johnson, who earlier in the year had in fact walked from Vézelay to Santiago ...

'On 1 September we checked our shiny, ten-speed bicycles into Victoria Station for onward transmission to the station at Avallon, the nearest to Vézelay, where we would collect them three days later. It was good to see them again as planned and for the next three weeks we cycled through south-west France averaging a modest 33 miles a day and awarding ourselves one rest-day per week. In fact we did a lot of walking up hills, including the Pyrenees when we could see nothing but fog and the road beneath our feet. While France was warm, sunny and relatively easy, Spain was often cold and wet, with numerous trials to test us.

'During the whole time we saw only one pilgrim on foot, a heavily-laden young woman, and no other cyclists. On 7 October we rode into the Plaza del Obradoiro in Santiago, in triumph and excitement. Mademoiselle had recommended a small bar/hotel called Suso's, where Señor Suso (senior) greeted us like old friends and locked our bikes safely out of harm's way. We had made no arrangements for the return journey and I had to be back at my desk in Camden on 12 October. Help was at hand however, in the form of Señor Ballesteros, the genial director of Santiago's tourist office, just up the road from Suso's. He introduced us to a travel agent friend who promptly enrolled us as members of the Spanish Family Circle, which qualified us for a cheap charter flight to London from La Coruña.

'... After the pilgrimage I found great difficulty in settling down to 'normal' working life again, something these days anthropologists call 'reincorporation'. The photos came back and were duly placed in an album, the diary was reread but for the rest of 1981 I felt as if I was in limbo of some kind. Mademoiselle Warcollier had told me that 1982 would be a Holy Year in Santiago (when St James's Day, 25 July, falls on a Sunday) but strangely I didn't feel any particular desire to return to Spain. I had no Spanish then, had been unwell in Galicia when on pilgrimage and had not coped well with Spanish mealtimes. Later that summer Mademoiselle, with whom I kept in touch, reported that she was receiving an increasing number of enquiries from Britain and that the Amis de Saint-Jacques now had five or six British members, including Mary Remnant, who had been in her Santiago group in July. ... Why didn't we, asked Mademoiselle, get together and form an association in England? Eventually, we did, on 13 January 1983, and it brought about great changes in my life.'

MARY REMNANT, FOUNDER MEMBER

'My first visit to Santiago was in 1967, as part of a Winston Churchill Travelling Fellowship to study the history of musical instruments as they are shown in the visual arts and to absorb the historical backgrounds in which they were played. Santiago Cathedral, with its musical Elders in the *Pórtico de la Gloria,* was of course a prime source.

'Later I became more interested in the pilgrimage as such, largely through taking part in a recording of pilgrim music and through seeing Mary Kirby's films on *The Road to Santiago.* These gave me the idea of constructing a lecture-recital about music and instruments on the pilgrimage, but time and money were needed for the journey itself. The opportunity arose in 1979, when the Early Music Network asked me to do a tour of lecture-recitals around England on a newly-researched subject and the Winston Churchill Memorial Trust very kindly agreed to give me a second grant to drive to Santiago in 1980.

'During the year of preparation I became aware of Constance Storrs's thesis *Jacobean Pilgrims from England from the Early Twelfth to the Late Fifteenth Century* (London University, 1964) and of the Centre d'Etudes Compostellanes in Paris, which had been founded by the Marquis Dr René de la Coste-Messelière. I wrote to him and received much useful information from Mlle Jeannine Warcollier, General Secretary of the Société des Amis de Saint-Jacques de Compostelle, which the Marquis had also founded in 1950.

'On 8 April 1980 my mother and I set off in our 1966 Morris Traveller, crossing from Newhaven to Dieppe and driving through Normandy (where the Abbot of Saint-Wandrille blessed the car) to Chartres. We then took the Tours route to Santiago, with deviations for particular reasons to Parthenay, Bayonne, Santo Domingo de Silos, Soria and Lugo. We arrived in Santiago on the evening of 19 April and, thanks to the grant from the Churchill Trust, were able to stay in the Hostal de los Reyes Católicos, which is so valuable for its closeness to the Cathedral and its own place in history. (However, my mother, who was then nearly 78, did pay for her own expenses so as not to encroach on the grant.)

'The 20th was a Sunday, and after going to Mass in the Cathedral at 10 a.m. and looking around it, we were shown other places in Santiago by Professor Miguel Morey, whose wife Isabel had been one of my mother's pupils in London soon after the war. (One of her sisters, Rosa, has lived in England since her marriage to Malcolm McGregor and joined the Confraternity at its first general meeting) ... Other people who were extremely helpful in Santiago included Professor José Lopez-Calo, SJ, one of the greatest authorities on Spanish mediaeval music, particularly that in the *Codex Calixtinus.* He showed us relevant books, drove us to Noya to see the musical Elders in the façade of the church of San Martín, wrote Spanish instructions in my notebook for a garage man to mend something which was wrong with my car and gave me an introduction to Carlos Villanueva, director of the Grupo Universitario de Cámara de Santiago. He in turn told me where to get bagpipe reeds. Last but certainly not least was Señor José-María Ballesteros, director of the Tourist Office. He took us into his sanctum there, gave us much useful information and got permission for me to photograph the minstrels carved in the banqueting hall of the Palace of Gelmírez. When one of my cameras jammed there, I went to the nearest photographic shop and was told that no-one in Santiago could mend it and it would have to go to LLa Coruña or Vigo, for which, of course, there was no time. Instead I went to Señor Ballesteros, who said, 'Come - I have a friend', and took me next door to the photographer Señor Guitián. He gently unjammed the camera and charged nothing, and I returned happily to the Palace of Gelmírez.

'After four days in Santiago my mother flew home and I started back, visiting the cathedrals of Orense and Jaca before zigzagging between the most appropriate places on the Arles, Le Puy and Vézelay routes and then meeting Mlle Warcollier for the first time in Paris. Among several providential happenings during the journey, the most striking was the discovery, through getting lost in the Pyrenees in the dark, of the village of Sos del Rey Católico. This was the birthplace of Ferdinand of Aragón, whose marriage to Isabella of Castile was so important, not only in the history of Spain and of music, but also of the pilgrimage to Santiago itself.

'For the next six months I planned the lecture-recital, sorting the slides I had made abroad, coordinating them with suitable music and, of course, reading more about the subject. My good friend from Oxford days, Dr Margaret Gibson (who was then a don at Liverpool University), told me about the work done by Professor George Zarnecki on the connection between the twelfth-century Herefordshire school of carving and the Santiago pilgrimage, and said that I should go to see him. I replied that I did not like to bother people who did not know me, to which she said, 'That's what he is there for', so I went to see him at the Courtauld Institute and he could not have been kinder or more helpful. About the same time Professor Jack Sage generously gave me a copy of the pilgrim tune 'Camino de Santiago', dating from c. 1500.

'During this period it occurred to me to have an organistrum made, based on the sculpted one at the top of the *Pórtico de la Gloria*, so I asked Alan Crumpler of Leominster to do it, as he had already made my mediaeval harp. He decided to use part of a walnut tree from the village of Lytchett Matravers in Dorset, where he grew up. This tree was already dead in a photograph taken in the 1930s and Alan had had part of the wood waiting to be used for 30 years. In 1991 I was able to visit his parents and they took me to the place where the tree stump was still visible. I played the organistrum to it, which was a great thrill, just as it had been in 1988 when I played it under the *Pórtico de la Gloria* which was then celebrating the eighth centenary of its completion.

'The lecture-recital finally took shape in October 1980 and I tried it out first, entitled *Mediaeval Minstrels on the Road to Santiago de Compostela*, at the Ursuline Convent School at Brentwood. The tour for the Early Music Network started in the Wigmore Hall on 30 October and, after taking the programme around the country I did it again independently in London's Purcell Room on 4 December. Sitting in different parts of the front row were Peter Johnson who was planning to walk from Vézelay and Pat Quaife who wanted to bicycle from there. None of us knew each other. Peter got in touch with me afterwards and came to see me about his journey.

'In July 1981 Mlle Warcollier was in London and came to dinner at my home, together with Peter who told us about his experiences. Mademoiselle told me about Pat Quaife, who had been in touch with her.

'During the Santiago Holy Year of 1982 I did the lecture-recital in Paris at the Val de Grace in the rue Saint-Jacques, coinciding with the exhibition *Paris: Carrefour des Routes de Compostelle* in June, before joining the Amis de Saint-Jacques at Santiago in time for the feast of St James on 25 July. On that day I met Jocelyn Rix who had just walked from Canterbury and her brother Paddy who had joined her at Ponferrada. She told me of the journalist Robin Neillands who had bicycled from Bordeaux to write it up for *The Times* but I did not meet him then. In October I returned to Paris to do my programme again at the Palais de Chaillot, before repeating it in the old pilgrim hostel at Saint-Léger-lès-Melle and for the Société des Concerts de Cognac. During that visit Mlle Warcollier said that the Amis de Saint-Jacques now had five English members and suggested that we should start an English branch. I said that it was a very good idea but that I had not got time to organise it.

'A few weeks later Robin Neillands rang to say that she had asked him to organise a meeting of the English members, so this was arranged for 13 January 1983 at my home in London, being the most central place. Conveniently it was also my birthday, so there was a double celebration at which the Confraternity came into being with the six founder members (Mlle Warcollier had by then put us in touch with Ian Dodd) and my mother Mrs Joan Remnant as the first ordinary member.'

JOCELYN RIX, FOUNDER MEMBER

Jocelyn, who walked from Canterbury to Santiago in 1982, was inspired by Edwin Mullins's 1973/4 TV programme about the routes through France, and the *Caminos Francés* and *Aragonés* in Spain. 'It was everything that interested me – religion and legend, history and geography, art and architecture, music and movement. For over 1000 years pilgrims had been making the journey and in some places, particularly in Spain, the tracks had remained unchanged. I fancied following in their footsteps.'

In the spring of 1981 a friend passed on to her two brochures, one on the *Camino,* and the other about the city of Santiago. They reminded her that when St James's Day falls on a Sunday, the celebrations are particularly splendid. 'I was thrilled to discover that that would occur the following year so resolved to make 1982 the Year of the Walk. In December 1981 I met a colleague of my father's. When I told him of my plans for the following year and their inspiration, he replied that Edwin Mullins had written a book about it, *The Pilgrimage to Santiago,* published by Secker & Warburg in 1974. What joy! My mother gave me the book for Christmas which I read avidly during January and February ... I was so keen to see those places for myself, I carried that book every step of the way from Canterbury to Santiago and at 1lb 6oz it was worth its weight in gold.

'I didn't become a member of the Société des Amis de Saint-Jacques de Compostelle, but Mlle Warcollier, the Secretary, was very kind, writing me letters with useful information including a list of places along the Paris route where I might stay, which I kept in my wallet. One entry in her neat handwriting read: 'M. le M. de la Coste-Messelière, Chateau ... Melle'.

'Finally, south of Poitiers, I came across a weather-beaten sign at about knee height and turned left off the road, along a drive with a slight rise. On reaching the brow I could see the drive ended at a real chateau, which somehow I hadn't expected, with a beautiful Paulownia in full bloom in front of it. Inside I discovered the M initials stood for Monsieur le Marquis who was President of the Société des Amis. He had a friend staying for the weekend and kindly allowed me to stay too.

I had good cause to celebrate in the drawing room of the *piano nobile*. Melle marked the spot on the fold of my Kümmerley & Frei map of the whole of France. Now I turned it over and found myself staring at a whole new territory ending at the Pyrenees and the tantalizing start of Spain. We drank a toast in Pineau des Charentes, my first taste of that delicious aperitif.

'Next day Monsieur le Marquis and his friend were going to visit the fabulous church at Aulnay, my next stop south and they kindly transported my pack there. They passed me en route and the last sight I had was of two arms, waving like wings, out of the windows of his battered white Peugeot. We met again in Santiago a couple of months later, Monsieur le Marquis having driven along the route to take part in the festivities around St James's Day, the French always having a special celebration on the 23rd. My brother Paddy and I met on the (modern) bridge at Ponferrada on 10 June and arrived in Santiago on 22 July so were able to take part. That's when we met Mlle Warcollier and her friend Mary Remnant for the first time, at an extremely noisy meal.

'I was delighted, six months later, to receive the invitation to meet some other people who had made the pilgrimage by different means and in different years at her home on 13 January 1983 and that's where the Confraternity began.'

STEPHEN BADGER (EARLY MEMBER, 1983; DIED 1997)

'I visited Compostela by chance in 1967. We started from Paris and unintentionally followed the old pilgrims' route fairly closely (which shows that it remains a natural route today). My camera was stolen from the car in León and so no pictorial record survives, but the consciousness lingered on to be fertilised by Edwin Mullins's book in the early 1970s. Secondly the prominent part which *The Canterbury Tales* play in most English school curricula is bound to raise the subject of pilgrimage and a subsequent chance visit to Lourdes proved so ghastly that it provoked an interest in trying to understand what it had all been (and perhaps still was) about ... and the interplay with medieval ecclesiastical art and architecture can only enhance this interest.'

(With thanks to Stephen's widow, Katharine Badger Croston, for making this account available.)

GOSIA BRYKCZYNSKA (EARLY MEMBER, 1983)

'I had already "done" the pilgrimage to Santiago in 1981, starting from Victoria Coach Station. My unorthodox approach to it haunted me for quite some time afterwards. Meanwhile, I was working at the Children's Hospital in Boston, Massachusetts and studying moral philosophy at Harvard University. To get into the way of thinking in England, where I was planning to return, I would periodically go to the Divinity Library at Harvard and read *The Tablet* or *The Catholic Herald*. It was while I was reading *The Tablet* in mid-April 1983 that I came upon news from Dr Mary Remnant about the foundation of the Confraternity. I immediately responded and became a member.

MOLLIE COVIELLO (EARLY MEMBER, 1983)

'I went to lectures on medieval architecture and ornament given by Linda Murray at London University in 1968-1970. My imagination was fired by the story of the pilgrims following the way for hundreds of years, the growth of the great churches, the slides showing the plans, the sculpture and stories in stone. I had essays to write so I read and studied many books.'

In 1977, after early retirement for Mollie and her photographer husband David, she was giving extra-mural lectures on medieval architecture for Aberystwyth University College, and they applied for a grant from the Welsh Arts Council and West Wales Arts to prepare 20 two-hour talks, with slides, for a future lecture series. 'We spent a £250 grant on films for David and a recorder for me and set off with a Volvo full of equipment, reference books, a large notebook, a small tent, coffee-making equipment and much enthusiasm and excitement. It took seven weeks to find our way ... We saw wonderful things, were accompanied by cuckoos and nightingales, and had five glorious days in Compostela staying at Suso's. We met a Dutch guide, Francis, who showed us places we would never have found by ourselves.'

PATRIC EMERSON (EARLY MEMBER, 1983)

'Returning to the UK in 1957 after 21 years abroad, apart from finding a job, one of the many things that interested me was finding out about my family history. By a stroke of luck I found such a history in the British Museum Reading Room. Therein I found that the person who started the family went on the pilgrimage to Santiago de Compostela in 1201 ... I knew nothing of Compostela, in fact I had never heard of it - and so started to read about it. As I am the last male in my particular line I thought that I would also visit Compostela to complete the circle, and so 770 years later I set out.'

Patric travelled from Biarritz to León by bus, meeting a scholarly Benedictine monk at a roadside bar in Sahagún where the bus had broken down. They continued westwards together, 'with a short bus ride to Astorga where we changed for a better bus for Lugo and then on to another rickety old one to Santiago de Compostela where we arrived late in the evening. Neither of us had any hotel arrangements which my monk solved easily by saying that if the Hostel at one side of the main square was good enough for *los Reyes Católicos* then it was good enough for us. It was a beautiful place and apparently the interior had been redecorated under the eye of the wife of the dictator, Franco. This was indeed comfort and luxury …

'The next day straight to the Cathedral and it was quite a feeling to think my forebear had walked up these stairs over 700 years before. We were fortunate enough to be there at the same time as a big French pilgrimage group and for them the famous *botafumeiro* censer was swung … My monk described it well as "One of the best ecclesiastical gimmicks I have ever seen" …

'Later, in talking to one of the cathedral clergy he mentioned that I was completing the circle as my ancestor had been there over 700 years previously. At this we were introduced to one of the more senior clergy and were given a comprehensive tour of the cathedral from the roof top and the bell tower right down through each level to the crypt below. We ended up seeing the casket containing the remains of St James about which both of us were sceptical – although we said nothing at the time out of politeness to our host. Out via the main door, embracing the statue of St James in the correct manner, and back to the hotel and a large dinner with much wine … I had closed the circle after 770 years.'

DAVID JARVIS (EARLY MEMBER, 1983)

'As a sixth-former I did part of the walk from London (St Ignatius College) to Walsingham with a large(ish) wooden cross. Later, but probably before 1960, a few lines in an obscure novel by Georges Simenon struck a chord. He mentioned a retired bank manager (widowed) – I am neither – walking from le Puy, preparing himself for the hereafter. Then a 'B' French film about a lady who vowed to walk the route from Paris to Chartres and was picked up each evening by the chauffeur. This encouraged correspondence with Captain T.A. Layton [author of the 1976 book, *The Way of Saint James*] and I read an article in *The Times* of 21 August 1982 by Rob Neillands, and I was hooked and thus joined the Confraternity.'

ROSA MCGREGOR (EARLY MEMBER, 1983)

'My reasons for joining the Confraternity from the very beginning are very different from everbody else's. My love of Santiago is nostalgic: I lived there for four years and my family lived there for 20 years. My father was professor of Spanish literature in Santiago for 20 years, so my younger brothers and sisters consider themselves *gallegos*. I have very fond memories of that time.'

JAMES MAPLE (EARLY MEMBER, 1983)

'In the autumn of 1983 I was granted a sabbatical for the next summer term. My brother had a house at Pauillac on the Gironde and I had become interested in the *Chemin de Saint-Jacques* through the Médoc and the Landes. I decided to do a little research into the possible routes of medieval pilgrims who avoided Bordeaux and may have left English ships at Soulac (where there is a fine Romanesque church) at the mouth of the Gironde and travelled along the west bank, joined as well by pilgrims rowed across the river by the monks from l'Ermitage St Martial at Mortagne-sur-Gironde and those using the ferry at Blaye.

'A friend drew my attention to a new book by Horton and Marie-Hélène Davies called *Holy Days and Holidays on the Road to Santiago*. The assistant in the bookshop in Sicilian Avenue (London), gave me a leaflet about the Confraternity. And so in November 1983 I rang Pat Quaife and joined the fast-growing new Confraternity.'

MARION MARPLES AND JAMES HATTS (EARLY MEMBERS, 1983)

'When I was a geography student at Bristol University in 1969, my new friends, historians as it happens, insisted that I should join them for a wonderful course of lectures on the development of Gothic architecture, and about this amazing pilgrimage. Fired with enthusiasm, my friend Jane and I applied for and received a travel grant to follow the route in the summer of 1972, after our graduation. Our sources of information were the lectures themselves and the sole book on the subject in the university library, *The Great Pilgrimage of the Middle Ages*, by the encouragingly named V. and H. Hell. The evocative pictures and lists of towns persuaded us to start our pilgrimage in Paris at the Tour St Jacques and then go by train to Poitiers to start walking. We had no experience of walking with heavy rucksacks, let alone a tent. We map-read our way along overgrown footpaths to idyllic campsites for about two days. We were not encouraged by the mockery of French schoolboys as we struggled through the rain, and soon resorted to catching a train at a well-placed station.'

On that occasion, using trains and buses, Marion and Jane reached Saint-Jean-Pied-de-Port, where they survived on onion soup for five days, waiting for money to arrive from Marion's mother to enable them to cross the mountains to San Sebastián and catch a train home.

'A condition of the travel award was to produce a report on our journey, which I did and was quite proud of. When I first got to know Leigh I was keen to show him the report, which he soon mislaid. This caused a certain amount of strain between us, but nevertheless we married in 1976 and our son was born in 1981. He was almost called Casimir, but my interest in the pilgrimage and the proximity of my birthday to St James's Day gave him the name James. The report had happily been found ...'

James was just two when the Confraternity was founded. He has literally grown up with the Confraternity, contributing enormously over the years to its development. His first appearance at a CSJ event was at Reading Abbey in May 1983, and he also took part, with Marion, in the first visit to Herefordshire churches in 1984. Ten years later, at the 1994 AGM he spoke about FEVE narrow-gauge trains in northern Spain, having already prepared an initial guide to FEVE trains and timetables. In between times he accompanied Marion on planning trips, took phone messages and acted as a one-man information point at AGMs on technical matters.

James was growing up as computer technology developed. He researched and recommended our computer requirements and taught himself word processing. He also has a sharp eye for design. Marion would produce draft CSJ documents and James would convert them into decent looking products. This has been a continuing process: he has been largely responsible for the cover designs for CSJ publications, as well as the design for more complicated projects like William Wey and the proceedings of the Canterbury conference. He now acts as production editor of the Bulletin and was able to advise Howard Nelson on designing the CSJ website and the development of the on-line bookshop.

At school and on visits to Spain James acquired good Spanish and helped Marion with translating and interpreting on CSJ trips she organised. It is perhaps hardly surprising that he chose to study Spanish and history at university where he says his knowledge of matters related to St James and the architecture of English parish churches has stood him in good stead.

BRIAN AND MARIJKE MORRIS (EARLY MEMBERS, 1985)

Brian decided in July 1984 that he would cycle to North Holland, where Marijke and their eldest daughter, Ingrid, were visiting her mother. He went via Dover, Ostende, Brugge and Zeeland. 'I paused in Westerham (Kent) making a photograph of the bronze of Winston Churchill on the Green. The sprightly grey-haired fellow who came over offering to take a picture of me alongside the statue was the late George Grant, and being cyclists we talked about the trips we had both made and I mentioned my new interest in cycling to Santiago with Marijke. George insisted that if we were contemplating such a journey we simply must become members of the Confraternity ... We completed our pilgrimage in 1985, travelling on a tandem from Santander over the Picos de Europa to León and on to Santiago - the first Confraternity tandem pair to make the journey.'

EDWIN MULLINS (EARLY MEMBER, 1983)

'I first heard of the city of Santiago when I was a student at Merton College, Oxford in the 1950s, and a Catholic friend of mine called Henry Mayr-Harting kept going there, I had no idea why. Appropriately he is now Regius Professor of Ecclesiastical History at Oxford University. As for the pilgrimage itself I first read about it in the most mundane fashion, in one of the Michelin Green Guides while I was travelling in south-west France in the late 1960s. It struck me straightaway as a subject I should love to write a book about. As a historian of art and architecture I grew increasingly fascinated by the subject the more I studied it, and even more so once I began to explore the pilgrim routes themselves, both on foot and in a car, and realised what an extraordinary social, cultural and historical phenomenon the pilgrimage had been.'

AILEEN O'SULLIVAN (EARLY MEMBER, 1983)

'Annual visits to relations in the small town of Killorglin, County Kerry, where generations of my father's family had lived, meant that I attended the Catholic church there, which had, for Ireland, an unusual dedication: St James (of Compostela). So one day in London I was most interested to read in my weekly Catholic paper that there was to be a meeting in the Wren Restaurant, St James, with the idea of founding a Confraternity of St James. Regrettably, due to work pressure, I was unable to attend. Later that week, I wrote to a Pat Quaife for information on the Confraternity and was pleased with her reply, which included a form to complete if I wished to join – which I did in March 1983 and also paid my annual subscription of £2-50. This has proved to be one of the best investments made in life by me, still a member 20 years on.'

RICHARD REECE (EARLY MEMBER, 1983)
'In 1964 I was teaching at St John's School, Leatherhead where one of the language teachers suddenly got the idea of going to Compostela and asked me to go with him because of my interest in archaeology and architecture. We took two sixth-formers to fill up the seats in the car which was the main means of transport, so there was only a little walking. Our journey was a bit before the recent development of the route, so we were rather encapsulated in our journey instead of part of something wider ... We carried with us a letter from the Archbishop of Westminster to say that although we were Separated Brethren he hoped any clergy would help us on our way. We did use it once or twice when requests to see the inside of locked churches seemed likely to be refused, but our welcome in general was very friendly, if slightly bemused: "What are these four English un-Catholics doing?"'

ROSEMARY WELLS (EARLY MEMBER, 1983)
'I taught in a large London inner-city comprehensive, and by every half-term would be feeling like chewed-up string. I realised that just to rest was quite inadequate: the meaning of 'recreation' is re-creation. So each half-term I took off for France to pursue my passion for Romanesque architecture. I chose a different region each time ... and it finally dawned on me that I was, in fact, following routes to Santiago, about which I then knew little.'

Appendix 2
The Quest for Constance Storrs

Something should be said about the quest for Constance Storrs. Professor Lomax had given me an address in Earl's Court where she had been in 1969 but he had no idea if she was still there; I went there on my bicycle and she had obviously gone. Then I rang University College, from which she had done her thesis, but they would not give me her address ... I also rang the two Storrs numbers in the London telephone directory but to no avail. By that time I was doing my Santiago lecture-recital a good deal, so I used to ask the audiences if they knew her, but they never did. Pat Quaife put an appeal in the Bulletin, again with no positive result.

In early 1988 I mentioned the problem to Dr Doris Jones-Baker of the Society of Antiquaries and she suggested that I should ask at the University Library. (I had not thought of that, considering her own college had lost touch with her.) So I went to Senate House and filled in an enquiry form. About a week later the telephone rang and a voice gave me her address: The Hill House, Badwell Ash, nr Bury St Edmunds, Suffolk, but with no telephone number. Directory Enquiries then provided me with the number. By that time I was almost shaking – something most exciting was happening!

I dialled the number but there was no reply. About half an hour later I tried again and an elderly lady answered. I said, 'Is that Mrs Constance Storrs?', and she said 'Yes'. (This was a surprise, as I was expecting someone of middle age.) I started to explain about the Confraternity and to say that we had been searching for her for five years but the telephone was making bad crackling noises and she could hardly hear what it was about. After all, whereas I knew absolutely what I was talking about, for her it was completely out of the blue and unexpected. I therefore said that I would write to her about it and did, and received a very interesting letter in return.

As luck would have it, I was soon going to a Music Week at Hengrave Hall near Bury St Edmunds, so it was arranged that I would go to lunch at Badwell Ash where she lived with her husband Mr Francis Storrs and an old friend of theirs, Dr Susan Tracey. (I think their ages were 77, 81 and 72 respectively.) This was of course a great thrill for me and Mrs Storrs was very glad to know that we had been looking for her for five years. However, she said that when her husband retired in 1969 they left London and said that they were never going back there, so she could not even return to meet the Confraternity. This was not an insuperable problem as the Committee had been discussing the idea of having a conference somewhere. Hengrave Hall was an ideal setting so we decided to go there, but as there was a long waiting list it could not be till 16 to 18 March 1990. However, that gave us plenty of time for preparation and during it I took Pat Quaife, Marion Marples and Laurie Dennett to meet Mrs Storrs at Badwell Ash.

Eventually the time came, and in perfect weather, and as the Marquis de la Coste-Messelière approached the Hall he said 'Superbe!'. Mrs Storrs was driven over by Dr Tracey and was able to meet some of the many people who had been waiting to see her. Our invaluable members Professor Derek Lomax and Professor Brian Tate agreed to arrange for her thesis to be published at Santiago, with the latter as the editor, and he accompanied her back to Badwell Ash to discuss the details.

As it turned out the Conference was only just in time, as Mrs Storrs got cancer and died on 24 August, but at least we were able to say 'Thank God we found her in time!'. She wanted to be buried in the cemetery at Badwell Ash, so the funeral service was held in the Anglican church there, conducted together by the Anglican vicar and the Catholic priest from Stowmarket. (The Storrs were Catholics and Dr Tracey was an Anglican.) The Confraternity was represented by Marion Marples, Doreen Hansen, Alfred Peacock and myself. Two weeks later, when I was conveniently on the way to Ely, there was a Requiem Mass in the Catholic church at Stowmarket and I played the organ for it.

A year later, on 14 August 1991, I did my Santiago lecture-recital in memory of Mrs Storrs at the Gershom Centre in the nearby village of Great Ashfield and several members of the Confraternity Choir took part.[1]

On 25 October 1991, the day that our 'hostel' was inaugurated at Rabanal, Francis Storrs married Susan Tracey, on the specific command of Constance when she knew that she had not much more time to live. Susan told me later that she would not consider it for over a year, but by then it was the obvious solution.

However, in February 1995 Susan herself died of cancer. I went to her funeral too and after the interment Mr Storrs, sitting in a wheelchair in front of the graves, said: 'There is just room for me between the two of them'. After that he insisted on living on his own, mainly in the kitchen, where he had his missal and rosary and could easily reach the food. I called on him once and he told me to help myself to anything from a box containing jewellery, etc., as the family had taken everything they wanted. At the bottom of the box I found a tiny silver shell brooch, embossed with the cross of the Order of Santiago, so that has become a great treasure.

Eventually we heard that Mr Storrs himself had died, so when I was near Badwell Ash one day I went to the cemetery to see the graves. He had been put on top of Constance (where presumably the place had already been prepared) and the inscription said that he had died on 25 July – THE FEAST OF ST JAMES!

MARY REMNANT

NOTES

1 By that time the programme was called 'The Musical Road to Santiago de Compostela'.

Appendix 3
Rabanal's First Pilgrims

Who were the first pilgrims to sleep in the Refugio Gaucelmo at Rabanal? There are competing claims, all of which have merits.

The first places in the Gaucelmo pilgrim register are claimed by two Spaniards, Ángel Luis Barreda Ferrer (Coordinator of the Spanish Federation) and José Ignacio Díaz (editor of *Peregrino* magazine) who booked in on 8 June 1991, the day the *refugio* was officially open to pilgrims (see Chapter Four).

A month earlier, on 9 May 1991, when the last works to the house were being completed, a group of three German pilgrims from the Peregrinatio Europae (or Europawallfahrt) organisation arrived on foot from Astorga on their way to Santiago. They were led by Msgr. Dr Gerhard Specht and included the Confraternity's good friend, Herbert Simon from the Santiago-Freunde-Köln. On their arrival in Rabanal they met the El Bierzo president, Porfirio Fernández Rodríguez, who was inspecting the recent work that had been done and who gave them permission to stay overnight. Asumpta and Charo also appeared and, with Porfirio, helped make the pilgrims as comfortable as possible in a house with no beds, no light, no kitchen and only cold water. There was, of course, no pilgrim register to sign. As true pilgrims, the three gave thanks for the hospitality during Mass at Santa María the next morning. To confirm their status Herbert Simon later sent an account of their stay which was entitled: 'Die ersten Pilgergäste in der Herberge Rabanal "San Gaucelmo"' (The First Pilgrim Guests in the Rabanal refuge "Saint Gaucelmo".

The previous year, during the first ever Confraternity working group visit to Rabanal in October 1990, two young Scottish pilgrims had appeared and helped with clearing the rubble out of the first floor (see also Chapter Four). The working group itself was staying in Molinaseca as the Rabanal house was not ready for occupation. However, John and Sarah were given permission to stay and the next morning, when the working group members returned, they found a scrap of paper which read,

For the CSJ members –
just for future information
the first two Pilgrims to stay at
the new Rabanal refugio
were John Budd and
Sarah Cumings from
Edinburgh. Thanks for your
welcome and your hospitality.
We had a surprisingly warm and
comfortable night! Hope the
work goes OK.

And that, I thought, was that until a visit to Strasbourg in the mid-Nineties with the Amis de Saint-Jacques when I met a Monsieur Guilpart who had been on pilgrimage in the summer of 1990. He told me that he had actually spent a night there, clandestinely, in August 1990, and was therefore Gaucelmo's first pilgrim.

The answer to the question posed above goes something like this:

- a Frenchman was the first person to spend a night in the parish house while restoration work was in full swing (August 1990);
- two Scots were the first to sleep there, with permission from the Confraternity working group, when conditions were slightly better (October 1990);
- three Germans were the first to sleep there, with permission from the El Bierzo president, when the works were almost completed (May 1991);
- two Spaniards were the first official pilgrims to sleep there, on the first day that wardens were there to greet them (June 1991), but before the inauguration had taken place.

In fact, it does not really matter who has the greatest claim; the four sets of pilgrims, from four different countries, typify the international nature of the Camino de Santiago at an early stage in the story of the Refugio Gaucelmo. And who knows how many anonymous pilgrims, needing just a roof over their head, may have crept in to sleep during the previous three decades when the house stood deserted and forlorn?

POSTSCRIPT

There is no doubt about the identity of the first pilgrim quadruped at Gaucelmo: Win and Val Buick's Welsh/Navarrese donkey, Peregrino, who wrote [sic] in the pilgrim register of 8 July 1991: *Thanks for the wonderful rest and the best grazing on the Camino.*

194

Appendix 4
1993 Holy Year Lectures

17 FEBRUARY
Dr Mary Remnant: Introduction: The Pilgrimage to Santiago and the Confraternity of St James

17 MARCH
Dr David Hugh Farmer: Saints and Pilgrimage with reference to St James

19 MAY
Professor Alison Stones: The Illumination and Decoration of the *Codex Calixtinus*

16 JUNE
Dr Annie Shaver Crandell: The Compostela *Pilgrim's Guide* and the Artistic Landscape of the 12th Century

15 SEPTEMBER
Professor Brian Tate: The English Pilgrimage to Santiago

13 OCTOBER
The Very Revd David Stancliffe: The Spirituality of the Pilgrimage

17 NOVEMBER
Ms Patricia Quaife: 'Camino de Santiago, Camino de Europa'

Appendix 5
Walking to Santiago
Things I did Wrong in 1982

1. No forward planning (apart from reading *The Pilgrimage to Santiago* by Edwin Mullins).

2. No training.

3. No detailed map (I had one of France and one of Spain).

4. No proper pack (I had one of Florence Nightingale's Crimean cast-offs).

5. No proper boots (but wonderful ones from New Zealand).

6. No proper waterproof (luckily 1982 was very dry).

7. No water-bottle (don't know how I survived. Now I wouldn't stir without a thermos).

8. No sleeping bag, but the only time I needed one for the consecutive nights at Rabanal and El Acebo I met a Spaniard who was carrying two! Not everyone is lucky enough to have such a good guardian angel.

9. No proper socks (100% nylon loopy ankle socks, but I did have more than three).

10. No compass.

11. My total inability to get up early. I lapsed happily into the Spanish way of life:
    - going to bed late;
    - getting up late;
    - seeing round the place;
    - setting off at midday or later;
    - walking through the hottest part of the day;
    - arriving late at my destination, 8 or 9 p.m.;
    - eating late, and going to bed late …

JOCELYN RIX

Appendix 6
Fragments from Rabanal, 1986-2002

It is a long way from Rabanal del Camino to the church of St Mary Moorfields in the City of London. But in June 2002 members of the Confraternity gathered in the crypt of St Mary's for what amounted to an evening assessing the ideals which originally brought the Refugio Gaucelmo into existence in 1991 and the inspiration which has sustained it since. Gaucelmo at Rabanal ranks as one of the foremost achievements of the Confraternity during its first 20 years. However, complacency was certainly not the order of the day for the team of seven – Laurie Dennett, Paul Graham, Mary Ivens, Walter Ivens, James Maple, Marion Marples and Joe May – who made their presentation that evening. From the very first video image of the former priest's house with its collapsed roof and awesome air of 'Spanish nowhere' dereliction, the panorama bounced from one panel member to another as the dream of the few became the reality of the many.

There are people more qualified than I am to write about Rabanal. I come upon the general scene more in the role of a receiver than a giver. In scanning the 20 years of the Confraternity's existence since the founder members convened in January 1983, there is a temptation to allow nostalgia to creep in. In his prologue to *The Go-Between* L.P. Hartley reminds us: 'The past is a foreign country: they do things differently there'. But Rabanal is an amalgam of the past, the present and the future.

I was one of the fortunate 19 who numbered themselves with Pat Quaife in the autumn of 1996 for the dual purpose of celebrating the Refugio Gaucelmo's fifth birthday and visiting some of the Maragato villages in the general vicinity of Rabanal. Late October can be cold in Rabanal but the sun favoured us throughout the week and the autumn colours glowed. Some of us stayed at the *refugio* and some at Antonio's *mesón* which at that time was the only non-refuge option in the village. And indeed some of us stayed in *both* places due to a miscalculation one night about the closing time of Gaucelmo! Pilgrims were still trickling through in small numbers, and their need for rest was of prime concern. The area around Rabanal – the Maragatería – is steeped in history and what was not immediately apparent in 1996 was the extent to which increasing interest in the Camino would bring about a regeneration of its fortunes. Laurie Dennett's account of her original passage in 1986 when, as she said in June 2002, such pilgrims as there were in those days would skip the bit between Astorga and Ponferrada and take the train because there was no accommodation, is a far cry from 1996, which in turn is a far cry from the present. I was back again in Rabanal in 1997 on my way from the Pyrenees to Santiago, and even then the nearby 'ghost' village of Foncebadón had yet to awake from its long sleep, which I gather is now beginning to happen.

So – past, present and future. As a wayfarer and a pilgrim my own thanks must go to those who had the foresight and the courage to create what the Refugio Gaucelmo now represents. And more recently to the seven who presented the unfolding vision so absorbingly. And – my own concession to nostalgia – to Pat Quaife who took us there in that golden October of 1996 and showed us a world which continues to delight the memory.

JOHN REVELL

Appendix 7
Confraternity Office-holders and Honorary Members, 1983-2003

President   H.E. The Spanish Ambassador

Chairmen   Robin Neillands, 1983 to 1985
James Maple, 1986 to 1988
Patricia Quaife, 1989 to 1994
Laurie Dennett, 1995 to 2002

Hon. Secretaries Patricia Quaife, 1983 to 1988
Marion Marples, 1989 to 1998

Secretary   Marion Marples, 1998-

Hon Treasurers Ian Dodd, 1983
Peter Johnson, 1984 to 1986
Rosemary Wells, 1986 to 1988
Stephen Badger, 1989 to 1994
Timothy Wotherspoon, 1995 to 2001

Finance &   Alison Thorp, 2001-
Systems Manager

Honorary   Jeannine Warcollier (1983)
Members   José-María Ballesteros (1983)
Marquis Dr René de la Coste-Messelière (1984)
(deceased)
Professor George Zarnecki CBE (1984)
PCC of St James, Stoke Orchard (Glos) (1986)
Constance Storrs (1988) (deceased)
D. José J. Puig de la Bellacasa (1990)
Mary Remnant (1992)
Asumpta Oriol (1992)
Charo Carrión (1992)
Alberto Morán Luna (1992)
Patricia Quaife (1992)
Herbert and Liliana Simon (1994)
D. Alberto Aza Arias (1999)
Moya Jolley (2000)